HAWAI'I CHRONICLES III

D1512259

HAWAI'I CHRONICLES III

World War Two in Hawai'i,
from the pages
of *Paradise of the Pacific*

EDITED BY
BOB DYE

A Latitude 20 Book
University of Hawai'i Press
Honolulu

© 2000 University of Hawai'i Press
All rights reserved
Printed in the United States of America

00   01   02   03   04   05   5   4   3   2   1

Photographs courtesy of the Hawai'i War Records Depository

Library of Congress Cataloging-in-Publication Data
Hawai'i chronicles III : World War Two in Hawai'i, from the pages of Paradise of the
Pacific / edited by Bob Dye.
p.   cm.
"A Latitude 20 book."
ISBN 0–8248–2289–7 (pbk. : alk. paper)
1. World War, 1939–1945—Hawaii.   2. Hawaii—History—1900–1959.   I. Title: Hawai'i
chronicles three.   II. Title: Hawai'i chronicles 3.   III. Dye, Bob, 1928–   IV. Paradise of the
Pacific.
D767.92.H376 2000
996.9'03—dc21   00–023410

University of Hawai'i Press books are printed
on acid-free paper and meet the guidelines
for permanence and durability of the
Council on Library Resources.

Printed by The Maple-Vail Book Manufacturing Group

In memory of Ma Boyle

"With a heavy hand and a soft heart, she beat her employees with
stern words and kind actions into production of *Paradise of the Pacific*
for many years. And under her dictatorship, at once both fascistic
and benevolent, they made a good magazine of it, a beautiful
and informative house journal of the Islands."
Excerpt from *The Honolulu Advertiser* editorial July 18, 1946.

Contents

Contents

Contents

Contents

Contents

Contents

Acknowledgments

❖ The editor and publisher gratefully acknowledge the permission of David Pellegrin, president and CEO of Honolulu Publishing Company, to reprint articles from *Paradise of the Pacific*. Thanks, too, to Barbara Dunn and her staff at the Hawaiian Historical Society for photocopying articles from *Paradise*. Russ Lynch of the *Honolulu Star-Bulletin* assisted in the search for biographical material on the magazine's editors. Nancy Morris of the Hamilton Library, University of Hawai'i at Mānoa, "discovered" and made available copies of *Paradise of the Pacific Weekly* and *Crossroads of the Pacific*.

❖ Readers may notice an apparent inconsistency in the use of the *'okina*—glottal stop (')—and *kahakō*—macron (ˉ). The contemporary Hawaiian *'okina* and *kahakō* appear only in the introductions the editor has contributed to this book, but the original orthography of the *Paradise of the Pacific* articles has been retained. Other kinds of inconsistencies occur (such as variations in capitalization and hyphenation); however, the editor chose to edit minimally and to follow as faithfully as possible the articles as they were originally published.

Introduction

Ma's *Paradise of the Pacific*

Ma must have been mad as hell. She had been putting out *Paradise of the Pacific* since the start of the century, and now the self-proclaimed military governor of Hawai'i told her to stop publishing the magazine. It wasn't fair. She hadn't started the damn war.

Within hours of the Japanese attack on Pearl Harbor, Governor Joseph B. Poindexter relinquished control of the government of the Territory of Hawai'i to Maj. Gen. Walter C. Short, commanding general of the Hawaiian Department. Short took complete control of government and suspended the writ of habeas corpus. Civilians would be tried for even minor traffic offenses in provost courts presided over by military officers.

Three days later, General Orders No. 14 was issued: "By virtue of the authority vested in me as Military Governor, I hereby order and prohibit, effective at 8:00 A.M., December 12, 1941, the publication, printing, or circulation of all newspapers, magazines, periodicals, the dissemination of news or information by means of any unauthorized printed matter, or by wireless, radio, or press association, except as follows. . . ." Ma scanned the list, finding that the exceptions included the *Star-Bulletin, Advertiser, Hilo Tribune-Herald, Hawaii Press, Maui News,* and *Garden Island* on Kaua'i. Her beloved *Paradise of the Pacific* was not listed. A casualty of war! *Paradise pau?*

Pau, indeed! Ma would see about that.

What Ma said to the military governor was probably a victim of censorship, not that her lips betrayed any military secrets but because of the ripeness of her language. Ma was as "pungent as a Bully Hayes," boasted an employee, referring to that foul-mouthed pirate.

Sure enough, on December 22, General Orders No. 40 was published and *Paradise of the Pacific* was added to the list of publications permitted to go to press. There was no good reason to keep the magazine from being a part of the official press. No one could find a more patriotic publishing company in all of Hawai'i. Jimmie Boyle, the manager, had been a marine, and the previous editor was Lt. Col. Edwin North McClellan, USMC (Ret.). The magazine had reported favorably on the U.S. armed forces in Hawai'i since the Spanish-American War.

There would be strict censorship, of course, but that mattered less to Ma than to editors at the two Honolulu dailies. So what if the monthly *Paradise of the Pacific* couldn't report the comings and goings of warships and troop strength? It never reported that kind of military news anyway. Ma knew that, as long as she didn't offend the censors, she could continue to document daily life in Hawai'i and to report the hopes of its citizens for a better life after the war in the Pacific was won. So that is what she did.

Ma's maiden name was Elinor Alice Veilleux. She was born in a Vermont village called Irasburg, a place so small that it doesn't appear on maps. She arrived in Hawai'i in 1900 and went to work for *Paradise of the Pacific*. The editor, Wray Taylor, was retiring in September and the magazine needed a writer to help William M. "Bill" Langton, the manager, who would take over the editorship as well. Bill was reputedly "one of the best pressmen in the West." The sixteen-page magazine displayed three-color work, tinting, and bronzing. There were five hundred subscribers in Hawai'i, and passengers on steamships, those arriving and departing, were provided with free copies. The Holiday Annual had proved so popular that the forty-eight-page December issue press run was five thousand copies.

Paradise first appeared in January 1888 as an eight-page monthly paper. Backed by Honolulu shipping tycoon Samuel G. Wilder, publisher Thomas G. Thrum and photographer J. J. Williams were coproprietors. The intent of the venture was to lure tourists to Hawai'i. Subscriptions were free and advertisers were guaranteed a circulation of fifteen hundred copies. The owners promised to disseminate "reliable information concerning the Hawaiian Islands, their climate, scenery, volcanic wonders, agricultural and commercial pursuits, as also the many attractions presented by life in the tropics. . . ."

King Kalakaua, impressed by the factual way readers were informed about the small country, sent copies to Hawaiian consuls in foreign cities. Most of them had never set foot in the Islands, and this was an inexpensive way of educating them about the kingdom they represented. As the Journal of the Kingdom, *Paradise* was granted free postage to any foreign destination. Kalakaua later provided public funds to wrap the paper in a cover, making of it a magazine of sorts.

Kalakaua died in 1891, the monarchy was overthrown in 1893, and the Islands were annexed to the United States in 1898. Government subsidies were a thing of the past, and Langton was struggling to pay bills and meet payroll. But that didn't keep Ma from falling in love with the boss. When she wed Bill in 1902, she married the magazine as well. After the honeymoon they became coproprietors, buying out other interests and expanding the printing business. Ma was a go-getter, and Bill didn't reign her in. Who could? Ma's byline began appearing regularly in 1903. Then, a single issue cost fifteen cents. An annual subscription was $1.50, half the weekly wage of a yardman. That year's Holiday Annual explained, "all household servants being Chinese and Japanese, keeping house [in Hawai'i] is less expensive . . . than in the east."

There are precious few scoops for an editor of a monthly magazine. In Honolulu, a town of fifty thousand people by 1910, everyone seemed to know everyone else's business and gossip traveled with the speed of sound. Frustrated as journalists, the Langtons decided to publish a weekly newspaper that would appear on Saturday. They hoped that in this weekly form, *Paradise of the Pacific* would increase its influence by keeping "in touch with the march of events." But to maintain "the tone and style" that they nurtured in the magazine, the Langtons decided not to besmirch the pages of the weekly with politics. This new publication would adhere to a promise of its parent, that "the strife and bitterness incidental to party politics will be rigidly excluded." On the very last day of 1910, *Paradise of the Pacific Weekly* first appeared. The price was ten cents. George Frederick Henshall, thirty-seven years old, was editor, and Bill Langton was associate editor.

Henshall's wife, Helen, was the widow of his elder brother William, a promising Honolulu attorney who had drowned in a shipwreck in San Francisco Bay in 1901. Helen, one of twelve daughters of Julia Afong, a socially prominent *hapa* haole, and the late Chun Afong, a prosperous Chinese sugar planter and merchant, connected her husband to kama'āina elite. A brother-in-law, Abram Stephanus Humphreys, supported the paper by advertising his legal services in each issue.

The editorial copy was well written, even literary. But without reports and comment on government and politics, the weekly newspaper lacked an edge. Readers of cultural news and reviews were affluent but their numbers too small to attract large advertisers. Awash in red ink, the decision was made, most reluctantly, to add politics to the editorial mix. Before doing that, however, to protect the good reputation of *Paradise of the Pacific,* the name of the paper was changed to *Crossroads of the Pacific Weekly.*

The first edition under the new masthead was published on July 15, 1911. Freed of the *Paradise* image, the paper turned crusader, running a series of articles that exposed "political rottenness" at city hall. Municipal government was then new to Honolulu. Joe Fern, the first mayor, was sworn in just two-and-a-half years earlier, in January 1909. A Democrat and unabashed proponent of the spoils system, Mayor Fern was unfailingly loyal to cronies. So there was much to investigate.

The stress and tension of investigative journalism proved too much for Bill Langton, who was ailing. He sold the paper to a thirty-six-year-old feisty editorialist and street fighter, Edward P. Irwin, who took over as editor and publisher of the weekly in January of 1912. A University of Kansas graduate and Spanish-American War veteran, he had come to Hawai'i in 1906 to be a reporter for the *Star-Bulletin.* To balance Irwin's aggressive prose, a genteel and genial writer was named associate editor. Will Sabin was a collegial fellow with a sense of humor. When he reported in the April 26, 1912, issue that there was a move afoot to establish a press club, he noted that dues would not be on a par with the Pacific Club because journalism did not pay that well.

Bill Langton died on January 25, 1913, from pneumonia, in Santa Monica, California. He had gone there a few months earlier to regain his health. Before departing, he signed the business over to Ma, who assumed the chair of both editor and publisher. One of her first acts after Bill's death was to cancel the printing agreement with *Crossroads.* Publisher Irwin found another printer to do the job, but soon gave up the project. The last issue of the weekly, eight letter-size pages, nine-by-twelve inches, appeared on March 28, 1913. Irwin moved to California to work on newspapers there.

Ma was remarried, in May 1913, to the magazine's business manager, James Edward "Jimmie" Boyle. She hyphenated her last name—Langton-Boyle. Jimmie, born in Morris, Minnesota, on St. Patrick's Day in 1881, had come ashore as a U.S. marine in 1910. Like so many other servicemen, when his enlistment was over he stayed in the beautiful Islands. He loved Hawai'i as much as Ma did, and was as tough. They made a formidable team at the publishing house.

Ma's toughness was legendary. A story was often told, that when James Dole notified Ma that he was reducing the size of a Dole Pineapple Co. ad from full page to half, moving it from the back page to the inside, and going from color to black and white, she would have none of it. Marching into his office, Ma pounded on his desk, "Jim Dole, you cheap blankety, blank, blank . . . what kind of man are you?" She handed him a contract for a full-page ad on the back page and in color. "Sign it," she ordered. And he did.

In January 1917, Ma turned over the editorship of the magazine to the genial Will Sabin, then forty-two. A frequent contributor to the magazine since the turn of the century, Sabin published a volume of poetry, *The Edge of the Crater and Other Poems,* with The Paradise of the Pacific Press in 1915. Under Sabin's editorship, the literary quality of the writing improved. A Brooklyn-born adventurer and world traveler, he had come to Hawai'i as a crew member of a sailing ship in August 1898. Dignified in manner and distinguished in appearance, a colleague described him as "a man of letters whose thoughts demanded leisurely formation and thorough expression." His writing forte was wit and satire. Another colleague wrote, "His best efforts were directed toward the lighter side of life; the amusement to be obtained from a well-turned, good-natured pun, the esthetics of a glorious sunset."

Each of Sabin's Holiday Annuals was eagerly awaited, and the daily press in Hawai'i and the Mainland reviewed that issue as they did books. With about a hundred pages of text and several full-color reproductions of paintings and other graphic art, the December issue alone was worth the then $3.50 yearly subscription price.

Ma continued to write an occasional article for *Paradise.* "Her style is vigorous, picturesque and her thought is true," wrote Charles Eugene Banks, editor of the *Hilo Tribune-Herald,* about Ma's report of a visit to Maui. He explained that her prose "escapes that sentimentality which is the weakness of most descriptive articles." Ma was straightforward in everything she did. And kind. Although most of the articles and photos were of Hawaiians and haoles, attention was given to immigrants. Photographs of Asians were flattering and the stories about them warm. An early example, in the October 1903 issue, was a story about the "first Japanese baseball team." A photo showed boys from the Japanese Boarding School in team uniforms posing in the traditional American way. The Japanese population was then more than sixty-one thousand and growing.

By 1924 the Japanese population had doubled and about half of the students in public schools were of Japanese descent, nearly twenty-six thousand of them. A debate over "Americanizing" these nisei children was heated. Sabin tried to calm the waters in the September issue by giving some humorous perspective to the oratorical pyrotechnics: "Is Americanized the right word, or modernized? All that is modern is not American. Paris gowns, for instance. And all that is American is not modern. 'Pep,' for instance."

In a radical departure of policy, that December Sabin published an incendiary article by Edward Irwin, his former boss at *Crossroads of the Pacific*. Irwin had returned to Hawai'i to become city editor of the *Advertiser* in 1917 and was named editor a year later. But after a number of lawsuits over his editorials, he left the paper in December 1920. At about that time he married a *hapa* haole schoolteacher in Honolulu, Bernice Pi'ilani Cook.

The article revealed Irwin's racist dislike of Asian children who were American citizens by accident of birthplace: "Even if it be possible, by education and training to give the American-born Oriental an American viewpoint, we cannot change his blood, alter his features or heighten his stature." He complained about their monkeylike "flat features, protruding teeth and short legs."

Irwin wasn't the only racist in town. A year earlier Honolulu supervisors changed the designation of streets named after Japanese, replacing them with Hawaiian words. Uemura Lane was now Mapu Lane. One meaning for "mapu" is ape. Irwin was relieved that Japanese "have shown little disposition to intermarry with other races and have not as yet materially contaminated the Caucasian and Polynesian blood of the Islands." The headline, "Ed Irwin More than Suggests that We Should Not Try to 'Americanize' Orientals in Hawaii, Even If We Can," made clear that the opinions expressed were those of the author and not the magazine. Sabin commented editorially: "Mr. Irwin's treatment is different from any we remember reading in Honolulu print." Irwin would continue to expound anti-Japanese views in the columns of his own newspaper, called the *Weekly Times* (later *Honolulu Times*). Fistfights and lawsuits followed some issues of that paper.

To counter vituperous Irwins and boorish supervisors, territorial officials emphasized a better side of Paradise—and advertised it on Aloha Tower, which was under construction in December 1925. Ma wrote: "Aloha! This beautiful word is to glow from the tower at the harbor entrance to Honolulu. . . . It cries welcome and love. It can do this in truth and sincerity because Aloha is the real spirit of these islands."

Charles Banks, who had written so flatteringly about Ma's prose style, became editor of the magazine in September 1925. He took over until Will Sabin returned from a lengthy vacation to Brooklyn, New York. Early in 1926 Sabin was back at work editing the February issue of *Paradise*. In April 1928 Ma again took over the editor's chair, holding it until the spring of 1935.

Ma never again wore two hats, leaving the editorship to younger souls, save the ubiquitous Will Sabin, who served a final hitch from November 1935 to April 1936. Ray M. Frisen, who edited just four issues, relieved him. Replacing him was Edwin North McClellan, a prolific writer and Hawaiian history buff. As an undergraduate at the University of Pennsylvania, he had been editor of *Punch Bowl,* a student humor magazine.

McClellan first saw Hawai'i in 1908 from the deck of the USS *Wisconsin,* one of the battleships in Teddy Roosevelt's Great White Fleet. That flotilla stopped in Hawai'i for about ten days before continuing a circumnavigation of the world. Later, in 1925 to 1927, he was executive officer of the marine barracks at Pearl Harbor. Stopping in Honolulu in 1935 on his way to Shanghai, to be second-in-command of the Fourth Marine Regiment, he prophesied enemy air strikes on Hawai'i and called for strengthening defenses of air bases: "The shocks caused by German submarines are nothing compared to those bound to happen in the next war by air ships."

McClellan retired from the Corps on June 30, 1936, and in August settled into the editor's chair at *Paradise.* Although he held a law degree from George Washington University, writing was his real love. The author of a history, *The United States Marine Corps in the World War,* and a Navy law book, he was a frequent contributor to military publications. McClellan's editorship of *Paradise* lasted four years and coincided with America's preparation for war in the Pacific.

The strength of the armed services in Hawai'i was 25,512 in 1936. McClellan had easy access to bases and had friends on them. His first Holiday Annual carried illustrated stories on the Marines, Coast Guard and Hawai'i National Guard. A single issue, then, cost thirty-five cents, and an annual subscription was four dollars. A copy of the Holiday Annual was a dollar.

McClellan was an expert on international relations and added such analysis to the editorial pages of *Paradise*. And his articles showed an understanding of military problems. He was unfailingly sympathetic to the needs of the services. But so too were stories appearing under other bylines. That result was not achieved because McClellan was an autocratic editor, insisting on a single viewpoint and a common style, but because he wrote those other stories under one or another nom de plume—Bailey S. Marshall, Shoemaker McDonald, Donald Dickson, Albert Wray, Richard Donaldson, Anne Oberlin, Neal O'Hara, Elizabeth Quinton, Ned North, Eddie Mack, Elsie Dinswood, and E. N. Bailey.

With a war about to begin, McClellan volunteered for active duty in July 1940 and his last issue appeared in August 1940. When the bombs fell on Pearl Harbor, the magazine's editor was Henry E. Dougherty. Up to that historic moment, Dougherty's biggest story had been President Roosevelt's visit to Hawai'i in 1934. Dougherty, an *Advertiser* reporter, then moonlighting as associate editor of *Paradise,* reported the president's promise that the United States would not be an aggressor nation in the Pacific, that the U.S. military presence in Hawai'i was for the national defense: "These forces must ever be considered an instrument of continuing peace for our nation's policy seeks peace and does not look to imperialistic aims." The Japanese military, of course, did not believe a word of it and made plans to let the president know that seven years later.

When Dougherty returned to the Mainland in October 1942, because of an illness in his family, Eileen McCann O'Brien, a graduate of Wellesley College who began her journalistic career as beauty editor of the *Boston Record-American,* replaced him. She later became the *Advertiser*'s woman's page editor, and just prior to joining *Paradise* was in the public relations department of Consolidated Amusement Company. Under her leadership *Paradise* shifted away from analysis of international events to coverage of the social and economic effects of the war on Honolulu, especially those caused by the increase in population. There were about 136,000 members of the armed services then in Hawai'i, boosting the total population to some 446,000.

Ma served as a buffer between the military government and her editorial staff, to give them as much independence as wartime patriotism and the censor allowed. To keep on the good side of the military government, the magazine printed in each issue "public information" pieces from and about the various services. These articles, though propaganda, were professionally written, most of the authors being journalists and writers who had been drafted. But some journalists, to their consternation, ended up as censors. One wrote in the November 1942 issue of *Paradise:* "No one has much aloha for censorship. It is accepted—rather gracelessly in some cases—as one of the necessary evils of war. Nor will the censor find many to help him prove that such unpopularity is not deserved."

By the spring of 1944 Ma was sick of body and tired of working seven days a week. Circulation was up, primarily because of the magazine's popularity with thousands of mainlanders stationed in Hawai'i—military and civilian. They collected copies as mementos and sent issues home to family and friends. There were then nearly 859,000 people in Hawai'i, with about 407,000 of those in the military. By comparison, when Ma began working for *Paradise* at the turn of the century the population of the territory was just over 154,000, with 293 of those in the armed forces. With the war almost won, the military and war-related civilian population would soon decrease. This was a good time for Ma to sell, and she offered the business—magazine and printing plant—to her beloved employees.

Taking control on All Fools' Day, the fourteen employee/owners announced that there would be no major editorial changes. However, they did promise to cover more of the Pacific "as the interest of millions of Americans develops in that vast area." A kahuna blessed the enterprise by drenching the offices on Beretania Street with coconut milk that gushed from a trinity of holes in the husk. This admixture of religious symbolism promised that Ma's blending of Hawaiian good will and Calvinistic hard work would continue at *Paradise of the Pacific.*

With the daily battles over, Ma and Jimmie stayed home a lot, seldom visiting with friends. Jimmie died first, on December 6, 1945. Seven months later, in July, Ma died. The *Advertiser* ran an editorial obituary that was simply headlined "Ma Boyle."

"So Ma Boyle is dead. That means to many residents of Hawai'i the departure from this life of a notable person. Hawai'i may have had, still has, many picturesque citizens, but it has never had one more picturesque than Mrs. Elinor Langton-Boyle. With a heavy hand and a soft heart, she beat her employees with stern words and kind actions into production of *Paradise of the Pacific* for many years. And under her dictatorship, at once both fascistic and benevolent, they made a good magazine of it, a beautiful and informative house journal for the Islands. When she retired from active command, she handed the publication over to those who had labored under her. She was a fine woman, was Ma Boyle."

Ma was cremated on July 17, 1946, and her ashes interred with those of her first husband, Bill Langton. The Reverend Henry P. Judd conducted graveside services at O'ahu cemetery.

I

Prelude to War in the Pacific

Only a decade after the U.S. annexation of Hawai'i in 1898, Congress authorized construction of a naval base at Pearl Harbor. From this strategic bastion the relationship between U.S. naval strength and American foreign policy would be demonstrated in the Pacific. As U.S. Adm. Alfred T. Mahan phrased it, "one of the functions of force is to give moral ideas time to take root."

The island of O'ahu was destined to become the best defended fortress on the Alaska-Hawai'i-Panama defensive perimeter. In 1907 Fort Shafter became the first permanent post for federal troops in Hawai'i, and 234 men were stationed there. Two years later Schofield Barracks was established near Wahiawa. Troop strength rose to about 600 men. During the First World War the number of soldiers increased to as many as 12,463. But after the armistice, the size of the force was reduced to fewer than 5,000 men.

Events in Asia during the next decade, however, brought about another military buildup in Hawai'i. Japan invaded Manchuria in 1931, quit the League of Nations in 1933, and opened undeclared war against China in 1937. On December 12 of that year, Japanese planes strafed, bombed, and sank the American gunboat *Panay* as it attempted to evacuate American and British officials from Nanking, China. Two crewmen were killed. A week later the infamous Rape of Nanking began.

Signs of impending war with Japan were ominous and civilians in Hawai'i began to prepare for that inevitability. Beginning in 1939 an annual blackout exercise to coincide with military maneuvers was conducted in Honolulu. And in Kailua and other rural areas near military installations, civil defense units were established.

In 1940 an emergency disaster plan was adopted. Honolulu women began making surgical bandages and dressings. The local Red Cross gave first-aid classes, formed a Women's Motor Corps, and made plans to establish a blood bank in Honolulu. The following year, Consolidated Amusement Company presented the Red Cross with its first ambulance.

The seven sugar plantations on O'ahu organized a Plantation Provisional Police Force in July 1940, and members began firearms instruction at the Honolulu police range. So valued was this paramilitary force that its 562 men were asked to participate in Army maneuvers. Troops in Hawai'i then numbered about twenty-five thousand. That number would grow to nearly forty-two thousand in 1941. Schofield Barracks had become the largest Army installation under the American flag. The primary mission of the troops there was to defend Pearl Harbor from Japanese raiders or invaders—and saboteurs and assassins.

Fear of what Hawai'i's Japanese population would do in the event of war with Japan had preoccupied military planners. Various plans were proposed, including taking local Japanese "hostages." In August, fingerprinting and registering of aliens was begun. A year earlier, the FBI had reopened its Honolulu office to investigate possible sabotage and espionage.

Civilians, too, worried that Japanese nationals in Hawai'i would act against them. At cocktail parties a joke was told: A nervous haole woman asks her Japanese maid if she would kill her mistress if Japan attacks Hawai'i. "No," the maid replies, "that's the gardener's job." John F. B. Stokes, a retired ethnologist from the Bishop Museum, expounded on his belief that Japan had infiltrated the Islands with saboteurs, and that Hawai'i had become a base for Japan's ambitions in the Pacific. At the close of the year a five-man Espionage Bureau was established in the Honolulu Police Department. Police Lt. Jack Burns (later an elected governor of Hawai'i) was assigned as the liaison between the police and the FBI.

In a plebiscite conducted at the 1940 election, 67 percent of Hawai'i voters called for eventual statehood for Hawai'i.

On November 22, Governor Poindexter drew the first number in the Hawai'i draft lottery. In December, the Navy activated the new Kāne'ohe Naval Air Station. Construction of another air base, to be the largest in the Pacific, on twenty-seven hundred acres at Barbers

Point was underway. The editor of *Paradise* commented: "Not since the wars of conquest, when Kamehameha the Great consolidated the island group . . . has conflict reared its head so close to this archipelago. We heard ominous echoes during the First World War, but they were echoes only. Today actual war clouds are just beyond our island horizon."

Along with more troops came civilian personnel and defense workers, which put the total of newcomers at about two hundred thousand. This sudden increase in the percentage of males in the population, most of them whites between twenty and forty, caused social problems—real and perceived. The Women's Christian Temperance Union in Honolulu asked that drinking fountains be provided in convenient places so that the men could quench thirst with water rather than beer. That failing, they advocated the establishment of milk bars. The real need was more police. On July 28 a civilian police reserve was formed on Oʻahu and 120 men began training on August 23. In three months they would be on armed patrol.

Honolulu civic leaders had warned residents: "The Army and Navy are not here to protect the population of Honolulu; their duty is to defend Hawaii as one of the most vital parts of the American Defense system. In case of emergency the civilian population must be prepared to care for itself." In April a Major Disaster Council was established.

Unbeknownst to people in Hawaiʻi, decisions had been made in Washington that placed them in harm's way. From late January of 1941 through the end of March, high-level American and British military staffs had met secretly in Washington, D.C., to develop war plans. Dubbed the ABC-1 Plan, it called for beating Germany before taking on Japan. A month later, American, British, and Dutch officers met in Singapore to plan strategic operations against Japan in the event it attacked the United States. On July 26 President Roosevelt nationalized the armed forces of the Philippines.

On October 1 the Twenty-fifth Infantry Division was commissioned at Schofield Barracks. The territorial legislature enacted the Hawaiʻi Defense Act, giving the governor great authority to act in case of an emergency. A Territorial Guard was established and recruitment was begun. On the twenty-first, the Navy sued to condemn 117 acres for expansion of Pearl Harbor.

On November 3 the American ambassador to Japan, Joseph Grew, warned Washington that Japan might resort to war measures "with dramatic and dangerous suddenness." That warning went unheeded, despite growing civilian consensus in Hawai'i that armed conflict with Japan was imminent. On November 27 Washington warned Hawaiian commanders that hostile action could be expected. That very day the Japanese attack fleet steamed out of Tankan Bay, in northern Japan. On November 30 *The Honolulu Advertiser* headline read "JAPANESE MAY STRIKE OVER WEEKEND."

The attacking Japanese fleet was twenty-three hundred miles northwest of Pearl Harbor on December 3. On that day Japanese consulates in the United States burned secret documents. On December 6 only 125 of the Army's 234 planes on O'ahu were operational. That evening, in a last-minute effort to prevent war in the Pacific, President Franklin Delano Roosevelt made a personal appeal to Emperor Hirohito. It was too late.

Pacific War?

❖ Never before has the Eastern Pacific faced the possible threat of a major war as this year. Wars between groups of Hawaiians, War of 1812, Mexican War, War with the Confederacy, Chinese-Japanese War, Spanish-American War, Japanese-Russian War, and the World War, all left impressions on the Eastern Pacific Area; but never in the past has Mars glared so personally toward that theatre as during this year.

Hawaii is the nearest American soil, that may be classified as continental, to the raw edges of the pirate-like, undeclared war, now raging in Asia. The Philippines and Guam may be defined as "temporary" possessions, and Wake Island is but a sand dot. In principle, America may be said to be in as much a state of war as either Japan or China, for neither has declared war, and the United States has not taken advantage of the Neutrality Act to affirmatively express a neutral status. American National Defense personnel—Army, Navy, and Marines—are present in many parts of the theater of war. American material, including liquid fuel and cotton, is reported as being received in Asia.

The bombing of the *President Hoover* and Flagship *Augusta*, the sinking of the U.S.S. *Panay*, violations of treaties, and other war-like acts, suggest the possibility that the United States may be in a state of quasi-war that might evolve into actual war. Indeed, it was reported that, at first, the survivors of the *Panay* believed that their country was at war with Japan, until they learned the horrible truth.

Hawaii of America looks westward, toward this vicious fury of chaotic killing, with confident hope that the United States will honorably avoid war.

American National Defense personnel in Hawaii and the 310,956 American citizens (including many dual citizens) here will be the first Americans to feel the scorching breath of war should it breathe eastward. So will the 85,759 aliens residing in Hawaii.

First published January 1938.

Look at the chart of the Hawaiian Islands extending about 1,445 miles from the Island of Hawaii northwestward to Kure (Ocean) Island—a royal coastline. These islands of Hawaii form an island-ladder approach for about eleven hundred miles from Kauai to alien islands that in turn lead right to the present conflict.

America must be ready if war should come. It may not come if we are ready.

America "On Defense" in the Pacific

❖ Will history repeat itself? In 1914, Assistant Secretary of the Navy Franklin Delano Roosevelt asserted that our national defense was unready for war and urged that his country prepare—the World War followed. Twenty-four years later, in 1938, President Roosevelt made the same assertion and the same urge. Will history repeat itself, and will the Second World War begin in 1938?

National defense means an efficient national offense. The United States cannot be defended by waiting on our coasts for the enemy. All of our foreign wars were "defensive wars"—even the Mexican War when Our Navy presented the Union with California and its hinterland. Vital phases of every one of our wars with foreign enemies occurred on foreign soil or water.

During the American Revolution (1775–1783), small naval squadrons harassed British commerce in European waters, landings were made in England, while France and Holland provided naval bases in Europe or the West Indies. We won the French Naval War of 1798–1801 because of naval victories in the West Indian area and other foreign parts. The War of 1812 (1812–1815) was an American victory due almost entirely to American naval achievements in seas removed from our coasts. It was during this war that the first American warship (frigate *Essex*) appeared in the eastern Pacific; that the first American warship (*Sir Andrew Hammond*) visited Hawaii; and that the first American naval base was established in the Pacific—at Nukuhiva, Marquesas. The Mexican War (1846–1848) was fought entirely beyond the boundaries of the United States. Even during our domestic quarrel of 1861–1865 vessels of the two American navies competed for supremacy on alien oceans. No battles of any character were fought on American soil or waters during the Spanish-American

First published February 1938.

War of 1898. Finally, during the grandest "defensive war" in American history, millions of American citizens went to Europe and Asia, in 1917 and 1918, to defend the United States.

"Invasion is not what this country has to fear," wrote Assistant Secretary of the Navy Franklin Delano Roosevelt in January of 1914. "In time of war would we be content like the turtle to withdraw into our shell and see an enemy supersede us in every outlying part, usurp our commerce and destroy our influence as a nation throughout the world? Yet this will happen just as surely as we can be sure of anything human if an enemy of the United States obtains control of the seas. And that control is dependent absolutely on one thing—the preponderant efficiency of the battle fleet.

"Our national defense must extend all over the western hemisphere, must go out a thousand miles into the sea, must embrace the Philippines and over the seas wherever our commerce may be. To hold the Panama Canal, Alaska, American Samoa, Guam, Puerto Rico, the naval base at Guantanamo, and the Philippines, we must have battleships. We must create a navy not only to protect our shores and our possessions but also our merchant ships in time of war, no matter where they may go."

That was twenty-four years ago. In 1938 President Roosevelt again feels that the army and navy are not adequate for war and recommends to Congress that the country be efficiently placed "on defense."

"As Commander-in-Chief of the Army and Navy it is my constitutional duty to report that our national defense, in light of increasing armament of other nations, is inadequate for the purposes of national security and requires an increase for that reason," wrote the President in a special message to Congress on January 28, 1938. The Chief Executive made it clear that he based his recommendations "not on aggression but on defense."

"Adequate defense means that for the protection not only of our coasts but communities far removed from our coasts we must keep any potential enemy many hundred miles away from our continental limits," explained President Roosevelt.

"We cannot assume our defense would be limited to one ocean or one coast," and "we cannot be certain the connecting link—Panama Canal—would be safe. Adequate defense affects therefore simultaneous defense of every part of the United States."

While urging Congress to appropriate adequate funds for the army, the President recommended that funds, approximated by officials at almost a billion dollars, be provided with which to improve the navy by one-fifth.

Vital as is Hawaii in American National Defense in the Pacific, her status is constantly becoming more valuable to the entire country, as well as receiving impressive recognition. The President's recommendation means much to Hawaii.

The chief mission of Our Navy (including aviation), in war, is to protect our maritime interests, such as the foreign trade routes over which a considerable portion of American national prosperity flows during war and peace. The navy must guard the trade routes when America is neutral, for otherwise our country would be economically strangled. Another naval mission is to aid the army in guarding, or preventing an invasion of, the United States, which, in the Pacific area, includes Hawaii, Alaska, and American Samoa; but probably not the Philippines and Guam.

In a "defensive war," in the Pacific against an Asiatic opponent, the mission of Our Navy would include control of the sea and air in the area between the American continents and a curved line (really the western boundary of the United States) from Panama, through Samoa and Wake, to the American Aleutians. The naval mission also would include keeping American trade routes open all over the world. Advanced naval and air bases, if not made available by allies, would have to be acquired by force. America should accelerate the speed of preparedness to the maximum.

Hawaii will be the powerful center of her country's defense in such a war.

Dual Citizenship and Expatriation
GEORGE SAKAMAKI

❖ There are five general ways in which citizenship is acquired. One is by birth, which groups the nations of the world into three principal classifications: (1) nations that observe the Civil Law practice whereby a child's citizenship is determined by the nationality of its parents, as in Germany, Japan, Norway, Sweden, Switzerland, and others; (2) nations that espouse the Common Law doctrine, which awards citizenship according to place of birth, as is the system in countries like Argentina, Denmark, the Netherlands, and Portugal; and (3) nations that combine the law of blood and the law of soil, including Belgium, France, Great Britain, Greece, Italy, Russia, and the United States.

These divisions are by no means clear cut, and a lack of uniformity produces confused and conflicting situations so as make it possible for a person to own two or more citizenships, knowingly or unknowingly. A person may knowingly become a dual citizen through naturalization, option, marriage, legitimation, and through other affirmative actions, if he gains his second citizenship without having divested himself of his original nationality. A person may unknowingly be dual, as in the case of a natural-born dual citizen claimed by the United States for having been born on American soil and at the same time by some foreign country holding to the law of natural descent. We are concerned in this article with the latter class of "mixed subjects" inasmuch as the problem of dual citizenship in Hawaii is focused on American citizens of Japanese ancestry.

Americans of Japanese parentage in Hawaii have been given a clean bill of health by the Congressional Statehood investigation committee (see Senate Document No. 151, 75th Congress, 3rd Session, Washington, D.C.). The verdict has not softened their desire to become better Americans and more deserving of the confidence placed in them. Notwithstanding this, there are those who are skeptical of these

---

First published April 1938.

young Americans, despite the fact that "the history of Hawaii and of America," to quote Samuel W. King, "shows how each racial group at first suffered under various restrictions and discriminations, only to win eventual full acceptance as fellow Americans."

The problem of dual citizenship has been raised in Hawaii with little regard to an essential fact in the situation—that double nationality and dual allegiance are not synonymous. Young Americans in Hawaii definitely do not owe allegiance to Japan; they are not serving two masters. Most of the Americans of Japanese descent born prior to December 1, 1924, and who have not yet renounced their Japanese citizenship are not aware they are unwitting victims of a conflict in nationality laws. Take my case as an example. Born in Hawaii, I had always regarded myself *ipso facto* an American without any obligation to Japan. Only a day or two before I testified before the Congressional Statehood committee last fall, I learned that all persons of Japanese antecedent born prior to December 1, 1924, were automatically citizens of Japan, according to Japanese law, regardless of whether their births were or were not registered with Japanese authorities. That left me technically a dual citizen, and it was with great embarrassment that I so testified. A few weeks ago, however, another member of my family had the occasion to check on her status and found that I had been expatriated back in 1925. Thus, I find now that I am not in possession of two citizenships and that I have not been a dual citizen for more than twelve years. I mention this to point out that registration of births and even expatriation are frequently executed without the knowledge of the parties most concerned and in no way imply divided allegiance.

In some cases duality continues because of inertia; in defense of this is the feeling that because they consider themselves loyal to the United States and to the United States only, they need not be concerned as to what the nationality law of some foreign country might be. Their position and attitude, although assailed, should be understandable to fellow Americans of other national strains that likewise do not bother to find out what laws might be in the land of their foreign ancestors.

Nations as well as individuals object to conflicting claims on citizenship, yet are powerless in most cases to alter the situation that is so much part of every nation's very existence. It is to "paradoxical Japan" that we must turn for an example of governmental action to end double nationality. By revising her laws in 1916 and again in 1924, Japan now offers every American-born Japanese the opportunity to divorce himself from Japan by presenting evidence the United States will take care of him after Japan lets him go. Necessary documents include (1) a copy of the family record; (2) an American birth certificate; (3) written approval of parents or guardian if the applicant is still a minor; and (4) written consent of the family council where step-parents make out approvals. These papers are filed with the Japanese Minister of the Interior through the local consulate together with an application in Japanese requesting separation from Japan. The Official Gazette published in Tokyo will announce all applications granted, and the consul in turn will notify each applicant of his estrangement. Thereupon, the head of the applicant's family should file a report of loss of Japanese citizenship with the registrar of the family's record in Japan.

The routine is not as simple as it sounds. The majority of our Americans of Japanese ancestry are handicapped by not knowing the Japanese language. The initial move to secure a copy of the family record frequently checks them into inaction. Many find they are not registered in Japan and so cannot obtain the all so necessary prerequisite, the family register. Failure of parents to record births with the Board of Health, inability to uncover living witnesses to testify to their birth in Hawaii, and other difficulties too numerous to enumerate here are faced by applicants for expatriation. Some cases, indeed, offer no solution under existing American and Japanese laws, rendering dual citizens utterly helpless before accusations of duality.

Granting that dual citizenship and expatriation, in their ramifications and in the light of extenuating circumstances, can be considered rationally and with sympathy, there is small doubt but that all our young American citizens in Hawaii will "win eventual full acceptance as fellow-Americans."

Speed! Congress! Speed!

❖ Speed! Congress! Speed! Swift speed is of the essence today on Capitol Hill. Our Country has owned Hawaii since 1898. For over forty years Congress—charged by the Constitution with the vital duty of preventing war, declaring war, and winning war—has been cogitating over the problem of National Defense in the Pacific. Acts must now replace cogitation. Immediate demand is being made now for the solution to the problem, which is more than complicated by an air-power so impressive that even a well-informed imagination can hardly believe what it knows to be a fact.

"There is a new range and speed to offense," said President Roosevelt to Congress on January 12, 1939. "Therefore it has become necessary for every American to re-study present defense against the possibilities of present offense against us."

"The Baker Board report of a few years ago is completely out of date," and "we cannot guarantee a long period free from attack in which we could prepare," continued the President.

Congress should start right now to provide adequate funds with which to create a perfect defense of the United States Pacific Coast Line (Aleutians-Hawaii-Samoa-Panama), of which Hawaii is the keystone. Protective power will radiate in all directions by air, on and under the sea, from this Pacific Stronghold. A zone will be formed through which no enemy can penetrate. If Hawaii falls, however, the Pacific Coast is invitingly wide open. Other parts of this curved defensive line need first-aid treatment by Congress, but today it is of Hawaii we write. Speed, and more speed, by Congress, is the requirement at this very moment.

Warplanes that can reach Hawaii from the Mainland in ten hours or less have thrown the minds of old-fashioned strategists into a tailspin. Air-bases in Alaska, along the United States Pacific Coast, at Panama, and on various isolated Pacific Islands force respect for

---

First published February 1939.

American airpower. Warplanes that fill the air, like an Army covers the ground, are a consternating reality. Mobility and power of aviation modify methods of war even though they cannot change the Principles of War. The warplane of the future may have such radius and speed that naval plane-carriers will be unnecessary for American defense in the Pacific. All this should accelerate the speed of Congress in efficiently facing the facts and solving Pacific Problems.

The United States Army guards Hawaii so that it will always be available to the Fleet when it arrives in Paradise. State Department and other experts, with their pacts, conferences, and reductions in armament, have created the present situation. Congress should, in this extremity, follow the suggestions of well-informed naval, air, and military advisers.

Times have changed mightily. Lots of money is required, but Congress will save money in the long run if it follows the advice of military, naval, and air officers who undoubtedly have prepared a master-plan for American National Defense in the Pacific. Piece-meal and muddling through spell defeat.

Naval, military, and air defenses of Hawaii must be created—or at least started—to resist modern methods of attack by modern material and equipped personnel. Dry-docks; mine base; destroyer facilities; hospitals; land plane and seaplane bases; light, power, and water supply systems for National Defense; fuel containers; and a lot more shore necessities must be created or strengthened. Every project planned must be secure against explosive, gas, and incendiary bombs from the air. Adequate communication systems are needed. An additional channel from Pearl Harbor to the sea would help. Comfortable housing—and sufficient—for commissioned, warrant, enlisted, and civilian personnel attached to National Defense is required if a victorious morale is to be maintained. These are only a few thought-producing necessities of the many that actually exist.

Aliens should be excluded by law from certain restricted naval and military areas. Possession of photographs, of drawings and other similar material, of banned areas and objects should be made legally punishable. Only loyal personnel should be allowed to view the National Defense of Hawaii. Counter-espionage defense is an essential.

A tunnel, through the Koolaus, and adequate highways for National Defense missions as well as for civilian use should be constructed. Adequate docking facilities in Hawaii should anticipate war.

Networks of aviation routes, with protected bases, should be created within the American sphere of influence in the Pacific. Hawaii should be made so close, by air and sea, to continental United States that the mooted and misunderstood problem of Hawaiian self-sufficiency (from the food and supply viewpoint) will be perfectly solved.

Civilian Hawaii should receive every consideration from Congress. That they possess perfect morale is imperatively essential to a successful American National Defense. Discrimination—withholding rights and privileges guaranteed to American citizens by the Constitution from the People of Hawaii—is a blow at the national security of the United States. Some attention should be paid to guarding civilians against air and gas attacks.

A war-government for Hawaii should be outlined by law and detail everything to be installed when war or serious emergency threatens. The area of the Territory of Hawaii should be logically defined and an efficient government provided for the remaining American territory in the Pacific. The Flag should be raised over all American islands—like Christmas Island for example—in the Pacific. If a Department of Territories is not created by Congress for this purpose, all the territories—except Hawaii—should be placed under the jurisdiction of that Executive Department that can most efficiently administer their affairs in both war and peace. The United States should withdraw from the Philippines as soon as practicable. Such a withdrawal will increase the power of United States National Defense. While Guam might be held in peacetime, it would be well to provide for relinquishing it upon the approach of war. However, until the United States withdraws from Guam it must possess some degree of defense regardless of alien criticism.

Speed! Congress! More and more speed! Congress!!

Our Hawaii Is Absolutely American

E. V. WILCOX

❖ Visit the Archives of Hawaii to secure information. In that building—Waikiki of Iolani Palace—is lodged the true story of Hawaii. Although the earliest original document is dated 1790, authent that Hawaii should be solidly and unquestionably American in feeling and action. By the same token it becomes the duty of us mainlanders to back up Hawaii in her resolution to keep her Americanism undefiled.

The amazing pranks of the buffoons and bullies who are turning Europe and Asia back into the Dark Ages may have the effect of directing our attention to our own affairs more realistically. Perhaps in so doing we may take occasion to ponder for a while on the meaning of Hawaii to us. The importance of these Islands is out of all proportion to their size. For the moment let us disregard the lure of their elysian climate, the leis, the hula, the aloha welcome, and the rainbows. Let us consider their military and political significance.

Hawaii is our western front, our occidental lanai. The latch key is out and leis and alohas are ready for friendly guests. But there are also the military fortifications, Pearl Harbor Naval Base, and other equally warm receptions for enemies.

As to the loyalty of the American and Hawaiian elements of the population of the Islands, there can be no doubt. It is only the large number of Japanese that introduces a moot question for argument. That point has recently been hotly debated. Hawaii's appeal for statehood has brought the matter of Japanese allegiance to the fore. The opponents of statehood for Hawaii have pointed to the occasional occurrence of strikes in which there appeared to be a sort of "Japanese front." We have been reminded that Japan, in general, considers all Japanese as citizens of Japan, even those born in the second or third generation in other countries. The maintenance of Japanese language schools in Hawaii and the alleged propaganda from Japan have

---

First published December 1939.

caused many to wonder where Hawaiian-born Japanese would stand in case of war with Japan.

Now I wish emphatically to deny that I am holding a brief for the Japanese. My natural bias is rather against that race. But let us try to look at the thing calmly. About 81 percent of the 415,991 population of Hawaii is native-born as compared with 74 percent in Massachusetts, Rhode Island, and Connecticut. Must we also question the loyalty of New England? Only 67 percent of the inhabitants of New York City are native-born, 64 percent in Hoboken, 70 percent in Boston, and 75 percent in Chicago. Perhaps these cities will bear watching as closely as Honolulu. A couple of months ago I spent a few hours of a Sunday afternoon in Lincoln Park, Chicago. But St. Gaudens' statue of Lincoln was about the only American thing in the park. In the throng of people I saw few American faces and heard but few English words in the Babel of European tongues.

Are the Hawaiian Japanese more intimately tied by sentiment to Osaka and Kobe than are the Chicago Hungarians to Budapest? Will the Italian Colony in New York make faces at Mussolini while the Hawaiian Japanese kowtow to Emperor Hirohito? In this whole controversy about the loyalty of the Japanese citizens of Hawaii, I fear we are dealing more with individual opinions than with facts based on substantial research. Personally, I believe that a considerable number of the foreign-born Japanese in Hawaii might side with Japan against the United States in the event of war. But only 9 percent of Hawaiian Japanese are alien-born, and from my own experience with them in Hawaii, I feel that the vast majority of the other 91 percent of them would not return to Japan if they had a chance and would join with their American and Hawaiian fellow-citizens to prevent Japan from getting a toehold in Hawaii. They know that if Hawaii was to be taken over by Japan, they would automatically become coolies in place of American citizens and would drop back to hoofing it in wooden sandals at a fifty-cent wage. They would look more than twice at the motor car and other luxuries they now enjoy before taking a blind leap into the musty feudalism of *Dai Nippon*.

Needless to say. I do not mean to imply that a Japanese or Italian or Pole or Greek becomes eligible for membership in the Mayflower Society by merely learning how to drive a Ford, or dial a radio, or get a job at five dollars a day. But the second generation of Japanese or other immigrant races at least begin to appreciate the advantages of the American system in liberty of action, speech, and in physical comforts. Realization of these facts is a start toward becoming American.

Perhaps we have worried more than was necessary over the persistent propaganda of Japan, Germany, Russia, and Italy in the United States, setting forth in rosy colors the special virtues of their kind of shackles, gags, and political murder for keeping their people in crouching submission to tyranny. But I for one refuse to believe that they have made many converts by such tactics. We should by all means continue to expose these tricks. The conflict between hokum and common sense is as old as mankind. However, let us not be too easily persuaded that the Japanese in Hawaii are too stupid to choose wisely between Japan and American Hawaii. So long as American-born citizens of foreign parentage cannot guess five minutes in advance the kind of political chaos in which the latest model of dictator may indulge, we may reasonably assume that these offspring of alien races will gradually come to prefer the governmental system of the United States to the messy goulash of European politics.

Anyhow, the men and women who, during the past hundred years, have made Hawaii what it is know better than the casual visitor how to fit the various human elements in these Islands into the American pattern. One must lick the *poi* from one's fingers more than once before one becomes a genuine *Kamaaina*. It is not easy for one race to understand the ways of another. Long, intimate association helps toward that end. That's why I have faith in Hawaii. Beyond question, Hawaii has a racial problem. So has Chicago and New York and Boston and Pittsburgh. I do not see why Hawaii should be singled out as being especially unable to find a solution to the problem.

Finally, my conception of Hawaii is that of a strategic American outpost standing boldly out yonder in the Pacific, two thousand miles from continental United States, rightly proud of her past history, as loyal as any state in the Union, and fully capable of maintaining law and order. Her political and economic affairs have long been in efficient American hands. As a source of sugar, pineapples, and other tropical products, she stands the United States—of which she is a loyal part—in good stead. Why not gracefully recognize these facts and help Hawaii to continue her progress along the traditional American route and cease losing sleep about the allegiance and trustworthiness of the American people who are domiciled in Hawaii?

Naval Power in the Pacific
JOHN WILLIS

❖ The United States fleet was never based in Hawaii for sentimental reasons. When the new arrangement goes into effect, creating three fleets—Atlantic, Pacific, and Asiatic—the Pacific fleet will still be based here. The reasons have been told and retold: to guard the western ocean approaches to the United States. But recently President Roosevelt said that America does not propose to lose control of any ocean touching American shores. Finally, therefore, the Pacific fleet will be created to control the Pacific Ocean.

Vast sums are to be expended on defense projects in this area, centering in Hawaii. That Uncle Sam proposes to control the waters from the Philippines to Panama and from Hawaii to Samoa, and perhaps farther south, is evident. The aggressor nations have brought about this decision. America must be protected. No aggressor will be permitted to get within an area of thousands of miles away, if the American navy is permitted to function properly.

All the building, all the improvements at Pearl Harbor, and all the naval air bases and other defense points in Hawaii point to continued presence of a huge force of ships and men in these waters.

Usually reliable sources have assembled impressive figures on proposed naval projects in Hawaii. Allotments for this district, available at the beginning of the New Year, show an unexpended balance of more than $60 million. The amount is more than double the $30 million unexpended appropriations at the end of 1939, the figures say. Appropriation bills passed by Congress for the fiscal years 1940 and 1941 included a total of more than $80 million for public works projects in the Hawaiian sector and Pacific waters.

This sum has been broken down into the following items: the navy yard at Pearl Harbor, $19 million, with $10.5 million for dry-docks, $2.75 million for a power plant, more than $2 million for industrial shop buildings, and $1 million for storehouses.

First published February 1941.

It is said that the fuel depot at Pearl Harbor will require expenditures of more than $7 million. There will be an outlay of nearly $300,000 on a medical supply depot. Various harbor improvements will run up to $12 million or more. The naval air station on Ford Island will be improved to the tune of $7.5 million. Barracks and administration buildings will demand nearly $5 million. The project at Kane'ohe, say the same authorities, will entail expenditures of $12.5 million.

On other Pacific island bases, $20.5 million. Incredible sums, had they been mentioned a few years ago. The projects under way are so vast and comprehensive that they seem almost fantastic and unbelievable.

Five years hence, the United States will have a navy, doubled in power, and perhaps many times the strength of any other aggregation of fighting ships in the world. The present administration is out to make Uncle Sam's defenses impregnable, and building the navy to double power is the first step in that direction. Figures on this effort are illuminating:

The navy has now in service or is building 645 fighting ships, a figure that does not include old destroyers being reconditioned for this service or that. Of the 645 there are 32 capital ships, 15 in service; 18 aircraft carriers, 6 in service; 85 cruisers, 37 in service; and 325 destroyers, 159 in service.

Back in 1873, or nearly seventy years ago, a board of army and navy officers came to Hawaii from the United States to obtain a cession at Pearl Harbor in exchange for admission into the United States of duty-free sugar from Hawaii. After looking over the Pearl Harbor area, the board made its recommendation, and in 1876 a treaty was concluded giving the United States certain rights there. It was in 1887 that this reciprocity agreement was extended to give the United States "exclusive rights to establish a coaling and repair station for vessels of the United States at Pearl Harbor, and to that end, improve the entrance of the said harbor."

All of which was a prelude to what was to come, for on August 12, 1898, annexation of the Hawaiian islands to the United States became a fact.

Old-timers—and there are many—who recall the Pearl Harbor of forty years ago and compare it with the Pearl Harbor of today, can only express their amazement. What was once a lagoon, with many inlets and shallow water, fringed by almost desert beaches is today one of the pulsing naval centers of the world.

When one studies the great expanse of defense improvements in that vicinity and tries to visualize what it will be after another $30 million, or $60 million, or even $100 million have been spent there, the mind becomes a bit confused. Yet we know that great dry-docks are to be built; waters are to be deepened, expanding the anchorage area; channels are to be dredged more thoroughly; there are to be thousands of residence units, new barracks, new shops and docks, and vast fuel storage depots—one of the greatest naval bases in the world. That will be Pearl Harbor of the future.

Into this area will come thousands of skilled civilian workers as well as enlisted and officer personnel. Aside from being a vital defense point, Pearl Harbor, in many respects, will be a humming industrial city.

Payrolls for the present twelve thousand personnel at Pearl Harbor, say the authorities, reach nearly $14 million annually. That, in the natural course of expansion, will be increased, maybe doubled or trebled. From 1940 to 1941, the total number of civilian employees doubled, the increase being from about three thousand for 1939 to six thousand during 1940. Figures in all instances are in round numbers.

No, the United States is not going to turn the Pacific over to other naval powers. It must always remain a barrier against attack from the west.

The Army in Hawaii

GRANVILLE BROWN

❖ The past year has been one of the most eventful of the Army's long history in Hawaii. The year has seen the continued expansion of the military forces in the islands, the first all-island blackout, the induction of Hawaii's first contingent of selective service men into the Army, the boosting of the rank of the commanding general of the Hawaiian Department to that of lieutenant general, and the change of the Army's top command in Hawaii.

The calling of the Territory's two National Guard units, the 298th Infantry and the 299th Infantry, for a year's active duty at Schofield Barracks; the sending of the 251st Coast Artillery (AA) of the California National Guard to Hawaii; the formation of the Hawaiian Air Force with a major general in command; and the raising of the rank of the coast artillery commander in the islands to that of major general are equally important high spots in the Army's history in Hawaii during the past twelve months.

Islanders were treated to a sight of military might last May 23 when the Hawaiian Division at Schofield Barracks, augmented by the aerial strength of the Eighteenth Wing of the air corps, staged a colorful review witnessed by some ten thousand spectators at the Inland Post.

Units participating in the review included the Twenty-second Infantry Brigade, including the Thirty-fifth and the Twenty-seventh Infantry regiments; the Twenty-first Infantry Brigade, composed of the Nineteenth and Twenty-first Infantry regiments; the Third United States Combat engineers; the Eleventh Medical Regiment; the Eleventh Quartermaster regiment; the special troops; the First Separate Chemical battalion; the Eleventh Ordnance company; the Eleventh Signal company; the Hawaiian Division Pack Train; the Eleventh Field Artillery Brigade, including the Eighth, Eleventh, and Thirteenth Field Artillery regiments; the Eleventh Tank company;

First published April 1941.

and finally, the massed might of the Eighteenth Bombardment Wing of the air corps.

The second division review of the year was recently held at Schofield with an even greater array of military units, including besides those mentioned above, the 298th and 299th Infantry Regiments (formerly Hawaii National Guard) and some seven hundred selective service trainees who had received their training at the Inland Post.

Last spring's division review followed on the heels of the first all-island blackout, which was staged on the night of May 23.

When the signal "Blackout Immediately" was given at 8:34 P.M., lights throughout Hawaii, which a moment before had twinkled out their cheery warmth, went dark. In a few minutes Army airmen high over all the major islands of the group reported the blackout complete. When the all-clear signal was given at 9 P.M., high-ranking army chiefs were quick to report their satisfaction with the response of the island community in making the vital exercise a success.

The blackout drill came near the end of the annual department maneuvers with the thousands of troops stationed in Hawaii taking part in the operation in close cooperation with the civilian population.

The island blackout was also marked by the playing of the "Blackout March," written by composer Johnny Noble. This composition is the first music ever written in connection with a blackout exercise.

On June 18 the Hawaiian Department launched an intensified program of field maneuvers, which are being continued at the present time.

The program resumed where the annual department maneuver had left off on May 25. This maneuver was marked by exercises looking toward the repelling of parachute troops and the studying of lessons learned from the war now raging in Europe.

Early last October Durward S. Wilson, then commanding the Nineteenth Infantry at Schofield Barracks, was promoted to the rank of brigadier general and later took command of the Twenty-first Infantry Brigade at the Inland Post.

About the same time, barracks began rising at Schofield and at the new Camp Malakola near Barbers Point to take care of the two Hawaii National Guard regiments and the 251st Coast Artillery (AA) units that began to arrive from California for duty in the islands.

The construction of the barracks city for the Hawaii National Guard units at Schofield was handled by the Third Engineers and was marked by speedy and efficient construction, the camp almost rising overnight.

In October the War Department announced that Maj. Gen. Frederick L. Martin would be ordered to duty with the Hawaiian Department. This was rapidly followed with the designation of the air corps units in the islands as the Hawaiian Air Force under command of General Martin and composed of the Eighteenth Bombardment Wing at Hickam Field and the Fourteenth Pursuit Wing at Wheeler Field.

On October 21, 22, and 23, units of the Hawaii National Guard regiments, the 298th and 299th Infantry, began arriving at Schofield Barracks to join the Hawaiian Division for a year's active duty in conjunction with the President's plan for augmented national defense. At the same time, preparations got underway to receive the 251st Coast Artillery Regiment of the California National Guard, which was ordered to proceed to Hawaii to augment the anti-aircraft strength of the department.

In the meantime, on August 2, Gen. Charles D. Herron, commanding general of the department, was raised to the rank of lieutenant general of the Army when the War Department announced its decision to have a general officer of that rank command the many and varied military activities that make up the island military garrison.

Gen. Fulton Q. C. Gardner, commanding in Hawaiian Separate Coast Artillery Brigade, was elevated to the rank of major general in November, in keeping with the expanding strength of the coast artillery command.

At the same time Brig. Gen. Jacob H. Rudolph arrived in Hawaii to take command of the Eighteenth Bombardment Wing of the Hawaiian Air Force, with headquarters at Hickam Field.

On December 9 some seven hundred selective service men put behind them their civilian endeavors to become trainees in a special camp erected at Schofield Barracks. Training of the men proceeded on schedule, so that on March 15 they were assigned to units of the 298th and 299th Infantry Regiments at the Inland Post.

Although confronted with many new problems in the induction into the service and the training of these men, the job was completed efficiently and thoroughly at the Schofield Barracks reception center.

Throughout the entire year, an accelerated construction program was speeded at all the major Army posts in the islands.

Command of the Hawaiian Division at Schofield was relinquished by Maj. Gen. William H. Wilson to Brig. Gen. Daniel L. Sultan when General Wilson sailed on March 4 en route to Savannah, Georgia, to become commanding officer of Camp Stewart, Georgia.

On February 7, Lt. Gen. Walter C. Short took over command of the Hawaiian Department from Lt. Gen. Charles D. Herron. General Herron sailed for the Mainland prior to his retirement, following the change of command ceremony.

The new commanding general of the department brings a long record of achievement with him to his new post and was quick to familiarize himself with all details of the large island command.

General officers of the Army now on duty in the Hawaiian department include: Lt. Gen. Walter C. Short, commanding general, Hawaiian Department; Maj. Gen. Fulton Q. C. Gardner, commanding the Hawaiian Separate Coast Artillery Brigade; Maj. Gen. Frederick L. Martin, commanding the Hawaiian Air Force; Brig. Gen. Daniel L. Sultan, commanding the Hawaiian Division; Brig. Gen. Maxwell Murray, commanding the Eleventh Field Artillery Brigade; Brig. Gen. Jacob H. Rudolph, commanding the Eighteenth Bombardment Wing; and Brig. Gen. D. S. Wilson, commanding the Twenty-first Infantry Brigade.

II

War!

On Sunday morning, December 7, 1941, Japanese aircraft attacked the recently arrived U.S. Pacific Fleet at Pearl Harbor, the naval base itself, and airfields on Oʻahu. So complete was the surprise that the enemy met only light resistance from Army defenders—only thirty pursuit planes managed to take off and but four of the twenty-seven antiaircraft batteries were able to go into action. Within two hours, the attackers sank or heavily damaged 18 of the 96 warships in the harbor, 8 of them battleships; destroyed 188 of 394 aircraft on Oʻahu and damaged 159. There were 2,403 American servicemen killed in action and more than a thousand wounded. Fifty-seven civilians died, including three City and County of Honolulu firefighters. Japanese raiders suffered far fewer casualties—they lost twenty-nine aircraft and five midget submarines.

Gov. Joseph B. Poindexter invoked the Hawaiʻi Defense Act at 11:30 A.M. At 3:30 P.M., Lt. Gen. Walter C. Short proclaimed himself military governor of Hawaiʻi. An announcement was broadcast soon afterwards, in English and in Japanese, that the U.S. military was completely in charge of the Territory. Strict censorship was imposed—including that of all mail.

That evening people prepared for another aerial attack and anticipated an invasion would follow. It would be preceded by an uprising of thousands of Japanese nationals living in Hawaiʻi, some people believed. Called to active duty was the Territorial Guard, many of whom were nisei.

"SABOTEURS LAND HERE!" was the banner headline in the morning *Advertiser*. Another headline stated boldly, "RAIDERS RETURN IN DAWN ATTACK." The story below reported that an enemy force had landed on northern O'ahu, that enemy troops had parachuted into Kalihi, and that there had been more bombing by the enemy. None of this was true and the newspaper's publisher, Lorrin P. Thurston, was told by the military government that the paper would be shut down if such irresponsible reporting ever happened again. The situation was chaotic enough without the morning paper falsely alarming the public.

On December 8 the United States declared war against Japan. Hawai'i civil courts were closed by military order. The FBI took 482 people into custody: 370 of Japanese descent, 98 of German or Austrian descent, and 14 of Italian descent.

Two days later Japanese forces invaded the Philippines. The following day Germany and Italy declared war on the United States, and the United States declared war on them.

On December 15 Secretary of the Navy Frank Knox claimed Japanese spies in Hawai'i had been responsible for the success of the raid on Pearl Harbor. "I think the most effective Fifth Column work of the entire war was done in Hawai'i," he told the wire services. There was no evidence to support such a reckless claim.

On December 15, a Japanese submarine shelled Kahului, Maui.

On December 17, Adm. Chester W. Nimitz took command of the Pacific Fleet. General Short was replaced by Gen. Delos Emmons.

On December 23, Wake Island fell to the Japanese. Two days later, Hong Kong was captured.

On December 27, registration and fingerprinting of all civilians in the Territory was ordered.

1942

On the first day of the new year, the *Advertiser* ran a photo of Hawai'i's Gov. Joseph B. Poindexter and Honolulu's Mayor Lester Petrie being fingerprinted. The entire population of the territory was to be registered by military authority. There was no objection by the white elite, who saw registration as a justifiable step to insure that authority would remain firmly in haole hands.

News arrived that Manila had fallen to Japanese forces on January 2. On January 20, gas masks were distributed on O'ahu. Next day twenty-two white civic leaders met to organize a civilian volunteer defense force. Within days about fifteen hundred men volunteered for service in seventeen companies. Official approval for activation of the Businessmen's Military Training Corps was signed on January 21. A primary mission of the BMTC was to immobilize enemy aliens in Honolulu.

On January 28, the army transport *Royal T. Frank* was sunk between the islands of Hawai'i and Maui by a Japanese submarine. Twenty-nine men died.

General Emmons ordered the 317 Japanese members of the Hawai'i Territorial Guard dismissed from the service. One hundred fifty of them went to work as laborers for the Army Corps of Engineers. Mostly university students, they called themselves the Varsity Victory Volunteers.

On February 21, the Businessmen's Military Training Corps was armed and ready for service. On the following day all civilians of Japanese, German, and Italian ancestry were ordered to turn in firearms and other weapons, ammunition, and explosives.

On February 24, bars were allowed to reopen.

In March the induction and enlistment of all nisei was stopped. The nearly fourteen hundred Japanese-Americans in the two battalions of the Hawai'i National Guard were reformed into the Hawaiian Provisional Infantry Battalion. They would be shipped to the Mainland for training before being sent to the European Theater.

On Wednesday, March 4, at 2:12 in the morning, air raid sirens in

Honolulu sounded an alert. People heard planes droning over the city and then explosions on lower Tantalus. Had the long-expected invasion begun? The raid was carried out by two Japanese flying boats that had flown two thousand miles from the Marshall Islands to French Frigate Shoals. After being refueled there by a submarine, they flew to O'ahu, planning to bomb Pearl Harbor. Heavy clouds obscured the target and their bombs fell into the sea and onto the hillside. The same clouds hid them from pursuit planes, and the enemy returned safely to base.

In late March, the *Advertiser* called for the suspension of all elections in the Territory: "Inasmuch as there can be no major civic issues at stake for the war's duration, the public can get along with what it has." Some local officials privately liked the idea of holding an elected post without having to run for it.

The Sand Island Detention Center closed in March. Some detainees were sent to the Honouliuli Internment Camp, a hot and mosquito-ridden place. The following month the public was barred from the Honolulu waterfront. During this period troops from the Mainland reinforced Hawai'i National Guard troops on the neighbor islands.

On March 24 Secretary Knox repeated his claim of subversive activity by Japanese in Hawai'i to a congressional committee.

A Japanese submarine brought the year to a close by shelling Hilo, Nāwiliwili, and Kahului.

The April edition of *Paradise* reminded readers: "Carrying a gas mask is not an idle gesture. Our enemy across the Pacific has no conscience. He will hesitate at nothing to annihilate every man, woman and child in these islands. . . . Keep your gas mask with you at all times."

On April 9, seventy-five thousand Philippine and American troops on Bataan surrendered to the Japanese. On April 25, selective service registration was extended to men between the ages of forty-five and sixty-four. On May 7, Corregidor fell.

On May 25, Japanese naval forces began an operation to invade Midway and capture the Aleutian Islands. U.S. forces converged on Midway and a massive sea battle took place. Americans lost the carrier *Yorktown*. Although the Japanese force intended an invasion, the Hawai'i Provisional Infantry Battalion was shipped to the Mainland. Called up to stand guard in Honolulu were members of the Businessmen's Military Training Corps, the mostly white civilian defense force. Japan lost four carriers and a significant number of pilots and planes. America had won naval superiority in the Pacific. Although Hawai'i was no longer a war front, the Territory remained under martial law.

At the end of June, the Hawai'i Tourist Bureau closed for the duration.

While on the Mainland protesting the administration of national defense policies, Governor Poindexter, whose second term had expired, was replaced. President Roosevelt appointed Ingram M. Stainback as governor of Hawai'i on July 23. He was sworn into office on August 24. The following day, forty Japanese families left Hawai'i in exchange for Americans in Japan. The strength of volunteer units of Hawai'i civilians reached twenty thousand men in August. They trained without pay and bought their own uniforms. Ex-governor Poindexter returned to the private practice of law in Honolulu.

In October the curfew hour was extended two hours, from 8 P.M. to 10 P.M.

The 1942 primary election was held on October 3. But the campaigns lacked the good fun of prewar political rallies—no hula, no music, no beer. Candidates had to submit any radio speeches to censors. The turnout was light. In the general election, Mayor Petrie was returned to office, despite his promilitary government posture. He said at a news conference: "We are capable of conducting our civil affairs without military interference but, in war, not without military assistance. We recognize that civil authority alone is not an adequate safeguard for ourselves or for the people on the Mainland who rely upon us here for defense. Martial law, reasonably administered, is a protection for both." Civilians suffering under it weren't convinced.

In December, the Twenty-fifth Division left Hawai'i for battle in the Solomons. The Honolulu Parks Board removed the Japanese fountain from Kapi'olani Park. During the year about twenty-four hundred persons of Japanese descent in Hawai'i petitioned to Anglicize their names. On these and other changes, *Paradise* commented, "Hawaii—which used to lounge like a lazy, graceful and beautiful woman—has discovered she has a backbone."

Out of the Night

❖ The President of the United States immediately denounced it as treachery of the worst order. Since then the entire nation has echoed in a great and growing crescendo the President's sentiments. While still talking peace with the United States, Japan struck without warning. And now the slogan has spread to the farthest corners of the United States: "Remember Pearl Harbor." The American people will never forget, and they'll never quit until the attack has been fully avenged.

The big majority of American citizens in Hawaii who are of Japanese ancestry feel the same way as Americans of Anglo-Saxon stock. Thus far they have been calm and, with minor exceptions, have contributed their share toward meeting the situation. We in Hawaii are vitally concerned. Naturally all citizens, no matter what their racial or national ancestry, are expected to be loyal to the American flag and American traditions.

In describing what happened at Pearl Harbor, we quote from the report of Secretary Frank Knox: "The essential fact is that the Japanese purpose was to knock out the United States before the war began. This was made apparent by the deception practiced, by the preparations which had gone on for many weeks before the attack and the attacks themselves, which were made simultaneously throughout the Pacific. In this purpose the Japanese failed."

Secretary Knox has told us of the number of casualties, has specified the vessels destroyed or put out of commission temporarily, and stated that American forces shot down forty-one Japanese planes and sank or captured three hostile submarines.

It goes without saying that during the days immediately following the attack on December 7, the air was filled to suffocation with all sorts of rumors. But as the days went by and calm was restored, Hawaii buckled down to the business of preparing for whatever emergencies

---

First published January 1942.

42

may await us in the future. Highest praise must be extended to every branch of our national defense in Hawaii, with the civilian holding a high spot in the picture.

The Days Ahead

The power of a seer is needed for one to penetrate the future in these troublous times and to forecast with any degree of accuracy what may be in store for us. In normal years, with the world comparatively free from major wars, the routine of business and relations between nations go along according to schedule. Deviation from a given program is the exception, and not the rule. At the beginning of this good year 1942, the world is so torn with turmoil, dissention, wars, death, and destruction that any attempt to forecast the events in the months to come would be akin to lunacy, utter folly.

Some of us, perhaps, think we know, and many there are who will offer their forecasts. Here in the Pacific the waters are roaring with trouble. The Pacific is pacific no more. It is stormy from the uttermost reaches on the West to the uttermost fringes in the East. There is feverish activity at Panama. There is war in Hawaii. And in all the seas touching the Pacific—the China Sea, the Yellow Sea, the Java Sea, and other seas—there is war. The waters are a-whirl with it. All these things we know. The present is portentous. What Japan aims to do, what China can do, what the United States and Great Britain will do remain for the days ahead to reveal.

With the entire civilized world in a jittery state, these islands will be more adversely affected, perhaps, than heretofore. Shipping to Hawaii will be more restricted. That goes without saying. Shortages in many commodities may develop. Whether we'll be called upon to endure extreme hardships is in the lap of the gods, a circumstance of the future. The days ahead will bring Hawaii more and more into the world limelight, no matter which way the fortunes of war may sway.

Remember Pearl Harbor

❖ Honolulu will never forget Sunday morning, December 7. The sudden, savage attack on Pearl Harbor and army posts by a nation then at peace with the United States, and at that moment still talking peace, immediately was labeled the basest of treachery by the President of the United States. Since then Secretary of the Navy Frank Knox has published to the world something of the extent in material damage and the number of lives lost. . . . Winged death, coming without warning—just as Japan has always attacked wherever she has waged war—naturally brought apprehension to the island population. . . . But not for long. It is not the American way to take it lying down. . . . Honolulu and all of Hawaii rose as a single person to take the situation in hand. . . . Governor Poindexter acted quickly with the powers vested in him. . . . Martial law was invoked, and martial law began to rule. That was as it should be. . . . False rumors, vicious rumors, were spiked and calm again prevailed. . . . Hurried, even drastic, changes were made in the routine of civil life . . . but Hawaii was soon in step and has continued in step. . . .

Much has been written about the situation as it has developed from day to day. . . . What betides no man knows . . . but whatever it may be, Hawaii will carry on. . . . Our people know the army and navy will meet with success every move by the enemy. . . . That is inevitable. . . .

Now it is up to us to live, act, and conduct ourselves as an acute emergency requires . . . a request that needs no urging. . . . The people of Hawaii will so live, act, and conduct themselves. They will render every aid demanded or requested by the authorities. . . . Hawaii is like that, because Hawaii is American . . . and Hawaii, with every other American community . . . will remember Pearl Harbor!

First published January 1942.

There Always Will Be Heroes

❖ In this department this month we have taken from the records, and from individuals themselves, stories of heroism performed during the early stages of the emergency in the islands. We'll lead off with that epic of Niihau, most isolated of all of the inhabited islands. It relates to Benny Kanahele, a powerfully built Hawaiian, descendant of Hawaiian warriors, and a Japanese pilot who was forced down there. Benny didn't get mad at the invader until the latter shot him three times . . . and then he picked up the little yellow man, dashed him against a stone wall, and Mrs. Kanahele finished him off by pounding out his brains with a lava stone. Now to Kanahele's story, as told to Mike Fern, who lives on Kauai:

"The Japanese plane cracked up. The pilot was found lying in the dirt where he had been thrown. We didn't know what to do with the man. Nothing like it had ever before occurred on Niihau. We did not know there was a war. We treated the Japanese flier as a guest. We took him to Aylmer Robinson's house and made him comfortable there. We allowed him to roam around. He made friends with Harada, American-born Japanese residing on Niihau. Harada got the pilot's gun back from Hawila Kaleohanu, who had hidden the weapon. Harada hunted around until he found it.

"The other Japanese resident on the island was named Shintani. Harada and the Japanese pilot asked Shintani to bribe Hawila into returning the papers. Hawila refused the two hundred yen the pilot had with him. Shintani became frightened and ran away to the woods. He thought his life would be worthless if he returned to the pilot without the war papers. And so Hawila became suspicious. Too much war talk, too much anxiety over the papers, coupled with bribery offers. He reasoned there must be war. He collected five cowboys, put off in a whaleboat, and rowed to Waimea, Kauai. That was on a Friday night. It was on this night that the pilot took the machine gun off the plane and set it up in a carriage belonging to Robinson. . . .

First published February 1942.

45

"Then they went out and burned Hawila's house and the plane. . . . And that same night Harada and the pilot went into the village and started shooting. They were trying to scare the people. They wanted those war papers. . . . I went to the beach and hid in a cave. . . . Everybody else in the village had run to hide in the woods. . . . Saturday, Harada and the pilot came to the caves and got me and my wife. They wanted me to find Hawila. I knew Hawila had gone to Kauai, but I pretended to hunt for him. I took them into the woods and we started yelling for Hawila. We hunted and kept yelling until we came to a stone wall. The pilot became suspicious. He bubbled with anger. He said he would shoot everybody on the island if we didn't reveal Hawila's hideout. He had the shotgun in his hand, and his pistol was stuck in one of his boots. . . .

"Harada's shirt was open. He seemed ready to kill himself. He was carrying the extra cartridges. He gave them to the flier and then took the shotgun. I jumped the flier as the shotgun was being passed. The pilot jerked the pistol from his boot and tried to shoot me. . . . My wife grabbed his arm and pulled it down. He called on Harada for help, so Harada grabbed my wife and pushed her away. In the clear, the flier started popping at me. The first bullet hit my ribs on the left side. I jumped him again, and he fired a second bullet into me. It got me in the hip. Before I could nail him, he fired into my groin. . . . Then I got mad!

"I picked up that flier and threw him against the stone wall. I knocked him cold. Then I turned to go after Harada, but Harada was using the shotgun on himself. His first shot missed, he was so clumsy. His aim next time was better. The gun went off and the charge took effect. He shot himself, all right. All this time my wife was going into action. She was plenty *huhu,* that woman. She picked up a big rock and beat that flier's brains out. She did a pretty good job."

Both were taken to Kauai, where Benjamin Kanahele at this writing is convalescing.

Daring American Pilots

Shortly after the attack on December 7, the commanding general of the Hawaiian Department released a story pointing out examples of heroism among army fliers:

"Second Lt. Kenneth M. Taylor, Hominy, Oklahoma, and 2d Lt.

46

George S. Welch, 906 Blackshire Road, Wilmington, Delaware, both flying Curtis single-seat pursuit planes, early in the raid attacked a formation of Japanese planes and each officer shot down two enemy craft. The other two Japanese planes escaped for the time being. A short time later Welch engaged two Japanese planes and, after maneuvers worthy of a veteran, shot them both down. This brought the two officers a total of six enemy planes destroyed in their first actual battle fight. Lieutenant Taylor's is a remarkable record and one of which he should be justly proud. He is a very recent arrival in Hawaii and the ink is scarcely dry on his commission as a fighting pilot. . . . First Lt. Lewis M. Sanders, 809 Pasadena Drive, Fort Wayne, Indiana, of another pursuit squadron, saw a dogfight between an American and a Japanese plane. As he banked to join the fight he saw the American plane go down in flames. In an avenging fury, Sanders relentlessly pursued the Japanese plane and shot him down. . . . Lt. Gordon H. Sterling, Jr., 56 Argyle Avenue, West Hartford, Connecticut, of the same squadron, upon attaining sufficient altitude, located a formation of six enemy ships. Undaunted by superior numbers he courageously attacked, cutting out one Japanese plane and destroying it. . . . Second Lt. Philip M. Rasmussen, 75 Westchester Road, Boston, Massachusetts, of the same squadron and flying the same type of pursuit ship, engaged a single Japanese fighter. There ensued a dogfight over Schofield Barracks, and anxious watching thousands thrilled as Lieutenant Rasmussen's superior maneuvering enabled him to bring the Japanese plane to the ground in a burning broken mass of wreckage. . . . Second Lt. Harry W. Brown, 1007 Monroe Street, Amarillo, Texas, a member of Lieutenant Taylor and Welch's squadron, searching for the attacking Japanese, unexpectedly found himself in the midst of a rendezvous of Japanese planes. Instead of a discreet departure he engaged one, out-maneuvered it, and shot the plane down in the Pacific Ocean just off Kahuku Point. . . . In none of these fights were the odds with the Americans. . . ."

Army Men Rescued

Somewhere off Hawaii an army plane made a forced landing. Nine men scrambled into the deep waters of the world's greatest ocean, carrying with them two small rubber life rafts, some Very flares, and scant provisions. They drifted hundreds of miles in a hectic period of four days and four nights, passing through two storms. . . . One raft was capsized, much of their provisions were lost, and sharks came and playfully flirted with them. . . .

On the fateful fourth day, the tiny speck on the crested sea was discovered by Ens. P. M. Fisler and his valiant crew, flying high over the scene in a navy plane.

The strong northeast trades had whipped up a rough sea, but Ensign Fisler decided to attempt a landing. He secured by radio permission to do so and he swooped low, bringing the plane into the trough close to the struggling army men and their life rafts. . . . After releasing most of their service loads the men climbed aboard the plane. . . . The pilot threw wide the throttles, the plane shot forward, took to the air, cut the crest of a few breakers, and gained altitude. In due time all were safely back at Pearl Harbor. . . . The men hauled from the deep were 1st Lt. Earl J. Cooper, first pilot, 24, Stevens Point, Wisconsin; 2d Lt. R. J. Eberenz, 24, Louisville, Kentucky; 2d Lt. J. A. Crockett, 23, Stephens, Arkansas; 2d Lt. Joaquin Castro, 25, Mission, Texas; 2d Lt. J. V. Buchanan, 26, Holly Springs, Mississippi; T. Sgt. J. R. Broyles, 23, San Antonio, Texas; Sgt. Lee W. Best, 24, Wendell, Idaho; Cpl. M. L. Lucas, 22, Fortuna, California; Pvt. D. C. McCord, Jr., 28, St. Louis, Missouri.

The fliers making the rescue were Ens. P. M. Fisler, first pilot, Ivanhoe, North Carolina; Ens. C. F. Gimber, Windber, Pennsylvania, second pilot; Aviation Machinist Mate L. H. Wagoner, Bakersville, North Carolina; Aviation Machinist Mate W. B. Watson, Gore, Oklahoma; Radioman 3d Class H. C. Cupps, Minneapolis, Minnesota; Radioman 2d Class W. W. Warlick, Lincolnton, North Carolina; Aviation Machinist Mate C. C. Forbes, Elizabeth City, North Carolina. Ensigns Fisler and Wagoner received the Navy Cross for heroism, and all others were cited for meritorious conduct by Adm. C. W. Nimitz.

The New Life

TIM WARREN

❖ Three months in Hawaii under war restrictions and emergency conditions have brought to island residents a mode of living unlike anything ever before experienced in Hawaii. That's natural, of course. Never before has Hawaii known a similar or paralleling situation. But, as has often been said, the miracle of it all is the willingness with which the residents have adapted life to these conditions. Our commanding general has said that discipline in Hawaii is better than what he observed in London.

What are the changes? We'll note a few. And we'll start with the lei custom. Long, long ago public announcement of arrival and departure of steamers was prohibited. When war came, the army and navy took over these arrivals and departures completely—and the former colorful, aloha-singing, lei-bedecked crowds vanished. There are no more public demonstrations at steamer arrivals and departures. So the lei-selling custom went into eclipse, and when it went into eclipse at the harbor, it began to fade elsewhere in the city. The lei-sellers are now employed in making camouflage for various defense outposts here and there on the island. Life, you see, has changed materially not only for the vendors of flower wreaths, but also for the public so closely associated with the custom.

The ghosts of yesterday are seen no more in Iolani Palace. Life there is real, tensely real. In the halls where King Kalakaua and his queen and his chiefs, legislators, ministers, attendants, and servants once laughed, sang, and danced, we find today the uniforms of the United States Army and Navy, defense workers, defense bureau executives, an intricate telephone system, the military governor—and the hundreds who come and go. It is a different life in the Palace. Sober faces, serious faces, determined faces are the rule. They have supplanted the

First published March 1942.

gay and smiling and holidayish faces of yesteryear. Out in the grounds are the air raid shelters—shelters that wind and zigzag beneath banyans, monkeypod, and other noted trees. At the entrance gates are sentries, guards . . . young fellows with orders; and at night, barbed wire entanglements aid the sentries.

Downtown are the thousands who stroll along with a small dun-colored bag dangling from their shoulders. It is a gas mask. There is a bit of grimness in the presence of this protector of life. The young chap who fitted a gas mask to my face and gave me instructions in how to use it ended his lesson by saying: "By having gas masks for everybody, the Japanese will be discouraged against using gas in Hawaii." Perhaps, young man; but it is for a greater reason that we carry them with us. It is to protect life against the possible savagery of a savage enemy. There is no guarantee whatever that the Japanese would spare us; none whatever. So it is a master stroke in defense to be prepared for them, no matter what weapons they may use in an attack. They'll bomb us, if they can—and hence the bomb shelters. They'll machine-gun us, too, if opportunity presents; and hence the protection being provided against this form of ruthlessness. So, to successfully meet all possibilities, another phase of life in Hawaii has been altered.

Blackout rules have aided materially in creating a different routine for all of us. We now go to the movies in daylight hours. . . . Public dances are held between the rising and the setting of the sun—any others, as was demonstrated at Punahou some weeks ago, will bring the police down upon patrons who have no passes for after-curfew prowling, strolling, or driving.

More of us now remain at home during the evenings. Families are getting better acquainted with various members. The old-time luaus in the open or beneath thatched sheds, at schools, or at any big gathering are no more. . . . The highways are not clogged with pleasure-seeking motorists. Strict gasoline rationing has halted the forays into the country and to the remote beaches on Saturdays and Sundays. . . . The holiday gatherings of months and years ago have, along with their gasoline supply, faded to a shadow. Your motorist, who once sped over the boulevards on his way to his office or store or shop, now sits in the bus or holds on to the straps, swaying to the rhythm of the rolling vehicle.

We go shopping about as usual, except the stores close somewhat earlier. Now that daylight saving time is in effect, we seem to find new hours during the daylight half of the twenty-four. Up early, to work early, always early everywhere; and when day is officially done, we still find the sun high in the heavens.

For a time the schools were closed. Now they are again functioning, but not with a total attendance. Thousands of young men of high school age are aiding in the defense effort, and they perhaps will not be back in the classroom until the war is over.

In all these changes, due to military necessity, there may be some inconveniences, but there are no hardships. Even the sense of inconvenience, due more to an upset in routine than to any other factor, is disappearing. Anyhow, the attitude of the Honolulu resident is one of patriotic endeavor to abide by all regulations and thereby lend help in every phase of the defense of the islands and the nation. Those who are careless, or not patriotically inclined, wind up in the provost court.

During the waning days of February, the military governor again permitted the sale of liquor in Honolulu, but under specified restrictions. There had been seventy-eight days of prohibition. Before one could purchase liquor in quantities beyond a single drink, one was required to obtain a special permit. Cafes, bars, and other "spots" were placed under strictest regulations. Frankly, reopening the bars was an experiment, with the warning that if regulations were violated, prohibition would again be enforced.

Warning—Take Heed

TIM WARREN

❖ It was a blustery morning in March 1942. The hour was 2:15 A.M. In the dead hours. A silver moon rode high above the scudding clouds. Blackout. A large majority of folks were asleep. Out of the deep night came a muffled rumble, accompanied by a quake. Another muffled rumble, more like an explosion than its predecessor. A third, even more pronounced, with doors rattling, walls creaking, and through it all the swishing of rushing air.

Scene is Honolulu. More immediate scene, the slopes of Tantalus. Immediate result: mystery.

Came the daylight hours, and residents living within a mile of Roosevelt High School talked and speculated on what they had heard and felt. Residents in the immediate vicinity of Roosevelt High School were taking inventory. Some found shell fragments on their porches and in their yards. One man said he scooped up some powder. Wandering a little farther from the doorsteps, they located newly made craters. Trees were torn apart. Branches were nipped off. The underbrush was parted, disentangled, pushed over. More craters—one, two, three—and then the fourth.

Army officers inspected the new holes in the Tantalus terrain. They were strung along, separated by short distances. They examined the fragments of metal that littered the scene. Undoubtedly a plane had been overhead. It had been flying high. A lone raider. Or was it alone? At least, only one got over the island. Searchlights had probed the sky. Residents had heard the hum of motors. But the unknown visitor went on his way. Where did he come from? Where did he go?

Lucky for Honolulu that the bombs fell in the woods and brush of the mountain. Lucky for Honolulu that clouds were floating between the plane and his supposed objectives. Lucky for all of us that the city

---

First published April 1942.

was blacked out completely. But a warning—a serious warning—that if one enemy bomber could slip in over the city in the dead hours, others may attempt to do likewise. Not that the plane surprised the authorities. The army and navy expect almost anything to happen. The fact that it got through does not mean that the trick can be repeated with facility. Nevertheless, we have had our warning.

However, that was one of scores of warnings. Every day brings a new caution, a new signal, something else again to whet our preparedness. Everything that is happening in Java, in the Philippines, in New Guinea, and in Australia is a warning fully as vital and as important as that of an enemy plane flying over our islands. Nobody doubts for a single moment but that Japan, unless crushed meantime, or crippled badly, will attempt an invasion of Hawaii. Every success in the Pacific Southwest brings her just that much nearer. We may not like to look at it in this manner, but the truth cannot be easily disputed. All opposition out of his way in Malaya, Burma, and the Netherland East Indies, why will the enemy hesitate to attack Hawaii? He will not hesitate, unless our islands are so strongly fortified and guarded by land and sea and in the air that any enemy would hesitate to come against them.

Every appearance of Japanese submarines in the Eastern Pacific constitutes a warning. Every movement of Japanese armed forces in China is a warning. The United States Army is not being fooled. The United States Navy is alert. No matter what force the Nipponese will send this way, it will be met savagely, squarely, and in devastating thoroughness. Don't get any other idea. The army and navy need no warning. It is the complacency that exists among certain residents that should be jolted into a realization of what portends.

"It happened once. It can never happen again," is a common expression. Perhaps so—and we hope so—even believe so—but we can't take anything for granted. The army and navy are not taking anything for granted. A majority of civilians are not taking anything for granted either. To those few who are, we would say: We are at War. We are in a strategic spot. The enemy desires that we be eliminated. Be on the alert. Be ready for anything. When warned, take heed."

Hawaii Territorial Guard Reserve

CAPT. ROBERT PATRICK

❖ "Ready for action," they fired back as Col. Philip Lindeman inspected the Hawaii Territorial Guard Reserves. The stuff men are made of, and the men who make America, is truly represented in the war training clan of Hawaii's enthusiastic, capable, alert, and "on the beam business men."

Not satisfied with standing by when things are happening and eager for a chance at constructive military training to enable them to perform efficiently and effectively through a recognized and authorized organization, these lively citizens are giving up spare time to work out regularly and rigorously in active combat tactics.

Having taken a physical exam and pledged their services for a year, and knowing that they will be called into active duty only in the event of an invasion or attack upon the Territory of Hawaii by an enemy force, or in the event of an uprising, revolt, or similar emergency, they are assuring themselves that they can carry on the dual role of civilian and soldier; but there is no imaginary assumption of soldierly skills because each man must qualify in practical tests and live up to the standards his uniform represents. School of the soldier, small-bore range practice, .30 caliber firing, extended order skirmishes, bayonet drill, and building up firing lines are only a part of the program.

"Them guys is smart; yardbirds all, but they learn fast," says Sgt. Harry "Joe Blow" Ward, as he surveys the Bank of Bishop's "vice-prexys" Irwin Spalding and Desmond Stanley, California Packing Corporation's superintendent Robert Newton, the *Advertiser*'s Danny Morse, the University of Hawaii's director of athletics "Pump" Searle, and many other prominent protégés.

In a short time the Regular Army personnel assigned to this duty

---

First published April 1942.

have converted the Ala Wai boathouse into a garrison providing training facilities from individually assigned lockers to a small-bore rifle range.

Records are kept of all attendance at both lecture sessions and practical drills and demonstrations. The only compulsory drill is for two hours on Sunday mornings, but the high percentage of daily attendance shows a keen interest in the daily program provided. Every afternoon forty to fifty members can be found stripping and assembling weapons, drilling, firing the rifle, or attending lectures. Already a majority of the men have fired the .30 caliber Springfield after having completed a rigid qualification on the small-bore shooting range.

And these men know the rigors of sentry duty because they have volunteered to learn guard duty by actually doing it, and when Tommy Tompkins, Ed Barret, Ben Seelig, or Dick Gurrey sound out with "Halt, who's there?" it's a hearty challenge that must be met.

"No, it ain't as comfortable as those innerspring mattresses you have at home," says Sgt. Ira Nelson, "but it will toughen you up for the job you'll have to do."

What impresses the casual visitor most is the keenly awakened sense of the men to the fact that preparedness through practice is absolutely essential, and that seriousness and willingness prevail in the entire program. These men seek nothing but the opportunity to condition themselves; rank doesn't enter the picture. They have a job to do, and quietly and earnestly they're whipping into shape to face the foe.

The Hawaii Territorial Guard Reserve is authorized to furnish all those properly enlisted with the necessary clothing and equipment and is providing this training program in the interest of the defense of the territory and encourages all individuals to call upon Lt. Ivan Wentworth-Rohr, adjutant, at the Ala Wai boathouse for full details.

Plans are drawn for the selection of officers and noncommissioned officers. Practical and theoretical exams will be given so that every man has a chance at leadership. It is the wish of the staff to provide facilities for the development of leadership, and all members are encouraged to get out in front and take hold of a group of men to gain confidence in command.

Yes, civilians, if you want to get into the "know" of Military Science and Tactics, and you want to get your hands around a weapon with which you can fight back, and you want to be a part of a military organization that functions as such, or if you just want to see an activity that is gaining momentum in developing stalwart defenders of our territory, drop in or around the Hawaii Territorial Guard Reserve headquarters at the Ala Wai boathouse on Sunday mornings or any afternoon.

The American Legion Goes to War Again

COL. ADNA G. CLARKE

Note: *Names of individual legionnaires are purposely omitted in this narrative, because each in his own way played a noble part, and obviously all cannot be mentioned by name.*

❖ Sunday morning, December 7, I had been enjoying my radio—having heard among other things a transcription of a nationwide sermon that my wife and I value very greatly—when strange and unusual Sunday morning messages began to come in, from both Honolulu stations, such as "All Army, Navy and Marine personnel report immediately to their posts and stations; all emergency police please report to police headquarters immediately; all civilians ordered off the streets; all steamfitters report to Pearl Harbor; all naval operators report for work; all firemen report for duty"—and then more unbelievable messages indicating that Pearl Harbor was under air and naval attack. One station announced that a bomb had been dropped in its immediate vicinity. Another announcer said: "This attack is the real McCoy." The other station emphasized it was a real attack. It was obvious that both announcers felt that many, if not most, of their listeners were still from Missouri.

I sat by my radio listening to big guns fire from the vicinity of Pearl Harbor, thrilled with the truly dramatic effect of what I was sure was an Army and Navy maneuver staged for the purpose of convincing us what the real McCoy would mean to Honolulu and Hawaii. I was still so sure it just couldn't happen to us that I joined a group of neighbors in the street in front of my house and assured them that it was all a most perfectly staged and dramatically executed maneuver. In fact I stated that, although a military man with no more information than any of them possessed, I could guarantee that it was not an enemy

---

First published June 1942.

57

attack. Then I went back to my radio and marveled at the vividness of the details of the show that was being put on. About this time my son-in-law, a doctor, called me up from his downtown office and stated that a bomb had dropped near the Governor's residence within a block of his office. I insisted that he must be mistaken and assured him that there was no reason for his being concerned about the safety of his wife (my daughter) and my three grandchildren, who live within a few blocks of me in Manoa Valley. Nevertheless, this began to shake my complacency, and I dug up my colonel's uniform and put it on just in case a call for retired personnel should come over the radio. When my good wife, who had suffered far more than I through three previous wars, saw me putting on a uniform she went to the kitchen and began making coffee and preparing sandwiches so that her soldier man would at least have a thermos bottle of hot coffee and something to eat; and I might add that that was all I did have to eat or drink until sometime the next day, and that to that extent I was more fortunate than many of my comrades of the legion during the first day and night of this war.

All morning I had a radio tuned on each station and the identical or similar messages coming from both stations were becoming ever more convincing. I might be wrong, but I still had my doubts about it being an enemy attack. At a few minutes after 11 A.M., both radio stations announced: "All American Legionnaires report at American Legion clubhouse, Kapiolani and McCully Street, immediately."

Without further delay I accepted the bottle of hot coffee and the sandwiches from my good wife and, assuring her that I still couldn't believe it was true, I kissed her good-bye and proceeded by automobile to the American Legion clubhouse.

As I passed near McCully and King streets I saw a block of frame store-buildings in flames. A few blocks farther I passed a stretcher, being carried by Boy Scouts, upon which was a woman being borne to Lunalilo School, which was being used for a temporary receiving station. I had barely reached the clubhouse four or five blocks away when, looking back, I noticed that the roof of Lunalilo, a large concrete elementary school building—the one I had just passed—was also in flames.

When I reached the clubhouse, I parked my car along with several score of other cars in the immediate vicinity and walked around to the front of the building where I saw a large group of legionnaires who had already assembled. Noting the large concentration of cars and men, my attention was called to the fact that an enemy bomber could not ask for a finer target should one come that way, so I returned to my car and moved it several blocks away and parked it under an algaroba tree.

I returned to the clubhouse and inquired who was in command. I was informed that the department commander, who lives in the Pearl Harbor navy yard, could not possibly get to the clubhouse and might even be a casualty. As a matter of fact, one of the enemy planes that had been shot down landed within a few feet of his house. No vice-commanders having arrived and the chairman of the disaster relief committee having been delayed by other disaster relief duty, it was decided to effect a temporary organization. A retired captain of the army, not a legionnaire, on his own initiative but with the tacit consent and approval of leading legionnaires present, had lined the men up and within an incredibly short time had effected an organization of a headquarters detachment and four provisional companies. Leaders of the companies were designated and they were directed to lead their companies in different directions, to include platoons, sections, and squads, with a leader selected and assigned to each, and a complete roster of the companies to be prepared.

Calls had already begun to come in from numerous sources asking for legion manpower. Even before the organizations were begun a detachment of men had been rushed to the fires at King and McCully streets and Lunalilo School to assist in fire fighting, do rescue work, and prevent looting. Two truckloads of men had been rushed to police headquarters at the request of the chief.

Having been deeply impressed with the danger caused by so large a concentration of automobiles, I had begun barking at everyone within hearing to get his car at least two blocks from the clubhouse and to park it a considerable distance from another car. Recognizing that this was a big order, unless off-street parking could be provided, I had gone across the street and was dragging out four-by-fours to provide ramps so cars could be driven over the curb into a large open park capable of holding all the cars present under the prescribed regulations. I was met by a past department commander, senior to myself, who informed me that a group of legionnaire leaders, including three past department commanders and another retired colonel, had decided that it was my duty to accept the responsibility of commanding the provisional organization that had been effected. I returned with him to the clubhouse, and after reminding the group that I had recently been inspected and condemned to limited active duty by army medicos because I was 67 years of age and had some kind of a heart ailment that no one, including myself, had ever previously discovered, I accepted the honor and responsibility thrust upon me, within the limits of my physical ability.

I designated the other retired colonel as second in command, the retired captain who had initiated the temporary organization as chief of staff, and I established headquarters in the legion clubhouse. What followed is included in my report, a portion of which I am incorporating in this article.

Even before the completion of the provisional organization, two truckloads of men had been sent to police headquarters to report for assignment for guard duty at wharves and docks, around public buildings, and over public utilities and other vital defense areas.

In this account all reference to race must be understood to be solely for the purpose of showing the cosmopolitan character of the American Legion and the solidarity of Hawaii's citizenry. All are of course Americans.

At 4 P.M. every man had been assigned to a relief of eight hours each or attached to headquarters to answer urgent S.O.S. calls of every possible kind or description. All reliefs had been directed to find their own food.

Early Sunday a squad of four men was sent in answer to a call for professional advice to investigate what was reported to be an unexploded bomb; the bomb proved to be a dud. It was properly guarded until disposed of by proper authorities.

During the early morning hours of Monday, December 8, an agitated citizen called for legionnaires to quell a disturbance a few blocks from the clubhouse. The report of the comrade in charge of the detail, a member of Omaha, Nebraska, Post, reads as follows: "A woman, middle-aged, fully undressed, with palms of hands together, same pointing heavenward, mumbling like a feeble-minded person. Reported as insane and turned over to military authority at the scene for observation and investigation."

Sunday afternoon a call from Civilian Defense headquarters was received for a detail to collect all high explosives from individuals, huis, firms, or corporations that had been licensed by proper authorities.

Soon after 8 A.M. Monday, December 8, a flying squadron of thirty-three cars or trucks, driven by legionnaires or other volunteers, accompanied by a Japanese interpreter and an expert powder man from Red Hill, left legion headquarters with the address or location of some 350 persons, or firms, who had been legally authorized and licensed to have and use explosives. Personnel of the highway department of the city and county had worked most of Sunday night providing a spot map showing the probable location of explosives and the address of the licensed owner.

By 4:30 P.M., 350 calls had been made, and large and small quantities of explosives and caps had been collected and deposited in a safe place under proper guard to await final disposition. In every case of confiscation, receipts had been made in triplicate on legal forms; one delivered to the owner, one retained by the legion, and one turned in to constituted authorities.

Two valuable non-legionnaire assistants to this powder detail were Jack Guard, Jr., who drove a truck, and Peter Dillingham, who served as a messenger and orderly. At 8:15 A.M., a detachment of thirty legionnaires was dispatched to St. Louis College to perform arduous labor all day in transforming that college into an Army hospital. A detail of three Catholic comrades was dispatched at their request to relieve three others who had been similarly selected on December 7 to guard the home of the Bishop at 1043 Spencer Street. A squad of nine men, all but the leader Filipino comrades, was furnished as a guard at the Children's hospital.

A squad of ten commanded by a past department commander, a high-ranking territorial official, was detailed for duty at the Central fire station. All were in addition to the scores of others who were still functioning under the chief of police as guards.

Monday night was a hectic period at legion headquarters. Calls for new details were coming in, especially from Queen's, Kapiolani, and Leahi, and the Children's hospitals. Rifle and machine-gun fire kept everyone alert and anxious. The clubhouse is a single-wall frame building. The car of the executive on duty during the early hours of Tuesday had two bullet holes in it when he went to use it at 8 A.M.

By 8 A.M. Tuesday, December 9, the third relief of all guards has been posted. A detachment of twelve men for duty at Queen's hospital was secured and dispatched. A similar detail of six men for Kapiolani Maternity hospital and four men for Leahi Tubercular home was also furnished. These comrades did all kinds of duty, from guarding the precious blood bank to quieting the nerves of anxious patients.

All day persons who had ammunition and explosives in their possession were turning them in to legion headquarters, and the "powder detail" continued to function the rest of the week. By Tuesday noon, word had been received that many of the legion guards could be replaced by other more permanent agencies.

Unforeseen trouble began to multiply. Legionnaires who had been using their own cars and providing their own gas, and many of them could ill afford it, could no longer get gas because its sale had been stopped. Arrangements were made by which they could obtain a few gallons each when urgently needed.

Many of the members were on essential defense work, which had been only temporarily suspended, and were being called back to their regular jobs. Some were breadwinners whose families needed their help. A few, unused to long hours of night guard duty in the rain, were showing signs of the strain. One member on special and extra duty had had his car badly damaged, allegedly by an Army truck.

One Filipino comrade called up and, after apologizing for quitting his post without being properly relieved while he went to a telephone, said he had been on his post in the "jungle" of Nuuanu Valley over a water reservoir for twenty-six hours and asked if he could be relieved. He was.

The department adjutant and his assistant did yeoman service throughout the week furnishing information, food, and material for blackout; receiving and storing arms and ammunition; contacting Civilian Defense headquarters; securing identification cards, arm bands, and car stickers, and in countless other ways helping to keep the headquarters functioning.

A letter received from the director of Civilian Defense, thanking the legion, contains the following statement: "As you know, all my shift directors are American legionnaires, and their handling of this extremely difficult position has been exemplary and most praiseworthy. Two other legionnaires have carried out instructions on gas masks and gas protection in many of our units. They have done a very fine job."

Elections—and War

TIM WARREN

Note: *Because an emergency exists in Hawaii of sufficient gravity to demand military rule, many believe that the regular and primary elections, scheduled for this year, should be called off. Others are of the opinion that the elections should be held. The military governor has announced that the military will not interfere with the election processes, unless the situation in Hawaii requires otherwise. Mr. Warren's article constitutes not only one man's opinion, but perhaps the opinion of many, and for that reason it is published herewith.*

❖ It was inevitable that someone should bring up the question of the autumn elections. It was inevitable that the politicians—out of office—should demand that the elections be held. It was inevitable that many of those in office, for the sake of appearances, should advocate holding the elections—as usual. As usual? A bit funny, that. Nothing in these islands can be done as usual—as it was done in pre-war days. That's patent—nothing. We are at war. Life's routine isn't the same. It can't be. Nothing is the same. It can't be.

Some favor omitting the primaries. Others favor omitting both primaries and the general election. Why an election, anyhow? Why try to change horses during an emergency? Besides, we are not living under constitutional government in Hawaii. We are living under military government. Justice is administered by martial law. Nearly every territorial officer is a figurehead of some sort. It is as it should be. In war, it is not the politician, the public officeholder, who directs military and naval strategy. So in an emergency, such as we have in Hawaii, it is the military that must take over, the military that must direct. The military is doing it—thoroughly and well. Why hamper a smoothly functioning, orderly government with a couple of hectic elections?

Military or otherwise, war or otherwise, elections this year can, and

---

First published June 1942.

will, if held, be just as hectic as formerly, unless restricted in some way. The military might censor the speeches—and I'm sure that would be a sensible thing to do in war time. They will prohibit night meetings, undoubtedly. Luaus will be curtailed. But even so, why spend all this effort on elections, on trying to throw somebody out of office in order to throw somebody else in when the effort could be directed toward winning the war. For the life of me, I can't see how two elections could help anything when the government is expecting an all-out war effort from everybody. All these men in office are functioning with military advice. New men, placed in office, would function likewise. Why make changes now? It doesn't add up.

I read somewhere that someone fears that our constitutional rights may be trampled upon if we do not have these elections. I do not know what the law is in the matter, but I do know that where other laws of the Territory have interfered with all-out defense, these laws have been placed on the shelf for the duration. We might go on and on, said the person interviewed, on and on, forever afterwards without elections if we call them off now. Tommyrot! Let us always remember this: The war is being fought that our form of government shall not perish from the face of the earth, that the freedom of all peoples of the earth shall not perish. Hence, it is rank foolishness to preach the doctrine that if we do not hold the elections we may by that omission create a precedent that will bar elections hereafter. The thought is too silly to harbor, even for a moment.

Why elect a new legislature, or go through the routine of returning the old to office? It is a hundred-to-one shot that the legislature is not going to hold any meetings while we are at war—certainly not until the military governor deems it expedient that, for defense or offense purposes, such meetings should be held.

Hawaii has no parallel in any Mainland community in this war emergency. Hawaii has actually been attacked by an enemy. Hawaii may be attacked again. It conceivably could happen on election day. Then, if the elections are held, and new faces appear at the city hall—what of it? As long as there is an emergency in the islands, will the present form of government exist? Let us concentrate on winning the war—and when it is won will be time enough to go back to the luaus, the public speeches, the festivals, and all the hoomalimali that goes with elections in Hawaii.

Thus we come to the conclusion of one man's opinion.

Analysis of Midway Battle

❖ The Battle of Midway, in which victor's honors were shared by both army and navy, is a cause for optimism. It demonstrated (a) that the Japanese navy is capable of the gross blunder of underestimation and (b) that air power, in which the United States is to be overwhelmingly supreme, is the vehicle to victory.

The Midway battle, at present writing, seems to have subsided to minor actions. These points in favor of the United States are now highlighted:

(1) To win the Pacific war, Japan must control Midway and Oahu. Her initial attempt is a costly failure. Japan's major wound is the blow to her seaborne air power. There is no official estimate as to plane losses, but it could conceivably reach two hundred. The real hurt is the loss of trained aviation personnel. Three to four hundred pilots, gunners, and radiomen may have perished. They are not easily or quickly replaceable.

(2) Loss of ships, men, and equipment may alter Japan's entire war strategy. Abandonment of offensive plans may be made because its sea strength is now very thinly spread. It is difficult to believe that Japan could maintain its position in the Philippines, Malaya and Singapore, the Dutch East Indies, Burma, the China coast, New Guinea, and its innumerable bases, old and new, in Micronesia and still launch a first-line offensive. Thus, *Australia and Russia may be temporarily freed of invasion threats.*

(3) Japan needs much of her sea power to hold what she has. This protective strength is thin, and an offensive from the south by General MacArthur might easily tear it away, chunk by chunk, as might drives from other directions. The turning point in the Pacific war could be at hand.

On the other side of the picture:

First published July 1942.

(Reprinted in *Paradise of the Pacific* from *The Honolulu Advertiser*)

(1) The blow off Midway was stunning, but not decisive. Overlooking losses, Japan has at least ten regular aircraft carriers and a number of converted carriers. Although the blow was heavy, it may not have accounted for all the forces available to Japan off Midway. Japanese forces are still at large in the North Pacific, in vicinity of the Aleutians. *Japan's navy, numerically, is not halved by either the Coral Sea or Midway actions.* Japan has launched or is on the verge of launching five forty-thousand-ton battleships. This gives her a first-line strength, eliminating the destroyed *Haruna* and the three damaged at Midway, of about eleven capital ships. A reassembling of her forces cannot be ruled out.

(2) In Japan's Micronesia, twenty-five hundred islands that stretch from Japan proper to Australia's fringe, there are innumerable bases, many of which hold both sea and air striking power. While U.S. raids on the Marshalls, the Gilberts, Marcus, and Wake no doubt hurt Japan's Midway effort, American forces must penetrate this dangerous maze before victory can be called near.

(3) Battles, especially sea battles, are packed with surprises. The Japanese navy is both persistent and resilient. It is proud, because previous to the Coral Sea and Midway battles it had never known defeat. It can be expected to come back for more. Japan knows that without Hawaii the Pacific war is lost.

The conclusion is that the U.S. advantage is unmistakably clear. There is a new power—the power of equality in numbers, superiority in equipment, the seasoning through experience of fighting men—that Admirals King and Nimitz, Generals Marshall, MacArthur, Emmons, and Arnold know is America's to hold and to use.

Politicos Are Worried

❖ Hawaii may hold an election this fall or it may not. It all depends on what is happening in the war about that time. This is the word that comes from Lt. Gen. Delos C. Emmons, military governor, who has the last say about all things civilian in the first American community to come under absolute military rule since the Civil War.

"You can hold an election if the Japs don't have you otherwise engaged this fall," was, in effect, the word given the people of the Territory by the military governor.

And Hawaii, where in ordinary times politics is the breath of life to man, woman, and child, just doesn't seem to care a hoot about whether it goes to the polls in 1942. It has plenty of other things to think about. This is heartbreaking to Island politicos. They are nonplused by a situation the like of which they never before have seen. Heretofore the merest whisper of their campaign drums has brought a countryside tumbling out joyously ready to gird its loins for a rough and tumble battle of the ballots. Today they are beating their tom-toms lustily and sending out mighty reverberations that roll tumultuously over the lava hillsides only to fade on the coral shores and die unheeded at sea. It's all wrong, brother, as any politician will tell you, sadly.

When the party leaders first sought out Brig. Gen. Thomas H. Green, who runs the military governor's office for General Emmons, and learned there was a possibility that the elections might be called off, they were aghast. Hawaii without politics! Incredible! Impossible! They would go to the people about this! There would be an ear-splitting roar of wrath!

They found the people strangely apathetic. What was the use of an election if there could be no campaigning? That was where the fun and interest lay. And who could campaign in a blacked-out community that goes to bed at nine o'clock in the evening? Auwe! Let elections wait until the Japs' ears have been pinned back.

First published August 1942.

This was not at all to the liking of the politicos out of office. To those already holding jobs, it sounded all right. But here again there was conflict of opinion. The Democrats control the city and county administration in Honolulu and the appointive governorship with its patronage, but the Republicans retain a firm grip on the legislature. So leaders in both parties had ideas they could better their position by a whirl at the polls, particularly because there are thousands of eligible Mainlanders here for war work who could be registered and, perhaps, voted right.

The Mainlanders, however, seem to be as little interested as are their Island brethren, and sweat as they will over their drums, the politicos seem to be making little progress in working up enthusiasm anywhere. They are going right ahead with plans for platform conventions, and election officials are readying themselves for the voting, if and when it shall come, and the county clerks are doing their share toward mustering the voters. But there is a noticeable lack of public interest, even though the clerks point out that it is an opportune time to register when one goes to the city hall periodically to renew his or her permit to purchase liquor.

What little interest that has been aroused is divided between the Democrats' ambition to unseat Samuel Wilder King as the Territory's delegate to Congress and the prospect of eliminating Americans of Japanese ancestry who have in recent years been showing increasing strength in the legislature and the county boards of supervisors.

There is only one Japanese-American in the territorial senate of 15 members. He is Sanji Abe, a holdover who would not have to campaign. Abe won his seat on the Island of Hawaii in 1940 over a vigorous opposition that capitalized on the fact that although he had made application, he was unable to shed his dual citizenship before the campaign began.

Six of the thirty house members in 1940–1941 were of Japanese ancestry. One of them, Thomas Sakakihara, also of the Island of Hawaii, has been interned, the Army announced, and it is doubtful whether the other five would enter a campaign now, although no word has been spoken against their loyalty.

Hawaii county also had two Japanese-American supervisors, but one of them, Frank Ishii, went to internment with Sakakihara. Kauai county also has two supervisors, on a board of seven, who are of Japanese ancestry. There are none in Honolulu and Maui counties.

Of the three Democrats in the senate, one is a holdover. The Democrats feel they have a chance to strengthen their forces in the upper house if an election is held, although strict party lines do not seem to count for much there. In the last regular and special sessions, both the senate and the house were divided nearly evenly between administration and anti-administration forces, strict party votes being practically unknown.

The issue that brings popular interest in Hawaii elections is quite a different thing. As has been intimated, the fun of a campaign with its flower leis, delectable *luaus,* unlimited liquid cheer, gay hula dancing, and night-long festivity is the mainspring of normal Island politics; a mainspring that today is broken beyond immediate repair.

A Gas Mask Graduation Class

LOUISE STEVENS

❖ The University of Hawaii is on a war basis. The longest summer session in its history will end August 29. An accelerated program that enables students to complete a standard course and receive a degree in three years instead of four was inaugurated following the commencement on June 4.

The only graduating class in America to receive their degrees in the war zone, the class of 1942 marched into the tropical garden of the University's outdoor theater, each student carrying his gas mask in its khaki case. The cumbersome masks, slung over shoulders by long brown straps, contrasted oddly with the black caps and gowns.

From an adjoining football field came the explosive commands of an officer drilling the Honolulu Businessmen's Military Training Corps.

An occasional airplane zoomed overhead.

An army colonel delivered the commencement address.

A degree was awarded posthumously to James Malcolm Topalian, who was killed on December 7 in the attack on Pearl Harbor.

Members of the graduating class publicly reaffirmed their faith in America by reciting in concert the Pledge of Allegiance.

Like all schools in the Territory, the University was closed by military order from December 7, 1941, to February 2, 1942. In the interval many students and instructors had taken defense jobs.

New courses designed to fit into the Territory's war needs were added to the curriculum at the time of reopening. Some of these were first aid, chemistry as applied to warfare, history of the warring countries, courses dealing with the economics of the conflict, and courses in nutrition to meet the increased interest in this science that the war has engendered.

A Chinese girl whose university in China had been moved from

First published August 1942.

Lingnan to Hong Kong while she attended it and who, when the war neared Hong Kong, had flown by Clipper to Honolulu to continue her education, received a bachelor's degree in agriculture. Her name is Fung Ting Fung. Bent on returning to China to help develop her country's agriculture, Miss Fung took her work so earnestly that when demand for war workers made it difficult for the University farm to get labor, she voluntarily herded swine and helped with the morning milking. Now she is taking graduate work at Cornell University.

During recent months University of Hawaii students have seen on classroom blackboards such instructions as this: "In case of an air raid alarm, go by way of the nearest stairway to the first floor, then to the center of the building, out by the fountain entrance, and left to trench 8-A."

The bomb shelter trenches that crisscross the campus were used twice during the spring semester, both times on Saturday mornings. Both times the alarm gave comfort to some of the students, for it interrupted examinations. Some faculty members continued their lectures in the trenches.

Army and navy uniforms are very much in evidence on the campus. Many service men use their leave for study at the University. Instructors have devised a tutoring-class-conference-correspondence system of instruction to accommodate the soldiers and sailors. The men come when they can and receive instruction individually, in class, in groups of two or three, or by correspondence. Several service men whose graduation from mainland colleges this year was prevented by the war expect to receive their degrees at the end of the summer semester.

The University of Hawaii has fitted itself into war conditions. It has enlisted for the duration.

Black Sunday and Thereafter

EARL M. THACKER

❖ It was hard to believe we had actually been attacked. Our family had just finished a leisurely breakfast and we were all planning to go down to Pearl Harbor, hoist sails on the *Panini,* and take a family group picture to be sent to our friends as a personal Christmas card. We aimed to get there before noon so that we would have the benefit of cloud effects with the coconut-fringed waters of Pearl Harbor in the foreground. The picture was changed. Here it is.

I shall try to describe how we have been living here in Honolulu since December 7. There are, of course, many things that cannot be told, but I am sure that a majority of readers have studied the Knox and Roberts reports. You have perhaps read in part or in full the series of articles by Roy W. Howard and the coverage in the Honolulu newspapers. In the latter instance I am addressing Mainland residents.

In the beginning I want to caution against reports of sabotage and fifth column activities in Hawaii. Not an instance of sabotage has been proven. Accounts in newspapers and magazines that have come back to us have been, for the most part, highly imaginative and without basis in fact. The horrifying details of arrows out in the canefields to direct the invaders, McKinley High School rings found on the Japanese pilots, obstruction of highways by Japanese gardeners—and the rest—are as inaccurate as they are fascinating. While it would be foolhardy to deny the excellent opportunities here for fifth column activities, authorities do not believe that a blanket evacuation of Japanese to a concentration camp or its equivalent is at all warranted. Precautions have been taken to prevent sabotage, and the proper agencies are constantly alert to detect fifth columnists.

I'll give you our experience and observation of actual events on December 7, since then named by some as "Hawaii's Black Sunday."

First published September 1942.

From our home on Diamond Head we had a ringside seat and a full view of much of what was going on. Like nearly everyone else, we thought the Army and Navy were being unnecessarily noisy in their maneuvers, especially on a Sunday morning. It was almost eleven o'clock when my driver returned from taking a Navy captain to his ship and confirmed that we were actually at war. We had heard the radio announcements—but that ships had been bombed and were ablaze in the harbor was still hard to believe.

By this time the noise was terrific. We could hear the rat-tat-tat of machine-gun fire, the sharper clap of anti-aircraft, and the roar of big guns and depth charges. The Waianae mountains were obliterated by the great masses of black smoke stretching from stricken Hickam Field and Pearl Harbor. Here and there dots of scarlet identified fires throughout the city. At first the planes flew low, and the roar of their engines was deafening. Later they climbed much higher, and the thinner sound, mixed as it was with the screaming pullouts from dives, was more terrifying than before. Towering geysers of water swelled up from the sea as the bombs dropped around ships that were the targets.

One bomb hit and destroyed a building on McCully Street, and shrapnel and anti-aircraft duds caused further damage in the city.

There seemed to be little any of us could do, so our family remained together throughout the day. Instructions coming over the radio were: "Stay off the streets. Do not use your telephone. This is the real McCoy. Oahu is being attacked by the Japs." Since then I have been serving as a block warden at Makalei Place. Each warden spends one night in each fortnight on duty, and every district in Honolulu is protected likewise. There is a constant alert throughout the city.

Martial law was invoked the day of the attack. As I write this Lt. Gen. Delos C. Emmons is military governor, with Brig. Gen. Thomas H. Green as executive to the military governor. All violations come before the provost court where decisions are rapid and penalties severe.

Physically, Honolulu and the island of Oahu have changed. The beaches are strewn with rolls and rolls of barbed wire. Guns, machine-gun nests, and anti-aircraft positions are everywhere. Sandbags and sand boxes protect many buildings. Trenches mutilate school grounds and the open spaces, such as parks. Bomb shelters are in every neighborhood. Signs indicating first aid stations are innumerable. In addition to the public shelters, almost every private home has its shelter, too. On many of these shelters are miniature vegetable gardens.

It probably is a toss-up between the blackouts and the gasoline rationing as to which is the more restricting. The blackout hours have varied with the changes in the rising and setting of the sun. In June, for instance, the hour was as early as 6:15 and as late as 8:15. Earlier in the winter and spring, it was 7 A.M. to 6 P.M.

Again, as I write—and I make this qualification because there may be changes in regulations—all cars must be off the streets by blackout time, except official cars and drivers bearing night passes. But we are permitted to walk outside until ten o'clock, at which time we are figuratively tucked into bed by the provost marshal. Automobiles used at night have their lamps painted black, except for a small round spot of dark blue and a tiny opening in the stop light to let the red peek through. While this arrangement warns another car of one's presence, it in no way lights the road; so night driving is hazardous.

As I said previously, the other major cross we have to bear is gasoline rationing. Each car owner is allowed a basic monthly ten gallons, and some of us, owing to the nature of our business, are granted extra gallonage; but never, in the opinion of many of us, in adequate quantities. We realize the importance of gasoline rationing and are glad to cooperate, but it is difficult to try to conduct our business interests without sufficient fuel for transportation.

A more minor cross, and one that we will be more than glad to bear if need arises, is the carrying of gas masks. We are supposed to carry them at all times, but they are a nuisance in more ways than one. But just one gas attack—may we never have it—will change our minds about that.

Because our curfew hour arrives at 10 P.M. if one is afoot—and earlier if in a car—it is necessary to leave for home with a safe margin, or one must stay overnight. As we do not always think of the curfew in time, we are becoming used to having a good night's rest on the too-short davenport, or in a bathtub that has been converted into a bed.

During the emergency—after several months of it—the theaters were given permission to remain open until later so that office workers and war workers, too, could attend an occasional movie. Moonlight dances at hotels became popular, the guests, of course, remaining overnight. That American institution, the cocktail party, began to disappear from the Hawaiian scene soon after the war started, due principally to a scarcity of liquor. Later, when prohibition was relaxed, the institution returned, more or less abbreviated.

All yachts and boats in Hawaiian waters were either taken over by the U.S. Navy or laid up for the duration, as were private airplanes. Our waters, once a happy fishing ground and a course for yacht races, became a war zone.

Hay and grain were almost impossible to obtain, and those of us who owned horses were compelled to turn the animals out to pasture. Perhaps it is just as well that all of us are so busy with war work because we no longer have the opportunities or facilities for play that we once enjoyed.

During the spring we were required to be vaccinated and inoculated against smallpox and typhoid fever. There was no escape for "conscientious objectors." It was a military order, so everyone sported a sore arm, except, in some cases, the women, owing to vanity, were vaccinated on their legs. And only God knows when they will wear evening dresses again.

The emergency wiped out unemployment. Many business concerns suffered due to unavailability of help. The defense jobs have paid such high wages that employees were lured from their former positions. A few stores closed due to lack of merchandise.

Ships to and from the islands, since December 7, have been operated in convoys. Women and children were evacuated as rapidly as possible. All travel operations have been strictly confidential. Due to limited freight space, most of which has been required for military supplies, only the most necessary commodities came through for civilian use. Perishable food, of course, has had priority, with canned foods also high on the list. There were times when there was a scarcity of butter, beef, eggs, and fresh vegetables and fruits—but there was never any danger of anyone going hungry. I note in passing that up to this moment we are all dressing about the same as usual. Men's trousers—if they are new—are minus the cuffs. Still newer clothes have a skimpy appearance—and if it keeps on for a long time, we may go back to malos and coconut hats (one for this and the other for that).

We had prohibition for several months. There were protests from the liquor interests, commendation from other cross sections of life. But the authorities relented, and the sale of liquor was again permitted under strictest regulations. Men who drank too much and too freely and then appeared in public places were hauled off to the police station to wake up next day facing a fine of five hundred dollars or a jail sentence. The provost court didn't fool in these drunkenness cases.

It was said by some that during the prohibition period it was impossible to buy hair tonics and vanilla extract. I do not know, not having been in the market for any of these commodities during that period.

What really happened to business? During the first few days after we were attacked, business was anywhere from 25 to 40 percent normal compared with corresponding days in 1940. This increased to about 85 to 100 percent normal on December 17, and on the three days before Christmas it went to 125 percent as compared with the same period in 1940. Before December 7, business was about 38 percent over last year.

During the emergency two major problems have confronted the sugar industry: One, labor, and two, equipment and supplies. Even early in December the industry was shorthanded due to attractive wages offered field laborers by the various defense projects. Since the war started the plantations have been called upon heavily, particularly on the island of Oahu, to furnish large numbers of men on vital jobs. A large amount of plantation equipment was, and still is, being used by the armed forces. If labor and equipment were available, it would be possible for the Hawaiian Islands to produce one million tons of sugar, so vitally needed.

In furtherance of war efforts, and as a result of extensive studies carried on by the Hawaiian Sugar Planters' Association, a program for diversified agriculture was developed, and considerable acreage was diverted to this purpose. Raising vegetables in Hawaii is not an easy matter, and as long as ships are coming here it is the opinion of many that it is more practicable to bring in foodstuffs. However, in the meantime, plantations have been carrying out pilot planting that may be expanded rapidly, if emergency demands. After the war had been about five months old, it appeared that it would be necessary to plant about forty-five hundred acres of cane land in vegetables.

Pineapple, our second largest industry, suffered from disrupted operations, and even now faces many new problems. Given that a substantial amount of the fruit is grown on the islands of Lanai and Molokai—and this involves the transportation of essential operating supplies to those islands and the bringing of fruit to Honolulu for processing—maintenance of uninterrupted interisland transportation schedules is of vital importance to the industry. Presence of enemy submarines in Hawaiian waters necessarily interrupted normal schedules. The industry also has been adversely affected by the diversion of manpower and equipment to war activities. Many problems arose during the peak operating period last summer, adjustments being in order because of prevailing blackouts and other restrictions.

On this subject, Henry A. White, president of the Hawaiian Pineapple Company, told me: "By accident of geography, essential American industries in this territory are faced with the unique necessity of continuing production in the midst of a war zone. Increased costs, such as freight surcharges and high marine insurance rates, unless government relief is extended, must be borne by the individual concern at consequent competitive disadvantage."

The Royal Hawaiian Hotel was leased to the U.S. Navy as a recreational and rest center for Navy personnel. The Red Cross and USO have units there, and the scheme is working out very satisfactorily. The Moana (as this is being written) continues to be operated as a hotel. There aren't any tourists, but local people, war workers, and military people keep it well filled. The Halekulani serves the same purpose, and the Pleasanton Hotel has been taken over by the U.S. Engineers. The Young Hotel roof and considerable other space has been similarly leased.

Regarding real estate, rents have always been considered high in Honolulu. It was generally expected they would fall right after the bombs did, but this has not been the case. Rental control went into effect, but in only a few instances were rentals brought down. This, of course, is not true of expensive properties, which used to be leased to tourists as rentals from five hundred to fifteen hundred dollars per month. There is no demand now for this type of property, but the need for moderately priced homes and apartments continues. The sales market is not exactly brisk, but there is some turnover each month, particularly in the four thousand to ten thousand dollar class, as well as transfer of some business properties. Many leases have been made on industrial and business properties to the Army, Navy, and war contractors.

Thus is one picture of wartime Honolulu.

War and Business in Honolulu

LESLIE A. HICKS,
PRESIDENT, HONOLULU CHAMBER OF COMMERCE

Note: *The figures representing retail and wholesale sales are prepared by the gross income division of the Territorial Tax Office and are not to be construed as representing the true picture of sales only insofar as sales can be reflected by the payment of gross income taxes. For example, 1941 wholesale sales to the government on defense jobs were not taxed, but in 1942 such sales were taxed; but unless the sales are taxed they are not reflected in the gross sales figures prepared by the tax office.*

It will be noted that all statistics in the accompanying article are based on figures up to and including June, the latest available as we go to press.

❖ Conditions of war have sharply altered many phases of Honolulu's business set-up, although the volume of retail and wholesale trade since the first of the year has mounted to the highest totals to date in the city's history. The gains have not affected all lines equally, and many establishments are doing less business as a result of restrictions now becoming nationwide. It is noteworthy that Honolulu is able to maintain a high level of trade while functioning as a front line in the Pacific war area.

One outstanding loss is the discontinuance of tourist travel, worth millions of dollars a year before the war. This loss can be said to have been made up by the sharp rise in gross volume of business from other sources. It is also noted that shipping conditions have improved, with the result that commodity and merchandise stocks, which were badly depleted within a short time after Pearl Harbor, have been replenished, and in some cases in proportions that are approaching normal.

Honolulu business interests, through the Chamber of Commerce of

First published September 1942.

Honolulu, are continuing to adhere closely to a policy of cooperation with the Office of the Military Governor and with other authorities in the war effort, and the program of the Chamber, and of business generally, for the current year is geared to that effort.

On the basis of gross income tax collections, retail trade in Honolulu in June totaled $19,306,844, compared with $13,864,758 in the corresponding month in 1941, an increase of $5,442,086. Wholesale business in June amounted to $10,923,904, against $10,832,728 in the corresponding month last year, a gain of $91,176.

In the first six months of 1942 the volume of retail and wholesale trading in Honolulu was $157,945,845, compared with $126,909,851 in the same interval in 1941, or an increase of $31,035,994. The volume of retail and wholesale trading in the Territory in the first half of this year was $176,218,019, against $144,226,736 in the corresponding period of 1941, an increase of $31,991,283.

Shipments of sugar have not been as large as during the corresponding interval last year, due to the war and the uncertainties of transportation. However, the showing is considered good, and indications are that, barring unforeseen circumstances, the whole of the 1942 crop will be landed at market. In June, shipments amounted to 91,060 short tons, compared with 134,440 in June last year. In the first half of this year, shipments totaled 338,612 short tons, against 527,943 in the corresponding 1941 interval. The task before the island plantations is to produce all the sugar they can as a vital wartime necessity. The current spot price for raws continues at the ceiling level of 3.74 cents a pound, or $7,480 a short ton.

Hawaii's pineapple canneries have been in full-scale production. The industry as a whole is on a wartime basis because the companies are packing to fill government contracts. Government procurement orders will require 34 percent of the 1942 pack and 14 percent of the canned juice pack, all to be set aside for the armed forces and other governmental agencies.

Immediate problems include not only labor supply but transportation of fruit between the islands. It is pointed out that the tin conservation order permits use of sufficient tin plate to take care of the current pack year. Shipments of juice in June totaled about 850,000 cases, compared with about 1,400,000 in June last year. In the first half of 1942, shipments totaled about 5,300,000 cases, compared with about 11,500,000 in the same interval last year.

Business increases in Honolulu are reflected in bank clearings, the total for June having been $70,369,740, as compared with $54,716,905 in the corresponding month last year. Clearings in the first six months of this year total $360,584,719, against $294,440,917 in the same interval in 1941.

There has been some improvement in volume of real estate transactions in Honolulu in the past few months, although totals continue far below figures recorded in the early months of 1941. Real estate transaction in the Territory in June amounted to $1,038,000, as compared with $1,284,500 in the corresponding 1941 month. In the first six months of this year, transactions totaled $4,505,500, compared with $8,164,500 in the corresponding 1941 interval.

Paladins of Paradise

MAJ. EDGAR RICE BURROUGHS, BMTC

❖ The old grey mare ain't what she used to be. Honolulu has changed. Do you see that buck private in khaki crawling along through the weeds on his belly, pushing a rifle in front of him? The sun is beating down on his tin hat. His hands and face are dirty. He is sweating like a horse. He is vice-president of the Bishop National Bank.

Five paces to his right, behaving in the same amazing manner, is the dignified manager of Remington-Rand's Honolulu office.

The young fellow with the .45 Colt strapped at his hip, the one who is signaling to them, is their boss. He is a grocery clerk.

They, with the rest of their platoon, are about to capture a command post with a major and his staff.

This is just one of the things that the Japs started in Honolulu on December 7.

These men and a thousand others like them are members of the Businessmen's Military Training Corps, better known as the BMTC. The organization was conceived early in January 1942 by a group of Honolulu businessmen for the purpose of defending their homes against enemies from without and within.

They took the idea to army authorities, who were not greatly impressed. They felt that not enough men would volunteer to make it worthwhile—that at best it would be a nine-day wonder that would fade out of existence as enthusiasm waned. However, they said that if five hundred men could be induced to sign up, the army would arm and equip them.

The last week in January a call for volunteers was issued through the newspapers, and on Sunday, February 1, a thousand men turned out in response. Training started within an hour, and it has continued, three days a week, ever since.

First published November 1942.

Many of the original volunteers have dropped out. Some have gone into the army, some have returned to the Mainland, some are doing equally important defense work in other organizations, and some were just plain weak sisters. But recruits come in a steady stream to replace losses, and most of the Old Guard who were in Kapiolani Park February 1 have stuck like the good and loyal citizens they are.

The army's interest in BMTC has steadily increased. On March 1, Lt. Gen. Delos C. Emmons reviewed the regiment—four battalions of partially trained men in civilian clothes. Just before General Emmons was to arrive, there was an air raid alarm, which found a thousand unarmed men in white shirts standing in mass formation in the open. A beautiful target for bombers. They were ordered to disperse and find cover. They evinced more curiosity than fear, and it was difficult to keep them under the trees. After the all-clear, General Emmons came and the review was held.

Shortly after this, four commissioned and four noncommissioned officers of the army were assigned as instructors, and rapid progress in training ensued. Two infantry and a coast artillery (AA) regiments are among the regular army organizations that have shown the keenest interest in the training of the BMTC. This training includes close and extended order drill, target practice with .45 caliber Colt pistols, and .30 caliber and sub-caliber rifles, guard duty, and hand grenade throwing.

Twice each month regimental field exercises are held in which actual combat situations are simulated, and on August 30 the BMTC took part in maneuvers with the regular army. The opportunity to do so stemmed from the second review held for General Emmons, on August 16. This time the corps was uniformed, armed, and equipped. It was led by a famous coast artillery band. It made a splendid and impressive appearance. So much so that General Emmons asked it to take part in the coming maneuvers.

The men were called out at midnight the following Saturday, and every post was manned within thirty-eight minutes. An excellent record when the extent of the BMTC front that night is taken into consideration. It extended from the Damon Tract to beyond the Blow Hole.

At the critique held at Fort Shafter a couple of days later, high-ranking army officers had only praise for the work done by the BMTC. The corps is now considered an important factor in the defense of Honolulu. It is here to stay for the duration. It deserves the active support of every organization and loyal citizen on the island.

The corps is, in a sense, elite. Not by the standards of the Social Register, but by a finer and higher standard—patriotism, responsibility, dependability. Every man must be passed by the corps' own intelligence officers and then by the Honolulu Police Department. He must be a descendant of non-Axis parents and vouched for by a member of the corps.

Half of the personnel of the BMTC are executives in civil life. Sixty-four percent have had some previous military training, ranging all the way from ROTC to West Point. The regular armies of the United States, Canada, France, and Great Britain are represented, as well as our navy, marine corps, and coast guard. Many fought in the First World War. The average age is a little over forty-two years of age. Ages range from the teens to the seventies. There is a place in the BMTC for every able-bodied man on Oahu who is not doing some other type of defense work.

No article on the BMTC would be complete without mention of the Auxiliary Corps, composed of housewives and employed women who give part of their time to the typing and office work of the organization and who furnish coffee and sandwiches when the men are on night duty.

Yes, the Japs started a lot of things on December 7. One of the best of them is the BMTC.

"Tourists" in Denim

DR. CLARENCE LEWIS HODGE

❖ The defense boom in Hawaii, with its attractive wages and island glamour, has caused thousands of war workers from the mainland and other parts of the world to flock to Hawaii to work on war projects. Skilled and unskilled labor, they come from all walks of life and from every state in the Union and many foreign countries. Several thousand come from the sugarcane and pineapple plantations of the outer islands, and others from Honolulu and rural areas on Oahu.

The number of war workers in Hawaii cannot be revealed for military reasons, but the islands teem with workers of all races, colors, creeds, and skills. They are here with one objective in mind—work to help Uncle Sam make this Pacific bastion safe from attack.

An adventuresome and picturesque group dressed in their blue or brown work clothes, wearing reddish tin hats and little round identification badges on their shirts—they are the men who service and repair and keep the armed forces in first class fighting condition.

Perplexing problems face these thousands of war workers who have come to Hawaii to help the government build a fighting fortress for freedom. Being thrown into a strange community operating under wartime conditions, away from home, family, and friends, and living in crowded construction camps, some of which are ill equipped to take care of the physical and mental needs of the men, have led to some discomforts and "gripes."

Inadequate housing and recreation facilities, poor food, delays in mail, costs of living, time off from work to shop, crowded transportation and shopping facilities, blackout and curfew laws, liquor, gasoline, and tire restrictions, lack of social contacts—these are only a few causes for complaints aired by war workers.

But war workers in typical American fashion have taken these

First published November 1942.

inconveniences in their stride, griped a bit, then laughed them off and gone on with their major task of helping to win the war.

War workers may be divided into two major occupational groups: those working for the U.S. government, and those employed by private construction companies. The majority are single men between the ages of twenty and thirty-five.

Because of the nature of the work, there are comparatively few women employed on war projects. Construction work is essentially a man's job, although there are several hundred efficient war working women employed in the offices of the army and navy and in private construction firms. They are engaged mostly as secretaries, clerks, typists, bookkeepers, telephone operators, nurses and nurse's aides.

These thousands of skilled and unskilled workers are employed on a hive of war projects: naval stations, army camps, marine barracks, industrial shops, radio stations, docks and yards, ammunition depots, and at a host of other defense units springing up like mushrooms throughout the entire Hawaiian archipelago.

Working twenty-four hours a day in three eight-hour shifts, this legion of men has, since the December 7 attack, literally transformed the topography of Hawaii into an arsenal for both defensive and offensive action.

They have built gun emplacements and machine-gun nests, air raid shelters and ammunition dumps, machine shops and warehouses, barbed wire entanglements, barracks and recreation centers, and in addition, have serviced and repaired war equipment.

Millions of dollars have been spent on war projects in Hawaii, and today with the nation at war, production, personnel, and payrolls have been accelerated in all departments to meet the needs of our fighting forces in action.

Without these men in overalls who service and repair, Hawaii would be useless as a military and naval base. War workers in Hawaii are as vital to victory as the men who man the guns.

To house and feed and provide recreation for the thousands of workers living at construction camps is a sizable task in itself. But the army and navy and private construction companies have handled the problem this way.

War workers (with families) who are employed at Pearl Harbor and Hickam Field live in civilian defense housing units that have been constructed for them by the army and navy.

The family units, built for permanent use, are attractively planned and are furnished with the most modern equipment. Since the attack, many wives and children living in these areas have been sent back to the mainland for safekeeping.

At some other projects single workers are housed in large dormitories of frame construction.

Thousands of war workers prefer to live in Honolulu and commute to work. They have become settled residents of the community. The largest concentration of war workers is found living in the Waikiki area, although they are scattered throughout the city wherever housing accommodations can be found.

At camps, the workers are fed in large dining halls that seat a thousand men or more. Electrically equipped kitchens manned by expert chefs, cooks, and bakers cater to the men twenty-four hours a day. In spite of food shortages and transportation problems, the meals served in these camps are well balanced and nutritious.

Blacked-out recreation clubs equipped with motion picture machines, reading and writing facilities, radios, pianos, stages, game rooms, canteens, and pool tables have been built at most camps for use of the men during their leisure hours.

Under the direction of entertainment and athletic directors, vaudeville shows, band concerts, movies, dances, sports, and tournaments have been organized for the men.

Giggie Royse, morale officer, and Joe Kaulukukui, athletic director at Red Hill, are only two of many recreation leaders at war worker camps who are doing an outstanding job in keeping the men happy and amused during their off hours.

The USO War Workers Committee, directed by Melvine H. Harter, provides mobile movies and variety shows at camps that request them.

Organized in June 1941 to provide recreation and entertainment opportunities for war workers on Oahu, the USO War Workers Committee is now operating nightly programs at fifteen camps. USO Camp Shows, directed by Don George, provide the talent for most of these shows, which are paid for by the workers.

A war workers' information center and lounge has been set up at Central YMCA, where the men may obtain community-wide information, secure housing listings, read and write, or play games and dance.

When in Honolulu, the average war worker generally shops a bit, takes in a movie or dance, maybe goes swimming at Waikiki, and most always drops into one of the bars with a buddy for a snifter and chat.

War workers in Hawaii, in addition to their jobs, are helping in other ways to win the war. Civilian defense battalions have been organized at several camps and thousands of volunteers are being given basic military training in the use of rifle and sidearms in the event of an emergency.

Millions of dollars in war bonds have been purchased by workers through war bond committees organized at the camps. Hundreds of workers have answered the appeal to give blood to the Honolulu blood and plasma bank.

Morale among the men is high. They feel they are making a definite contribution to the defense of democracy by taking a swing at the setting sun with spade, spike, acetylene torch, and hammer. They are setting the pace for war workers throughout the United States. They, too, are fighters.

Honolulu Today

LORNA ARLEN

❖ Complexities of living brought about by war are, like Cleopatra's charms, "of infinite variety." Among them is the difficulty of getting the simplest things done in Honolulu these days. Take the matter of a shoe shine. A friend of ours approached a young shoeshine boy on a downtown corner and was startled when the boy refused to clean his shoes. "No can, bud. They brown and white, see? It's fifteen cents for a shine, and I can do two pairs of all brown or all black while I'm doing your one. I'm too busy."

Then there's the problem of getting a watch repaired. For a routine cleaning and check-up, they tell you it will take nine weeks and they can't even guarantee that. And there's the sign in the plumbing shop, "We can't accept any new work at present." Memorable was the advertisement placed in newspapers by a local laundry. "We're completely exhausted, pooped, whipped down. We're closing for a couple of weeks, so don't come near us." If you want to get a typewriter repaired, you have to get a 1-A priority.

A friend of ours went to a radio shop to buy a new tube. "That will take a couple of weeks," he was told. "But look. All I want is a new tube. I know the number and I will insert it myself. All you have to do is sell me the tube, now." But it wasn't that easy. "Listen, Mac, you see all these radios here, waiting to be repaired? We take them in the order they came in. Put your radio at the end of the line and when we get to it, you'll have your new tube. Not before."

We bought an electric fan the other day, and it had to be mounted on a piece of plyboard before it could be placed in the living room window. This involved cutting two round holes a couple of inches in diameter and putting in four screws. Not being very mechanical, and not possessing a saw, we decided to take it to a well-known manufacturer

---

First published November 1942.

of furniture. It would be a ten-minute job for a carpenter. But when we reached the furniture shop there was no sign of a masculine employee. There were a couple of women sitting disconsolately amid the few odds and ends of furniture left in the store. We explained our simple request and were told blankly, "No can. No got anybody to work here. All with the Engineers." (We finally got a nine-year-old boy in the neighborhood to do the job.)

We went to the dentist a couple of months ago, expecting him to be concerned about our long absence. He made a couple of dabs at the teeth, like a worker on a Ford assembly line, and said, "Don't come back until school opens. I'm too busy." Then there's the business executive who smiled patronizingly when an old customer asked him by telephone to send over some merchandise. "We haven't had a delivery boy for months," he said. "You'll have to come and get it."

A girl we know misplaced her car keys the other day, discovering the loss at four o'clock after a hectic day in the office. She knew she couldn't leave the car on the street all night and called the police for advice. They were quite vague but said, "If you don't find the keys by blackout time, give us another call." Then she had a bright idea, called the agency for her make of car, and asked for a duplicate key. "Yes, we can get you another key," she was told, "but you'll have to have a priority from the military governor!" What she would have done if she hadn't found the key is something we have not been able to figure out.

We used to use white iodine on our nails, to overcome brittleness. But this practice has been abandoned because, in order to buy a fifteen-cent bottle you have to go to the office of the military governor for a priority. Little did we realize how simple life used to be.

Territorial Government at War

JOHN SNELL,
EXECUTIVE SECRETARY,
HAWAII EQUAL RIGHTS COMMISSION

❖ Japanese bombs—dropping December 7, 1941, on Oahu, first American soil to bear the brunt and suffer the scare of the initial Axis' aggressor attack upon the United States—unified the American people into a single indomitable purpose: "Win this war—get it over as soon as possible!"

Likewise, within two hours after the first explosion at Pearl Harbor, which transformed Hawaii from a vacation "Paradise of the Pacific" into the center of an active combat zone, all resources of the territorial government were dedicated to the achievement of that single objective of our fellow citizens on the mainland of the United States.

Since that memorable moment on the morning of December 7—a year ago—when Gov. J. B. Poindexter proclaimed a "Defense Period" throughout the Territory under the "Hawaii Defense Act" passed by the Legislature in the Special Session in September–October, the work of all territorial departments has been devoted—some in greater, some in lesser, degree, but each to the maximum of its potentialities—toward aiding in winning the victory that ultimately must be that of the United Nations. And this policy of all-out assistance will continue, under the administration of Gov. Ingram M. Stainback, for the duration.

Under the Hawaii Defense Act, which granted to the Governor all-embracing powers (he is limited only by the Constitution and existing federal statutes), the Office of Civilian Defense, already organized, has functioned magnificently to a degree that is described elsewhere.

Of the regular territorial departments there has been, for example,

---

First published December 1942.

90

the Attorney General's office, which began its "war work" back in September 1941. From that time until November 1 all available resources of the department had been devoted to expediting and facilitating the work of the Special Session of the Legislature, which was called largely because of the international crisis. The department had drafted the Hawaii Defense Act, with amendments and modifications as suggested by the military authorities. It had prepared the Hawaii Territorial Guard Act to create a home guard to defend the Territory in the event the Hawaii National Guard was called into active federal service, a measure that proved to be invaluable in the light of subsequent events.

Within an hour after the initial attack on December 7, the staff of the Attorney General was on duty to assist the Governor and public authorities in drafting the orders, rules and regulations, proclamations, and other documents to meet the territorial emergency and to carry into effect the proclamation of a defense period and a state of martial law.

Thirty rules and regulations, under and pursuant to authority granted under the Hawaii Defense Act, were drafted covering transactions in foodstuffs and feed, blackouts, liquor transactions, closing of certain businesses, regulation of business by food dealers, transactions in vegetable seeds, suspension of certain laws as to emergency employees, prohibiting the use of rice for liquor manufacture, emergency purchases and projects, registration and identification of the civilian population, enumeration of essential materials, safekeeping and custody of certain public securities, suspension of certain territorial holidays, etc.

Besides the drafting of such rules and regulations and appropriate executive orders, numerous legal problems relating to defense and emergency matters had the attention of the office. During December practically the whole staff devoted its entire time to such defense and emergency matters. Thereafter, as the strain and pressure became relieved, all of the time of two attorneys and part of the time of two more attorneys was taken up with such matters.

Immediately after the declaration of martial law on December 7, Col. T. H. Green, Executive of the Military Governor, established his headquarters in the office of the Attorney General. Three offices, with necessary furniture and equipment, were made available to his executive staff, together with space and equipment in the outer office.

Every assistance and cooperation were rendered the military governor in establishing his staff in Iolani Palace.

The Territorial Highway Department is another that has cooperated to the fullest possible degree in the nation's war effort, its principal activities, both before and after the December 7 attack, having been concentrated on road improvements and betterments particularly desired by Army and Navy authorities as a means of increasing internal communications on Oahu from the defense viewpoint.

The outbreak of war, and the emergency defense preparations preceding it, imposed new and additional duties and responsibilities upon the Board of Health, particularly on Oahu where, primarily as a result of the national defense program, there had been a rapid increase in population.

Additional public health services had been required in environmental sanitation, communicable disease control, food inspection, restaurant sanitation, public health nursing, supervision of water supplies, and problems related to housing.

Immediately following the President's declaration of a national emergency, plans were made for expanding public health functions for the increased protection of civilian and military health. Reserve supplies necessary for emergency use were obtained to keep adequate supplies on hand. Biological supplies, certain drugs, and laboratory supplies and equipment were recognized as especially important items. Measures for protecting water supplies and managing the sewage disposal system were carefully planned. Provision was made for satisfactory sanitary inspection under varying types of emergency conditions.

With the actual outbreak of the war, a close liaison was established with the medical departments of the Army and Navy, governmental departments, and other interested agencies to coordinate and correlate services. Appropriate measures for the prevention and control of communicable diseases were instituted. Routine sanitary, food, water, milk, and other inspection services were intensified, and provision was made for expanding other regular public health functions, including bedside nursing and obstetrical care.

The Board has continued to cooperate closely with the military authorities and private agencies for the mutual protection of the military and civilian health and it has collaborated with the department surgeon in the preparation of a number of military orders. Two such orders are worthy of note—the first requiring the immunization against typhoid fever and smallpox of the civilian population of the Territory who had not been vaccinated since January 1, 1941, and the second making venereal disease control measures more stringent.

The immunization program was organized and administered by the Territorial Board of Health, with the cooperation of the Medical Department of the Army, the Office of Civilian Defense, and various voluntary organizations. Vaccination against smallpox was required for all persons over the age of six months and against the typhoid fevers for all beyond the age of three years, except for the aged and infirm. Although immunization against diphtheria was not required, it was urged for all children between the ages of nine months and ten years not previously protected. Diphtheria toxoid was furnished by the Board, and the typhoid vaccine, smallpox virus, and incidental supplies were provided by the Army. As of September, records list 361,342 persons vaccinated against typhoid fever, 366,067 against smallpox, and 18,017 children protected against diphtheria.

In addition to its regular duties, the Territorial Treasury was designated as a depository for the safekeeping of the securities of residents of the Territory for the duration under a plan prescribed by the Department of Interior, with the approval of the President and the Treasury Department of the United States. General Orders 123 of the Office of the Military Governor and regulations relating to securities by the Acting Governor of Hawaii accelerated the depositing of securities to such an extent that a good portion of the regular office work was practically at a standstill during all of July.

Under ordinary circumstances, one of the primary functions of the Board of Agriculture and Forestry is the planting of hundreds of thousands of trees in the forest reserve land. This function was thrown into reverse, however, by the Japanese attack; instead of devoting its efforts to planting new trees, the Board is permitting the cutting and scaling of small timbers and saw log for use in the current war effort by the U.S. Engineers and to reduce the strain on shipping facilities from the mainland.

Inmates and parolees of the various establishments under the Department of Institutions—Oahu Prison, the Kawailoa Girls' and Waialee Boys' Training Schools, the Territorial Hospital, and Waimano Home—have engaged in work of various projects essential to national defense during the past year, including cutting firewood, of which several hundred cords have been donated to various units of the Army and Marine Corps for use in field kitchens; digging trenches and bomb shelters in public parks and school grounds; working as stevedores unloading freight from various vessels carrying cargo vital to national defense; working in warehouses and storage dumps; cultivating and preparing various plots of land for "victory gardens"; and cultivating and maintaining vegetable gardens at various institutions of the Territory.

They have also donated to the blood bank; and a large percentage of the prisoners have purchased War Bonds to the amount of ten thousand dollars. Women prisoners, since December 7, have made more than fifty thousand surgical dressings for the Red Cross, in addition to making a large number of hospital gowns and pajamas for children.

In the majority of cases, the morale of prisoners and inmates has been exceptionally high since the declaration of war, many having signed petitions volunteering their services where they could be used to the best of advantage.

Among the territorial departments most vitally affected by the war has been that of Public Instruction. The public schools were closed for several months immediately after the December 7 attack. Some of the school classrooms, cafeterias, laboratories, storerooms, garages, dispensaries, restrooms, gymnasiums, auditoriums, and lavatories were given up for the use of the armed forces or other agencies associated with the war effort. These units were distributed among the schools generally, and included all or nearly all of the facilities in twenty-six schools. Principals and teachers, and children and patrons have willingly shared school facilities as a part of the effort to meet urgent war needs. Classes have been conducted in temporary quarters such as private homes, churches, temples, social halls, storerooms—in fact any kind of vacant space that could be made available.

Principals and teachers and other members of the Department staff devoted virtually their entire activities to assist in registering the populace of the Territory and other operations of the Office of Civilian Defense, and they aided the war effort along various other lines.

The University of Hawaii likewise was turned topsy-turvy by the Japanese attack and held no classes from December 6 to February 2.

"The University has functioned only as an agency of the military," the president of the institution reported. "Some of our buildings were

On December 7th blast-damaged cars had their windows shattered and tires blown out.

From a midget submarine grounded near Bellows Field in Waimanalo, the lone Japanese survivor swam ashore and became the only prisoner of war from the December 7th attack.

Within days of the initial attack, civilians lined up to obtain cards when the military instituted gas rationing throughout the islands.

Fearing food shortages for their families as much as they feared bombs, housewives rushed to grocery stores to stock up on the morning after the attack.

Dogs and barbed wire helped soldiers guard the beaches.

Barbed wire was strung across the gate to Iolani Palace.

The civilian fingerprinting committee included UH professor Paul Bachman (far left) and Sheriff Duke Kahanamoku (far right).

Territory Governor Joseph B. Poindexter is fingerprinted as Honolulu Mayor Lester Petrie awaits his turn.

All island residents were issued gas masks, including the keiki.

Clerks at the Honolulu police annex display weapons confiscated from non-U.S. citizens living in Hawaii.

taken over; Hemenway Hall made a good evacuation center; the gymnasium was prepared for evacuees, and later was occupied by the Hawaii Territorial Guard as a barracks. The entire personnel of the R.O.T.C. volunteered and were accepted for service in the Territorial Guard. The men and women of the faculty engaged in many activities: among others, censorship, fingerprinting, chemical and bacteriological analyses of potable water, guard and police duty, and lecturing. In brief, the Board of Regents and the faculty subscribed completely to an all-out war effort, whether such effort should demand their time, their abilities or the physical plant."

Various other territorial departments also cooperated with the military authorities to the utmost degree of their potentialities during the first year following the Japanese attack. And, as has been stated, this fullest degree of cooperation on the part of the territorial government, as well as the civilian populace generally, with the military and naval forces, who are in the center of the active combat zone that now is Hawaii, will continue—for the duration—in conformance with the sentiments expressed by Governor Stainback in his inaugural message: ". . . When the history of that period (since December 7) is written, the activities of the civilian volunteers—men and women— will be a record of which Hawaii may be justly proud. We must continue this complete cooperation with the armed forces to defeat the common enemy; and in this cooperation we must be prepared to sacrifice, freely and cheerfully, comfort and self-interest in furtherance of the common cause."

The Year in Retrospect

LaSELLE GILMAN

❖ The old cliché to the effect that "you wouldn't know the old place now" applies today to Hawaii perhaps more fully than to any other American community. After the first year of war in the Pacific, the Islands have been turned upside down—revolutionized. It has been a bloodless, social revolution (bloodless, that is, except for the opening day), but it has changed not only the manners and customs of the people, and their mental and physical habits, but it has also altered the very face of Hawaii itself to an extent that would probably astonish any Mainland resident who had ever visited the Territory in the past.

Former tourists and business visitors, who once arrived in Honolulu and received all the traditional trimmings of a big boat-day aloha—the off-port greetings, leis, the band, hula girls—would have a difficult time reconciling themselves to the welcome they would receive these days, if they were fortunate enough to be able to obtain passage to the Islands at all by the strictly-war-business Army Transport Service. There are, of course, no pleasure tourists at all, now. The few who arrive from the coast are grim war workers, or transport-loads of troops. Even established Island residents who happened to be traveling on the Mainland when war began have been unable to return home unless their presence here was proved "necessary to the war effort." They have settled down in rather disconsolate little colonies along the west coast, apparently for the duration.

Travel to Hawaii is by convoy and involves no frills. There are no gay send-off parties, no lights at night, no frivolities. And when the ships slip into port at the end of a quiet, nervous voyage, they discharge passengers and war cargoes hastily, and as hastily reload for the return trip. The new arrival, whether here for his first or his tenth visit, faces a Hawaii of which he had not dreamed, even though he has been a careful reader of newspaper accounts during the past year.

First published December 1942.

Hawaii was not changed all of a sudden on that sunny December morning last year when the gray planes of Japan, with their identifying circular blood spots on the wings, dove without warning from over the Waianaes and Koolaus to drop death and destruction on Pearl Harbor. The change had been going on for more than a year. It probably started when the Pacific Fleet, without much fanfare, moved into Hawaiian waters and made headquarters here. It was given momentum by the creation of a national emergency. The war in Europe had broken the spell, and for many months between September 1939 and December 1941 Hawaii was going through a metamorphosis. The nature of the city of Honolulu was gradually changing with the slow, steady influx of war workers (we called them defense workers then), soldiers, and sailors. Big defense construction projects were being started. But the war did not touch Hawaii except by passing travelers' tales. There were various alarms, particularly because of Hawaii's geographical position midway between America and the war-torn Orient. The Islands kept their eyes on Japan. Hawaii knows Japan better than does most of America because of her close proximity and because of the thousands of Japanese residents here.

In the autumn of 1941 there was an intensification of defense preparations, particularly through the creation of a civilian emergency program in which volunteers were enlisted for key jobs should anything happen. But even the most pessimistic did not really expect the thing to happen as it actually did. Hawaii was in the position of knowing pretty well that a storm was coming, but when the torrent suddenly began to fall, her umbrella was still folded.

The facts of December 7—a black Sunday in the history of the Islands—are too well known to bear much repetition now. The attack was made, and there was a terrific toll taken in lives and property, especially at Pearl Harbor, which bore the brunt, and its vicinity. A few bombs, mainly incendiaries, were scattered across the city, starting fires, but the residential areas were largely spared, and the deaths were mainly among Navy personnel. The Army also suffered, but civilian casualties were comparatively light.

The attack stunned every person in the Islands. Yet they had made their preparations for it carefully, and when it came, residents almost automatically went to work with preconceived plans. After the first astounding concussions, the Army and Navy were on the job, and from then on Hawaii started all over on a fresh page.

On that long-dreaded, long-anticipated "M-Day," one of the first acts was one that was the farthest reaching: the civil governor of the Territory wisely placed authority with the military commander, who immediately placed Hawaii under strict martial law. This military government has continued for the past year, a virtually unprecedented system of governing in the United States, but one that has been regarded by authorities as best for an isolated island stronghold whose primary purpose is to stand as an outpost in the Pacific war zone, serving as a base for the embattled Fleet and defended by the Army. Nature may have created Hawaii as a picturesque South Seas tourist haven in the times of peace, but nature also placed the Islands in such a strategic position, geographically, that in time of war they could serve America best only as a bristling fortress and front line of defense—and offense.

Martial law under the military governor has worked extraordinarily well in Hawaii. There have been local chafing under it, local complaints and grumblings, but in general the Island residents have accepted its various prohibitions and inconveniences philosophically, although they realize that this is the only American community thus far upon which martial law has been imposed. Population of the Territory has expanded amazingly in the last two years, the increase being largely from the flood of war workers and their families who came into the Islands just before war began and the families of Service personnel. This population increase, of course, does not include the actual armed forces, the number of which is not made public. But any casual observer on the streets of Honolulu, Wailuku, Lihue, or Hilo could see that uncounted thousands of soldiers and sailors have arrived here to man the ramparts.

Under the general orders of the military governor, Hawaii changed overnight after December 7. There were the total blackout and the strictly enforced curfew. Neither have been relaxed since war began. The blackout has been a considerable discomfort in Hawaii because of the warm climate, making it unpleasant to remain indoors behind windows and doors barred to the evening trade winds, but once the residents realized that nobody was fooling, they blacked out their homes and liked it.

The curfew was imposed largely because of the obvious necessity. Only people who must be on the streets during night hours by reason of necessary war work are allowed to go unmolested by reinforced patrols of police and soldiers. The burden placed on Island police forces by the war has been very heavy, considering the many new and stringent military orders that must be enforced, but the police have taken it in their stride. So have the citizens for the most part.

For several weeks "after Pearl Harbor," a liquor prohibition was imposed, and the Islands ran dry, a hardship on war-jangled nerves, especially for kamaainas accustomed to their usual long cool ones on the verandah, and for malihini workers. Later, this was relaxed and liquor was carefully rationed. The system has worked well. Bars open at 10 A.M., close shortly after 3 P.M.

Civil courts were closed under martial law (they have recently reopened under certain restrictions), and the provost marshal established provost courts under Army judges. These courts operate without benefit of jury, closely resembling night police courts in metropolitan Mainland cities; justice is dispensed rapidly and impartially to all offenders or violators of military orders, whether they happened to violate the blackout, or robbed a sailor, or drank more than was good for them. The fines have been generally rather heavy; the "take" has gone into a special fund that is being held by the federal Treasury. There has been some serious criticism of the provost courts, and various changes have been made, but the Territory has accepted them as necessary, for the most part.

After the first month or so of uproar in Hawaii, the Territory settled down to the serious business of war. There were no further attacks made in the area save for "nuisance raids" by enemy submarines. Hawaii, however, is so deep in the war zone that other events in the Pacific appear to be happening in her own back yard, and the people of the Islands watched with careful, personal interest Japan's initial advances through the Philippines and Malaya, the East Indies, Burma, and the southwest Pacific islands toward Australia. Guam and Wake had fallen; many of Hawaii's wandering sons had fallen with them. But in those months the Army perfected its Island defenses and the Navy began a series of widespread operations that were launched with the raids on the Marshall Islands. Then came the great Battle of the Coral Sea, followed by the decisive Battle of Midway, after which American forces drove strongly into the Solomons and, as the weeks went by, the Japanese offensive seemed to be rolling slowly to a stop, and an Allied offensive began to gather momentum.

All this was noted in Hawaii with absorbed attention. Here the coast gun emplacements were built, the barbed wire was strung, the deep air raid shelters dug. Camouflage began to change the appearance of town and country. Troops swarmed everywhere. Civilians were issued gas masks. The office of civilian defense swung into action. Toward the end of the year there was hardly a citizen in the Islands not enrolled in one type of war work or another—from Red Cross volunteer to air raid warden to business men's training corps. Gasoline was strictly rationed months before it was on the Mainland. There were periods when there were shortages of various items of food, but there was never a time when the convoys failed to bring enough to stave off hunger. Potatoes might be hard to obtain at one time, eggs at another, beef at another, and candy or cigarettes now and then.

In short, Honolulu has passed through a boom year. There has been a terrific housing shortage, now eased by additional war worker housing suburbs. Everybody works—there is not enough help to go round. Domestic help is unobtainable, plantation labor is hard to get because men of all nationalities have flocked into lucrative war work, and even husky Hawaiian girls are now doing manual labor for good pay. Money is one thing of which there is no shortage, although the cost of living has likewise skyrocketed despite official efforts at price control. These war workers spend money as freely as the tourists of former days, and for small-business men life is pretty good, despite the many merchandising restrictions.

So far as Hawaii's big business is concerned—which means, mainly, sugar and pineapples—both products have continued to be shipped in large amounts to the Mainland. Plantations, however, have reduced their acreage considerably in order to grow quick food crops, and also because plantation labor, as well as equipment in the way of heavy machinery, has been loaned to the Army for defense purposes.

There has been, additionally, a certain shipping shortage, which has resulted not only in the periodic shortages of food supplies and equipment sent here from the Mainland, but also a strict priority system because of the prime necessity of sending war material to Hawaii. This has occasionally resulted likewise in long gaps between the arrival dates of important mail.

Soon after the attack a year ago, many so-called non-essential persons in the Territory whose homes were on the Mainland left. There were mainly women and children, at first largely the families of Army and Navy personnel, but also including many others. This evacuation program has continued for many months, and the result has been that the Territory's population is today predominately masculine; this "men without women" hardship is felt, particularly by the armed forces.

Pleasures have been drastically curtailed. The early closure of bars and cafes drives the population home long before dark, and the blackout and curfew keep them off the streets. Nightlife has vanished from Honolulu, a city once noted for its gay evening entertainment. Theatre patrons and dancers must find such relaxation in daylight hours; only in rare instances may dances or shows be found after dark, and then strictly behind blackout curtains.

For the goods they buy, the pleasures they find, Hawaii residents today pay with "Hawaii series" currency—U.S. paper currency stamped with "Hawaii." All other currency has been withdrawn. If Hawaii was by any chance invaded, the enemy would find little use for such money because the government would immediately invalidate it.

In short, Hawaii is a far cry at the end of 1942 from the Paradise Isles it was only a year or so ago. No one, in fact, expects to see the Territory ever to return exactly to the conditions that prevailed here before the war. The change is not only constant, it is permanent. What the future holds for the Islands few would hazard a guess. Yet in many ways it is the same Hawaii: the trades still blow over the green mountains, nodding the tall coco trees along the beach and ruffling the surf out on the reef. From a distance at sea, the hills and the flower-bedecked towns look almost as before. Man-made war cannot alter certain indestructible aspects of life in Hawaii. This is a fact upon which most of those who remain here through times of peril base their future in the inevitable days of peace to come.

1943

In mid-January a prominent Honolulu businessman, John A. Balch, proposed that at least a hundred thousand Japanese in Hawai'i should be sent to the Mainland. The proposal was made in a privately printed pamphlet entitled "Shall the Japanese Be Allowed to Dominate Hawaii?" At the close of the month a plan to induct fifteen hundred volunteers of Japanese ancestry in Hawai'i was announced. The Varsity Victory Volunteers requested to be inactivated in order to volunteer for combat duty.

Guadacanal was recaptured by U.S. Marines in February. In the Battle of the Bismark Sea, U.S. and Australian planes sank eight Japanese transports and four destroyers, hurting the enemy's chances of holding New Guinea. A month later, U.S. aviators destroyed or disabled three hundred Japanese planes and killed hundreds of pilots and ground crew at Wewak, New Guinea.

In May the Chamber of Commerce launched a program for postwar planning.

On July 9, at age seventy-three, ex-governor Poindexter was appointed as a Bishop Estate trustee.

On July 24, the Twenty-fourth Division left Hawai'i for battle in New Guinea.

In September, First Lady Eleanor Roosevelt spent several days on O'ahu. Later in the month, the first rubber produced and processed in Hawai'i was shipped to the Mainland.

On October 17, a Japanese plane reconnoitered Pearl Harbor.

The Gilbert Islands were captured by U.S. forces on November 23. The wounded from there and other battlefields were evacuated to Honolulu. A Red Cross Gray Lady told *Paradise:* "On several occasions, thousands of night-blooming cereus, one for each patient, were gathered late in the afternoon. They'd only last the night, but what real joy they brought those sick men."

Ke Kauwa Nei O Kauai
(Kauai at War)

EILEEN O'BRIEN

❖ The residents of Honolulu, absorbed in the complex problems of wartime conditions, are seldom aware that, on the outside islands, life presents an even more complicated pattern. A special Pearl Harbor anniversary edition of *The Garden Island* presents a fascinating summary of the year's events on Kauai.

From a newspaperman's point of view, the biggest story of the year from Kauai was the story of the battle for Niihau, an editorial states. "The story was not hampered by censorship to a great extent and was promptly printed in all the newspapers here and on the mainland. An article on the battle, in which Ben Kanahele and his wife killed an enemy aviator, states that after Kanahele recovered from his wounds, he and his wife returned to their simple life at Niihau. "Being heroes has not changed their way of life." The article also states that Blake Clark's story in the *Reader's Digest* for December "carries considerably embroidery, which places it in the category of legends."

The biggest story of the year for Kauai itself has never been published, the editorial states. "In newspaper parlance, we are still sitting on it. It can be partially but not entirely told now. The arrival of mainland troops on Easter Sunday is the story. During the first three months of the war, Kauai was defended by a handful of men. Today there are more soldiers packed in the Lihue theater on leave any afternoon of the week than there were defending this island the first three months of the war.

"The troops which poured off the transports that Easter Sunday arrived in a downpour of tropical rain and they had no idea of how happy the people of the island were to see them, since the Kauai people could not gather in crowds to hang leis about their necks and demonstrate their joy."

First published January 1943.

The story of Kauai's civilian defense activities has many interesting chapters. Unlike Oahu, where there are several separate and sometimes conflicting organizations of "last-ditch fighters," the men of Kauai have only one. Early in February 1942, just two months after Pearl Harbor, the organization of the Kauai Volunteers was authorized by Lt. Gen. Delos Emmons. Paul H. Townsley of Lihue was selected to organize and enlist three thousand men for the Kauai Service Command. Mr. Townsley was commissioned a colonel for the task.

Within one month's time Colonel Townsley had enlisted two battalions and a regimental headquarters company, and in two months he had brought the regimental strength to two full battalions. The Volunteers supply their own uniforms of khaki, with a blue necktie and blue and gold shoulder brassard, and are trained by carefully selected men of the regular army.

Kauai's Major Disaster Council formed the nucleus of what became the Office of Civilian Defense and has accomplished gargantuan tasks during the year. Hundreds of workers from all parts of the island have been trained, and among the wardens are large numbers of women. Charles J. Fern heads Kauai's OCD. The Kiawe Kommando Korps is a thriving patriotic organization, with a record turnout on one day in November of 1,624 persons. The Kauai Morale Committee has made an important contribution by its work among residents of Japanese ancestry, and the Sons of Mokihana have made a record as OCD volunteers, their latest project being the Kauai Farmerettes.

Oahu's food shortages seem trivial when compared with the situations that have existed on Kauai. Rice was rationed last January and rationing of butter followed. Other essential foods were rationed by the merchants themselves. As food supplies became scarce during February and March, the food administrator was forced to ration feed stocks, which resulted in the wholesale slaughter of chickens, pigs, and some cattle.

Kauai housewives were asked to practice meatless days twice a week, but this plan was abandoned when it was discovered that there was an even greater shortage of meat substitutes. When the troops arrived in April, the island had only a three-week supply of food left in its stores. Disaster was averted by the shipments that began to come through in abundance after the arrival of troops. Now, although food supplies are limited in variety, they are so abundant there is sufficient for all.

Kauai's best rumor of the year was started by women and caused a stampede on the beauty shops. "According to reliable sources," it was whispered that all beauty parlors would be closed in April. OCD Coordinator Fern came to the rescue with soothing words that the rumor was without foundation. Some observers decided that the run on the beauty shops was due also to the presence of the handsome young malihinis . . . the soldiers.

Honolulu Today

LORNA ARLEN

❖ Entertainment-starved Honolulu had its first taste of Mainland entertainment since the war began when Capt. Maurice Evans gave his spell-binding lecture at McKinley auditorium last month. Although in Hawaii for active duty with the army, Evans generously agreed to appear before an audience of civilians.

In spite of a downpour of rain, the auditorium was packed. It was an audience such has not been seen in Honolulu since darkness fell on the Islands. "Everyone" was there . . . the University crowd, the Manoa set, those familiar faces that used to be seen at the Symphony, the Academy, the Community Theater, the campus lectures. And plain Mr. and Mrs. George Spelvin who, like everyone else, were thirsting for entertainment from that remote other world, New York—the Big Time.

They were not disappointed. Maurice Evans stood before them in his regulation army uniform, without the lights, costumes, and trappings that make the world of the theater glitter. But through his supreme mastery the stage seemed peopled with living actors, and the magic words of Shakespeare created an unforgettable panorama of deathless pageantry.

Captain Evans' assignment in Hawaii is with the D.S.S.O., four letters that stand for Department Special Service Office. This is an intricate organization charged with providing educational and recreational facilities for soldiers off duty. He plans to take Shakespearean plays to soldiers in remote outposts by means of a caravan theater built on a four-and-a-half-ton chassis. The famous actor helped build the theater himself, incidentally, proving that he can wield a sharp hammer as well as cast spells from the footlights.

The caravan theater has a stage thirty-four feet long and thirteen feet from footlights to ceiling, with props and scenery that appear like

First published February 1943.

magic from the depths of the truck. Such a theater is an interesting throwback to the days when Shakespeare's plays were originally presented in open fields and courtyards, with a minimum of the trappings of modern theatricals.

Capt. Evans' plan for bringing the "flesh" theater to soldiers in Honolulu is but one of the many phases of D.S.S.O. activities. One of the biggest of its new projects is the huge recreation building now under construction just inside the main entrance to Fort De Russy in Waikiki.

The new building will have two connecting wings, one of which will be a two-story structure with a terrace similar to that of the second floor of the Army-Navy Y in downtown Honolulu. There will be a large dance floor, an auditorium with stage and projection room for USO shows, hula troupes, and special movies. On the upstairs lanai there will be lounges, game rooms, and other recreational facilities.

Adjacent to the new site are the present recreation facilities that have been open for nearly six months. These include a beer garden, movie, library, pool room, lounge, and complete hotel service.

Army officers have to relax, too, and their recreational needs are a part of the D.S.S.O. The Willard Inn, in Waikiki, is now an officers' club, and the Haleiwa Hotel was re-opened recently as a fun spot for army officers and their guests. In addition, they will soon have a recreation spot of their own at the former Judge Steiner home at Waikiki Beach.

❖ Meanwhile, the navy is by no means neglecting the fun department for its personnel. Their favorite spot for the lads in white is The Breakers, the navy's new recreation center on the beach at Waikiki, opposite Kapiolani Park bandstand.

Attendance at The Breakers has exceeded even the expectations of Commander Hickey, genial head of fleet recreation in Hawaii. When he drew up the plans for this spot, which is his pet and brainchild, he figured that a capacity of three thousand would be more than generous. However, he has had daily attendance up to thirty-six hundred and now wishes the place were twice as big.

The headline attraction at The Breakers these days is Artie Shaw, whose new band of navy men is strictly out of this world. Artie is proud of the fact that he enlisted in the navy as an ordinary sailor and now wears the uniform of a chief, instead of angling for a commission as other topnotchers of the show world have done. The new band is called Artie Shaw's Rangers and plays at the Waikiki spot every Sunday and Thursday. On Mondays music there is by Carey's Mustangs, and on other days of the week it's the Breakers Commandos.

Attendance at The Breakers is restricted to women and service men, the latter being about equally divided between the army and the navy. There's a section of tables reserved for officers and their guests.

Besides accomplishing its chief purpose of providing a place where service men can really enjoy themselves, The Breakers has done two other things. It has reduced attendance at less desirable bars in downtown Honolulu and has cut in half the traffic jam during peak hours at the Army-Navy Y.

❖ The arrival of Joe E. Brown last month marked the first personal appearance in Hawaii of a Hollywood star since before the start of the war. Although troops in Alaska, Iceland, and other outposts have had considerable entertainment by the film colony, the men in Hawaii had none until the appearance of the jovial wide-mouthed comedian.

Islands Await Effects
of New Regime

❖ An announcement that stirred Hawaii was the one from Washington, D.C., stating that citizens of Japanese ancestry would be permitted to volunteer for combat duty with the Army of the United States. The mainland was to provide three thousand men for the new unit, and the Territory of Hawaii would provide fifteen hundred.

The demonstration of loyalty given by AJA's in the Territory in meeting the quota and then exceeding it fivefold and more is heartening proof of the unity of all sections of the population in Hawaii. No more sincere display of patriotism can be asked of anyone than combat service because, while it is easy enough to talk Americanism, it is hard indeed to practice it.

AJA volunteers deserve recognition for their display of devotion to the United States. That is only fair. But they must expect no exaggerated gratitude, for they are doing no more than any and every American eligible for military service. They must expect only to be treated as American soldiers fighting for the preservation of the Four Freedoms.

That Americans of Japanese ancestry should have been regarded with some doubt on the part of the general population may not have been absolutely fair. But it was unavoidable, and the Administration deserves all the more recognition for its eminent justice and far-seeing tolerance.

It has given Americans of Japanese ancestry the sword with which they can cut every last tie, real or imaginary, binding them to Japan. The rest is up to the people themselves.

First published March 1943.

114

A Unique Experience in Government

WILLIAM EWING,
STAR-BULLETIN COMMENTATOR OVER KGMB

❖ In the throne room of Iolani Palace last month, ceremonies were held observing the restoration of civil government in Hawaii. Civil government was suspended, for all effective considerations, on December 7, 1941. Last month the powers given over to the military on that day were restored to the authorities who originally held them, the civil government.

The change was ordered at Washington by the departments concerned at the capital—the war, justice and interior departments—the agreement being reached on the advice and with the consent of their representatives here. In practically all cases the regulations that have applied under military order will be continued, the only difference being in the source of administrative authority.

At the "restoration" ceremony in Iolani Palace, the room was filled with people wearing leis and the smiles that go with them. The string section and singers from the Royal Hawaiian Band and other musicians of Representative Bina Mossman's troupe completed the setting by playing the "Song of the Islands." The house held a brief session to transact the day's business, and then the music, without which no Hawaiian ceremony would be complete, began again. The only note of war that sounded during the transfer of authority was the thud of anti-aircraft guns in practice firing. It served as a reminder that although the scene in the capitol was peaceful, the war is still near, and vigilance has not relaxed.

General Emmons was represented by General Burgin, who expressed the thanks of General Emmons to all for their cooperation,

---

First published April 1943.

particularly those on the outside islands. He asked the same cooperation with the civil governor, and the same support. Admiral Nimitz paid a compliment to General Emmons and said that the harmonious relations that have existed can be attributed as much to his wise administration as to the hearty cooperation of the citizens.

The man who took over during these ceremonies, and on whom devolves the responsibility for continued efficient administration—Governor Stainback—made his position plain in a brief address, offering the military and naval authorities the fullest support from him and staff. When he had concluded, a resolution, signed by every member of the House of Representatives, was offered, directing thanks to Admiral Nimitz and his staff and to General Emmons and his staff for the manner in which, since December 7, 1941, the defenses of the territory have been made impregnable, the safety of the people assured, and the welfare of the civilian population well cared for.

So ends a unique experience in American government. Under the pressure of military necessity, military rule was exerted in this territory. Now the principle of representative government has been upheld by returning this authority to the civil administration. Martial law has been in effect for more than fifteen months and, for that matter, still is. The greatest civil liberty our Constitution guarantees, the right of *habeas corpus*, is still suspended. But this does not depreciate the changes that have been made; rather, it underscores the willingness of the military authorities to go only so far in relaxing their control, and the ability of the civil departments concerned to understand this necessity.

It would be idle to contend that everyone in Hawaii has demanded the restoration of civil government. Agreement on the matter was reached in Washington. It has now been done, and the responsibility has passed to Governor Stainback and his administration. He not only deserves the same support the military authorities have received, it is imperative that he should receive it. We are all in this war together; our government requires our support; and the overall leadership is the same it has always been. We have merely changed the command.

"G.I." Hawaiian

MILLY LOU DONNELLY

❖ Little brochures have been issued by the Army telling our soldiers the proper way to ask for a spot of tea in London and what not to say to a veiled lady in Algiers. Perhaps a couple of colloquialisms would make them feel more at home in Hawaii, where East is sometimes Ewa, and West depends on where you stand at the time. Then, too, consider the sad sailor, to whom the pretty Hawaiian maiden said "Ae, No!" Things would have been so different if he had known she didn't mean "I? No!" but "Yes, indeed!" Therefore, I have assembled some everyday words and phrases into groups, which I hope may be convenient and useful for our visiting fighting men, and present them with my aloha.

The alphabet has only seven consonants—H, K, L, M, N, P, W— pronounced as in English. In the middle of a word, W has the sound of V. Every syllable ends in a vowel. Pronounce the five vowels like this:

A—Say Ah
E—Like the E in Hep
I—Like EE in Jeep
O—Plain old O
U—Like OO in Yoo! Hoo!
AE and AI—Like the AI in middle-aisle!
AU and AO—Like the OW in chow
EI—Like the A in hay-foot

THE SOLDIER
(Ko-a)

Airship	mo-ku-le-le
All right in rear	o-ho-pe-lae

First published April 1943.

117

Aviator	ka-ne-le-le
Battle, war	ka-u-a
Can do	hi-ki no
Cold	a-nu-a-nu
Dig	e-li
Dirty	hau-mi-a
Done, finished	pau
Government	au-pu-ni
Gripe	nu-ku-nu-ku
Halt!	uo-ki!
Hat	pa-pa-le
Help	ko-ku-a
Hot	we-la
Hurry	wi-ki-wi-ki
Mosquito	ma-ki-ka
Muddy	u-ke-le-ke-le
No can do	hi-ki o-le
Okay	po-lo-lei!
The Old Man	a-le-ma-ku-le
Red tape	"humbug"
Sleep	mo-e mo-e
Sleepy	ma-ka hi-a mo-e
Tired	lu-hi
Tobacco	pa-ka
Top Kick	lu-na ha-na
Trouble	pi-li-ki-a
Walk	he-le wa-wae
Wet	pu-lu
Win, victory	la-na-ki-la
Work	ha-na
Worry	ma-na-o pi-li-ki-a

THE PASS

Bottoms up!	o-ko-le ma-lu-na!
Buy	ku-ai mai
Club, group	hu-i
Costs too much	ma-ke-he-wa

Damn-fool	ka-ma-pu-lu
Dance	hu-la or a-na-pau
Drink	i-nu
Fight	ha-ka-ka
Gamble	pi-li-wai-wai
Garland, flowers	lei
Good bargain	ma-ke-po-no
Gossip	ho-lo-ho-lo o-le-lo
Guardhouse, brig	ha-le pa-a-hao
Headache	na-lu-lu
Intoxicated	o-na
Liquor	o-ko-le-hao
Lose money	po-ho ka-la
Off duty	mo-e mo-e
Out of bounds	ka-pu
Pay	u-ku
Pay day	u-ku la
Policeman	ma-kaʻ-i
Ride, in auto	ho-lo-ho-lo ka-a
Ride, surfboard	he-e-na-lu
Shoot the works!	"go for broke"
Sing, song	me-le
Swim	au
Thirsty	ma-ke-wai
Whoopee	we-la-ka-hao

KITCHEN POLICE

Beans	pa-pa-pa
Beef	iʻo pi-pi
Banquet, Hawaiian	lu-au
Cake, cookie	me-a o-no
Coffee	ko-pe
Come and get it!	he-le mai e ai!
Eat	ai, or kau-kau
Food	me-a ai, or kau-kau
Good grub	o-no lo-a
Hungry	po-lo-li

Pig	pu-a-a
Slightly smelly	pi-lau!
Spam	i'o pu-a-a
Spuds	ua-la (wah-lah)

HOSPITAL
(Ha-le la-pa-au)

Arm, hand	li-ma
Back	ku-a
Bathe	au
Bed	hi-ki-e-e
Be quiet!	E ha-mau!
Blanket	ka-pa-hu-lu-lu
Doctor	kau-ka
Ear	pe-pei-ao
Eye	ma-ka
Foot, leg	wa-wae
Head	po-o
Heart	pu-u-wai
Lie down	mo-e
Medicine	la-au la-pau-au
Mouth	wa-ha
Nose	i-hu
Nurse	ka-hu-ma'-i
Pain, ache	e-ke e-ke
Pillow	u-lu-na
Sick	ma-i
Sit	no-ho
Sore	e-ha
Stand	ku
Stomach	o-pu
Tooth	ni-ho
Well	mai-kai

THE CONVOY

Battle-wagon	ma-nu-wa
Captain	ka-pe-na

Deck	o-ne-ki
Sail	ho-lo
Sailor	lu-i-na
Sea, ocean	kai (or mo-a-na)
Seasick	ho-o-pai-lu-a
Ship	mo-ku
Submarine	mo-ku ma-la-lo kai
Voyage	ho-lo-mo-a-na

AROUND THE ISLAND
(Mo-ku-pu-ni)

East	hi-ki-na
West	ko-mo-ha-na
North; right	a-kau
South; left	he-ma
Toward the sea	ma-kai
Toward inland	mau-ka
Toward P. H.	e-wa (eh-vah)
Toward the Royal	wai-ki-ki
Cliff	pa-li
Heaven, sky	la-ni
Island	mo-ku pu-ni
Moon	ma-hi-na
Mountain	mau-na
Path, trail	a-la
Rain	u-a
Rainbow	a-nu-e-nu-e
Road, highway	a-la nu-i
Sun (day)	la
Wind	ma-ka-ni
Chinese	pa-ke
Filipino	pi-li-pi-na
Foreigner (white)	hao-le
Half-white	ha-pa hao-le
Japanese	ke-pa-ni
Native, old-timer	ka-ma-ai-na
Newcomer	ma-li-hi-ni

THE GIRL FRIEND
(Ku-u i-po)

Beautiful	na-ni
Beloved	hi-wa-hi-wa
Clever, smart	a-ka-mai
Crazy!	pu-pu-le
Desirable	mi-li-mi-li
Don't forget me!	mai po-i-na oe i-au
Dress	lo-le or ho-lo-ku
Fickle	ka-na-lu-a
Flattery	ho-o-ma-li-ma-li
Grass skirt	lo-le pi-li
Happy	hau-o-li
Honeymoon	ma-hi-na me-li
Jealous	lau-ko-na
Kiss	ho-ni
Lonely	me-ha-me-ha
Love, hello, good-bye	a-lo-ha
Pleasant memory	ha-li-a
Sad	kau-ma-ha
Shy (shame eye!)	ma-ka hi-la-hi-la
Some-day	i ke-ka-hi la a-ku
Sweetheart	hu-a-pa-la
Until we meet again	a hu-i hou

LETTER HOME
(Le-ka ho-me)

Answer	pa-ne
Baby, child	kei-ki
Daughter	kei-ki-ma-hi-ne
Father	ma-ku-a-ka-ne
Friend	ai-ka-ne
Gift	ha-a-wi-na
How are you?	pe-he-a o-e?
Husband	ka-ne ma-le
Mother	ma-ku-a-hi-ne

Ol' lady	lu-a-hi-ne
Sister	kai-ku-a-hi-ne
Thanks a lot	ma-ha-lo nu-i
Today	ke-i-a la
Tomorrow	a-po-o
Wife	wa-hi-ne ma-le
Write	ka-kau

TALK-TALK
(Ol-le-lo)

Alas!	au-we!
Good-night	a-lo-ha au-mo-e
How much?	e-hi-a?
Maybe, perhaps	pa-ha
No	ao-le
Where?	au-he-a?
Why?	no ke a-ha?
Yes	ae
Yes, indeed	ae no!

❖ A newcomer's statement about "sitting on a lei, with a lanai around his neck" is an old but favorite gag among kamaainas. There are many amusing anecdotes about the way malihinis mix up their Hawaiian phrases and say something quite different from what they had intended. The "Malihine Mele" ("Newcomer's Song") garbles Hawaiian delightfully, telling of "strolling along the shore in my muu-muu made of koa" (Hawaiian dress made of wood); "and I played a tune on my sweet okolehao (on my sweet whiskey); "as she danced her sweet kapu" (her sweet Keep Out); and "he softly told her how he'd seen a great big bad luau (feast) with a red opu (stomach) and a great big hakulau (net fishing)."

For the amusement and edification of servicemen in Hawaii and for others who may be interested, the *Paradise of the Pacific* presents "G.I. Hawaiian," by Milly Lou Donnelly, author of "Me Spik English" and other publications.

It's Their "Right to Fight" for America

AJA's Abandon Jobs and Security for Combat Duty

❖ "I am very happy. It is an honor for my son and for us," Harue Doi, Kauai yardman, said when he was informed that his only son, Mitsuru, eighteen-year-old Lihue garage attendant, was the first volunteer in the Territory to be inducted into the U.S. Army combat regiment created for Americans of Japanese ancestry. That typified the reaction of parents of the twenty-six hundred AJA volunteers inducted in the Territory during the past month.

"I'm just waiting to begin training and get into action," young Mitsuru, Harue Doi's son, said as he was congratulated on being the first AJA volunteer inducted in the Islands.

And that typified the reaction of the AJA volunteers themselves. It is in their reaction that lies the chief interest of the whole story of their entry into the armed forces of the United States. There were many outstanding cases among the volunteers—cases of men prominent in civilian life, brothers inducted together, married men voluntarily leaving behind their families, war veteran fathers encouraging their sons to volunteer as they themselves had done once before.

But the biggest story of all lay in the reaction of the AJA John Doe—the young mechanic, ambitious college student, horny-handed plantation worker, or average white-collar employee. The big story lay in the eagerness of these Americans to prove their loyalty and devotion to the United States. It lay in their willingness to abandon high-paying war jobs and security at home in the Islands for combat service on a distant battlefront.

Washington had announced on January 28 that Americans of Japanese ancestry would be given the opportunity to volunteer for

First published April 1943.

124

army combat duty. By February 28, one month later, the Territory of Hawaii's original quota of 1,500 volunteers had been met—sixfold and more. Of a total of 25,000 AJAs eligible for service by reason of age and citizenship, no less than 9,507 had volunteered.

They showed that they had been awaiting just this opportunity from the day the Japs had written a new page in the world's annals of treachery. They knew they were "on the spot" by the very circumstance of their birth—and they manifested, clearly and decisively, that they understood this opportunity to be the one for which all thinking Americans of Japanese ancestry had been waiting.

As Lt. Gen. Delos C. Emmons, commanding general of the Hawaiian Department, said before final results were tabulated: "This would be a most creditable showing among any other group of Americans anywhere in the country. My confidence in them is being justified."

To Volunteer or Not?

Whether It Is Better to Wait
for Uncle Sam and the Draft

*What does a boy of Japanese ancestry think about when
he wonders about joining the United States army? The
following was written by an American student of Japanese
ancestry at the University of Hawaii, shortly after the
announcement about AJA volunteers drove from his mind
all thoughts of the next day's examinations.*

❖ Examination Week had finally come when out of the clear came the announcement that the Army was going to accept fifteen hundred volunteers of Japanese ancestry from Hawaii. This important message was given to the students at the University before it had leaked out to the local papers. The announcement came at a special assembly held for the purpose. And of all times, it had to be given on the day before examinations were to begin. The instant it was announced, exams became secondary.

After the assembly, and at the assembly, most of the boys were enthusiastic and raring to go. I thought to myself: It's a good thing that the boys want to go, but I wonder whether they have given it any serious thought. If they are planning to volunteer on the spur of the moment, or because their friends are volunteering, it isn't being done properly. It isn't intelligent; it's just plainly stupid. Such a type of volunteer will make a poor soldier. I'm sure the Army wants us to think it over before we sign up.

. . . And yet our country has deemed us fit to serve her! She has called upon us in her need. Shall we refuse help? I should say not! All these years, the Japanese youth in Hawaii have said "We are loyal. Give us a chance to prove it. It isn't fair to doubt us without giving us

First published May 1943.

a trial." But is loyalty something that is only shown or proven by a trial, or only on a battlefield? No, loyalty is something that goes deeper than merely superficial action; it is a complex set of attitudes and ideals. Yet, how are people to know us? They can't see through us; they judge by what we do."

That night as I futilely tried to study, two "me's" begged and pestered to be recognized. Finally, in desperate effort to gain peace of mind, I let them in. One was light, the other was dark. The dark "me" spoke first and was answered by the other.

"Ah, what do you care about the things people think of you? As long as you believe in yourself, forget about the others."

"But you do care about what people think of you. You know that public opinion is important. Do the right thing."

"Sure, do the right thing. Remember, your life, your ambition, everything is at stake. Besides, this is a call only for volunteers; you can always do your share later. Maybe the draft, maybe a defense job."

"No, that's not the right attitude. Look at all the other American boys. They're giving their lives; they've forgotten their old ambitions; they know that they are needed. Volunteer; that's the only noble thing a man can do. Don't let the other fellow carry your share of the burden. It isn't fair."

"Fair, huh! It isn't fair for you to give up what you have planned for years; it isn't fair for you to ignore your parents' cherished ambitions for you. Participating in the post-war reconstruction period will be just as important as taking part in this war. Trained leaders will be needed. Stay and bear whatever comes your way."

"Why should you think about the post-war period when the present isn't secure. Remember, other boys are dying—dying for you."

"Sure, let them die. They haven't suffered as you have; they haven't been discriminated against as you have been. Their parents aren't 'kicked around' and looked down upon as your parents are. Let them die; they should be willing to die; they have everything to be thankful for."

"What would have happened to you if you had been born in Japan? Why, you'd be a farmer, a low-down, ten-sens-a-day farmer. You wouldn't be attending a university as you are doing now. You'd be a soldier, or even dead and rotting in China, or in the Philippines, or in the South Seas. A soldier you'd be, and a soldier with no choice but to die for the Emperor—an ordinary human being! You wouldn't have had any choice as you are having now. If you die now you will die for a concrete idea, not for a near-sighted human. You'll be dying for democracy, dying for the equality of man. Be a man by taking your share of the responsibilities."

"Be a man! What's a man if he doesn't stand for what he believes? Be a man; think about yourself. After all, this is a democracy, and you have your choice. And in a democracy the individual is paramount. You know what that means. You have the right to think about yourself first, last, and always."

"Is that what you want to do? Do nothing but think about yourself? It's selfish, that's what it is. And you don't want people to think that of you, do you? There's only one way out of this. Your country needs you; forget about your own selfish self."

"There are other ways out. Think about yourself . . . yourself . . . you———. Forget about volunteering and the war. Think about yourself and the tests you'll have to face tomorrow. Start studying, and forget about it, or you'll be a wreck tomorrow."

"Sure, study, study hard! *But don't forget . . . you can't run away from it!*"

"That's right, think about yourself. Forget about the tests, forget about volunteering, forget everything. What do you care if you 'flunk' and are 'kicked-out' of school; you can always 'sponge' off the old man. He's good enough for many more 'squeezings.' Take it easy, pal, take it easy."

"Don't take it easy that way. Relax with a clear conscience. Remember you can't escape it; it will always haunt you. . . . Don't be a man with a guilty conscience, a man who won't be able to sleep, a man who won't be able to meet his friends. You'll be a man in the psychopathic ward. That's what you'll be."

"Sure, you go ahead and join up and be a goddam buck private. You know what they're going to use you for—ditch digging and as a source of cheap labor. You with a college education; you deserve a better break. Don't sign on the dotted line; don't be an ass."

"Do be an ass, an intelligent ass. You want to go, don't let him hold you back. The Army'll make a true man out of you. You're going to go eventually; why not go now? You're going on combat duty, not ditch digging. Besides, you'll have your choice of Army service. You know what you're good for; you'll make good.

"Remember, it is one of the prime duties and obligations of a citizen to bear arms in defense of his country. You don't want to be a member of a conquered nation; you don't want to be shut up in a ghetto; and you certainly don't want to have your sisters used to bring forth more 'supermen' or even forced to be prostitutes. Remember what's happening in Europe and China. Remember you're fighting to preserve decency and the right to a peaceful pursuit of life for all mankind. It is your duty to fight for home, country, and humanity.

"Don't listen to him, big-head. Don't listen to him. I tell you. He's waving that same old flag. Don't fall for it, you lug. . . . Okay, okay, go ahead. Don't come crying to me later saying that I didn't warn you. So long, you wonderful ass."

. . . And so did I volunteer.

Lei Day, 1943

❖ Nimble Hawaiian fingers that once wove flower garlands now use their skill in making camouflage nets to conceal military fortifications. Men and women who once made their living growing flowers are doing more vital work. Land that once grew blossoms is now planted with vegetables so that the islands may become more self-sustaining.

This is typical of every phase of life in Hawaii, which has put aside its light-hearted mood of the past and has pitched into wartime activities more seriously, perhaps, than any American community.

Lei Day is now Bond Day in Hawaii, and the pageantry, except for an informal program and display of leis at the City Hall and celebrations at the University and schools, has been put aside for the duration. Last year Bond Day netted Uncle Sam more than a million dollars and the amount this year is expected to exceed that. The campaign, sponsored by the retail board of the Honolulu Chamber of Commerce, will feature a souvenir Lei Day-Bond Day stamp on every bond purchased that day.

It is pleasant, however, to look back into the past when the first of May was occasion for a celebration unique in all the world. Some have said that it was the happiest, gayest holiday ever celebrated in any land. The islands literally became a walking rainbow, when men and women of every age wore leis and presented them to their friends.

Although it seems like decades ago, it was as recently as May 1941 when Hawaii had its last big Lei Day celebration. There were festive events, music, pageantry, a Lei Day queen and her attendants, and special dancing parties at the Royal Hawaiian Hotel, the Young Roof Garden, and other night spots.

Official recognition of Lei Day dates back as far as 1910, when a festival was held at the home of Governor Cleghorn and a queen was given a floral-lei crown. From that day on, the observance grew more elaborate every year. Highlights included the pageant at the Univer-

---

First published May 1943.

sity of Hawaii, with the Lei Day queen and her pretty attendants, and the display of leis at Thomas Square, with awarding of prizes to the most beautiful and most original garlands.

Added impetus to the celebration was created by Don Blanding, Hawaii's "poet laureate," who is now in the army. In 1928 at Blanding's suggestion, Lei Day was officially added to Hawaii's calendar, and since that time it has become known as the holiday that has no counterpart anywhere in the world.

OPA—Hawaiian Style

❖ Uncle Sam's bulldog effort to stabilize the cost of living, and to distribute fairly and equitably those things that war makes scarce, definitely has reached these out-post islands in the Pacific. OPA, which in the past year has become a household word on the Mainland—affecting, as it does, every single one of America's 134 millions—is rapidly becoming a real, tangible something to those of us who saw the American-Japanese death struggle unfold in our own backyard.

The history of Hawaiian price control differs radically from that of its counterpart on the Mainland. It was the military government—not OPA—that swung into action against inflation when war suddenly came upon us. There just wasn't time, equipment, or trained OPA specialists available to carry out the functions for which the Office of Price Administration is responsible on a national scale.

Lt. Gen. Delos Emmons, commanding the Hawaiian Department in his capacity as military governor, delegated to the commanding officers of the various islands the task of administering price control and rationing within their own jurisdiction. The men chosen to perform these duties were young, energetic officers whose civilian background fitted them for the job that was to be done.

Starting from scratch, and with only one thought uppermost—that of immediately curbing the disastrous rise of prices they knew was sure to develop in an area suddenly peopled with thousands of defense workers making unprecedented wages—they went into action.

Taking only those Mainland OPA regulations that seemed applicable to the economic structure of the islands, they adopted them in principle as "military orders." In instances where Mainland regulations did not cover a specific problem, the military quickly and effectively adopted its own "rule-of-thumb" measures.

The army had a man-sized job on its hands preparing the islands against another possible return of Mr. Tojo's henchmen—but it

First published May 1943.

wavered not a whit in its determination to carry out as efficiently as possible this civilian task that the fortunes of war had thrust upon it.

Happily, this army-administered price-control unit did a fine overall job. Prices, generally, stayed in line. Of course, there were chiselers and "I-can-get-away-with-it guys," but many of these, the records reveal, soon felt the quick, precise, and uncompromising power of the Provost Courts. Violators learned that the army "wasn't fooling." Fines often in excess of those imposed on the Mainland for comparable offenses were levied with dispatch.

Gradually, though, the ever-changing trend of Mainland prices, together with the critical shortages of most commodities, resulted in an abnormal, complex, market condition that, in itself, permitted a field-day for certain types of opportunities. On one hand, legitimate merchants were being "squeezed" on fair profits; on the other, some items—cheap jewelry, for instance—were selling for three, four, and five times their true values.

General Emmons' "price boys" had fought a valiant "holding battle" against inflation, but now, it was generally agreed, the time had come to relieve the military of this highly specialized job of price control. Thus, on March 10, supervision of price control and rationing officially returned to OPA, to be administered by a civilian war agency under the same general pattern as that developed for the Mainland.

For several months prior to the date of transition from military to civilian agency control, General Emmons had had the assistance and advice of Karl Borders, a seasoned OPA executive from the Washington headquarters. During the later period of military control, Mr. Borders served in the dual capacity of territorial representative for OPA and as officer on the staff of the military governor.

On March 10, as Territorial Director for OPA, Mr. Borders assumed full responsibility for the program.

The turnover, from military to OPA, was accomplished with astonishing smoothness and a minimum of inconvenience to the general public.

Gradually, Mr. Borders built his organization by retaining most of the civilian help who had served under the army officers and supplementing this structure with price and rationing specialists from Mainland OPA offices—men whose actual experience in this unprecedented profession has contributed immeasurably to the operation of the program throughout the territory.

Mr. Borders, it is told, had one standard speech of welcome ready for these malihini OPA workers. It went something like this: "You now are in the Hawaiian Islands. You'll soon realize that life really is different here. People have a different outlook on life; businessmen do business a bit differently. We are here to stop inflation and we will, with the continued support of the merchants and public. But we must, at all times, remember that we are not on the Mainland—that we must make this program work with a minimum of hardship and inconvenience to trade and public, alike."

Proof that Director Borders and his staff have not forgotten that they are "off the Mainland" is contained in the fact that of more than four hundred regulations issued by the national OPA office—and that could have been applied to Hawaii—fewer than forty have been adopted for the islands.

This isn't to be taken as meaning that price and rationing violators will be dealt with more leniently than those of the Mainland.

"There will be violators," Mr. Borders has said, "but there will be far less, comparatively speaking. I have been here long enough to realize that the people of the islands take very seriously their duties and obligations of all nature in this mighty war effort."

In short, it seems that the plan is to make this anti-inflation program with the least disturbance to the tranquil life of the islands.

That's OPA—Hawaiian style.

Mental Disturbances Caused by the War

EDWIN E. MCNEIL, M.D.,
DIRECTOR OF THE HAWAII MENTAL CLINIC

❖ Emotions developed in wartime are anger and aggression. These natural emotions are directed not only against the enemy but at the leadership in our own group. This runs the gamut: Congress—capitalists—labor—bureaucracy—military leaders—promotion by seniority—the soft life of the age—the sugar plantations—the kamaainas—the press—and almost anything or anyone that has power or influence.

In this present war, most people are, in varying degrees, mad and scared—and because both of these feelings are very uncomfortable ones, people want to do something so that they will feel different. Unfortunately, from a psychological point of view, most people cannot do something directly against the enemy. There is a lot of satisfaction in giving the "dirty so-and-so" a "sock in the jaw" or in "taking a pot-shot" at a Jap.

But for most of us, this is not that kind of war. The wear and tear on the personality of the average individual is much greater in this kind of war. There are greater feelings of insecurity because of the speed and intensity of the war and the fact that, as a nation, we are in greater danger than we have ever been in our history. The facts of this situation cannot help but bring some feelings of fear and apprehension to any intelligent person.

Remarkable changes have come in almost every phase of our living here in Hawaii. Food is higher and there is a limited variety. Gasoline and tires are rationed along with liquor. The blackout has changed our eating, social, and work habits. The sending of women and children to the mainland has brought about tremendous changes in the habits

First published June 1943.

and in the sex lives of the remaining men and women. The repercussions of this one situation alone will be evidenced for generations. The high percentage of Japanese in the territory presents many other problems.

Mention of these well-known factors is sufficient to indicate the sources of many emotional and personality problems. Practically everyone in Hawaii has been under considerable emotional tension since the attack that started the war.

This tension is a normal reaction for the intelligent, sane individual. It may be evidenced in a loss of weight; loss or increase of appetite; increase in rate of liquor consumption; poorer sleep, with an increase in dreams, particularly of the fear or catastrophic type; development of gastro-intestinal difficulties such as hyperacidity and gastric ulcers; depressive feelings; unexplained irritability; and other complaints that are best described as anxiety symptoms.

Many people evidence a decrease in efficiency or show instances of remarkably poor judgment, as contrasted with their usual even-tempered level-headedness. Others will do things they cannot explain, except perhaps on a neurotic or daydreaming basis.

Since the war started we have seen the most disturbed group of patients of my five years in Hawaii. The largest group falls into the schizophrenic classification, with the catatonic and paranoid types predominating. In these cases, difficulties of adjustment under wartime conditions have been too great for the individual to meet successfully.

Although reasons for fear in Hawaii have lessened during the past year, due to the increased security of the islands, relaxing of martial law, and the return of many island families, mental disturbances have increased rather than decreased. This may be due to prolonged tension, limited recreational facilities, and factors such as the curfew, blackout, and general insecurity and uncertainty.

Some of our patient load is composed of the kind of rural, small-town, home boys who have never before been away from the protection and security of a familiar scene. Life here may become too complicated and difficult for them, requiring more stamina and flexibility than they are capable of giving. Another group shows strong paranoid trends with delusions, hallucinations, and a typical panic state.

Strangely enough, there have been few manic depressive cases, and we have not made a single diagnosis of war neurosis or war psychosis since the onset of the war. Nor have we seen any patients with what some are prone to call "shell shock." Some cases of toxic psychoses have been seen, the most dramatic being cases of alcoholic hallucinations occurring several days after the individual had stopped drinking, perhaps at sea on a ship where no alcohol was available.

I would like to suggest several steps that would help the situation among war workers. 1. A more careful selection of the workers on the Mainland. 2. A more satisfactory labor-relations program between contractors and employees. 3. Improvement of living conditions and recreational programs for war workers. 4. Increased facilities and personnel presently available for the care of psychiatric cases in Honolulu.

Night Life in the Twilight

EILEEN O'BRIEN

❖ Mainlanders no doubt laugh when they hear about Hawaii's new night life—from six to nine, with no liquor served. But to the fun-starved residents of Honolulu even a simple pleasure such as this is a welcome blessing. The people of Hawaii have had to learn many new things in the last year and a half, and the latest is that you can have a surprising amount of fun during an evening when you go home at about the time you used to go out.

At first they had to learn to stay home—and like it if possible. The blackout was complete and the curfew was strictly enforced. There was no place to go, and if there had been, you wouldn't have been allowed to go there. Because of the liquor shortage, bars closed at two or three in the afternoon, or else didn't open at all. On Sundays bars served only beer and were so crowded that most civilians didn't even try to get in.

So, for more than a year the residents of Honolulu confined what fun they had to their own homes and the homes of friends. The after-work cocktail at a bar, the dinner dance, and the leisurely dining out of the past had completely vanished.

Then, gradually, some of the restrictions began to be lifted. Dimmed-out lights appeared on the main streets, and people were allowed to drive until 10 P.M. Buses ran until this hour, and the movies started a "late" show from seven to nine. It seemed almost like an orgiastic revel.

Return of night clubs was the next logical step, but it took a lot of courage to consider such a venture. Curfew remains at 10 P.M., so such a club would have to close at nine or shortly after. Liquor still may not be sold after 6 P.M., so the night club would have to be dry. The need for fun was obvious, but would a nonalcoholic, six-to-nine night club succeed?

First published June 1943.

138

The answer was found by Ray Andrade, who had the courage to open La Hula Rhumba, Hawaii's first wartime night club. The golden-voiced singer has an excellent band of his own, but apart from that he started his venture with nothing but a lot of determination. He finally chose for his location the former Foresters' Hall on Lunalilo Street, near the Robert Louis Stevenson School.

The main hall, cleverly re-decorated in a blue and white color scheme, magically achieved a night club atmosphere, which is helped by an addition that was built at the rear. This is a low-ceilinged room, large enough for the band and the dance floor. Hangings on the walls from ceiling to floor, brightly colored paintings, and potted cactus give this patio a Spanish flair.

Andrade soon discovered that his faith in his plans was justified. Honoluluans pack La Hula Rhumba nightly, reveling in the fact that they can now have the sort of good time they had done without for more than a year. Women joyfully go to the back of their closets for dance dresses that have had no place to go, and men are digging out their white suits and dinner jackets.

There are no complaints that the fun ends at nine, because the people of the Islands have learned to accept philosophically all kinds of restrictions since the start of the war. When much has been taken away, simple pleasures are doubly enjoyed.

Honolulu's other night club is Kewalo Inn, which resumed its dinner dancing shortly after the opening of La Hula Rhumba. Under new management since the start of the war, Kewalo is ideally suited for blackout fun because the dimmed-out colored lights make it possible to leave open to cooling breezes the side of the patio facing the garden. The excellent music here is provided by Don McDiarmid and his orchestra.

The new ruling that permits the sale of liquor until 6 P.M. makes it possible for Kewalo Inn to offer a cocktail hour from five to six, for those with dinner reservations. Sitting in such a pleasant atmosphere and sipping a long cool one is an almost forgotten thrill for Honoluluans. Genial Al Brannen is the host here, and his account of his trials and tribulations make an interesting commentary on wartime Hawaii, his problems being the same as other restaurateurs, and, in a manifold way, of housewives.

First, there's the problem of getting adequate help in a community where there is more work than workers. Then there's the matter of getting food. In order to maintain the high standard he has set for cuisine, he has to shop around from one place to another, getting a few pounds of fine grade meat here, a few more there. And he has to transport it all himself because delivery service has practically vanished from Hawaii.

But the effort must be worthwhile because here, as at La Hula Rhumba, the place is packed every night and it is necessary to make reservations several days in advance. Hawaii's equivalent of "a hectic whirl of the night clubs" (both of them) today means a surprising amount of honest-to-goodness, much-missed fun.

Dinner dancing is not the only form of night life in Honolulu now, for recently the Civic Auditorium brought back night-time wrestling matches. This is a boon, especially for the men who, no matter how devoted, like a change of scene now and then from family and hearth. The huge attendance at the matches proves once again how thirsty for entertainment is hard-working Hawaii.

Most of the restaurants now stay open until eight or shortly after, so that it is possible to have a moderately festive evening now and then by going out to dinner to a place such as the Moana, Lau Yee Chai, or the Wagon Wheel. A lot of people have this idea, however, so here too reservations in advance are necessary.

Trader Vic's, with its delightful Hawaiian atmosphere, is still one of the most popular spots in town. Right after the war started they discontinued their luscious barbecued and Chinese dinners because of the scarcity of the necessary ingredients. Now, however, the dinners are back and are served until 8 P.M. The cocktail hour at Trader Vic's was from noon to three when this was written, but a shipment of mainland liquor may make possible the lengthening of these hours.

Another favored spot for eating and drinking is the South Seas, which also has a pleasant Polynesian atmosphere. In all of these places, and more especially in the downtown restaurants, pressure has been relieved considerably in recent months by the opening of the Breakers, Maluhia, and other recreation centers for service men.

At the start of the war there was little they could do on days of pass or liberty but crowd the restaurants and bars, leaving little room for hungry or thirsty civilians. Now, due to the great accomplishments of the army, navy, and USO, there are dozens of other places where service men can find rest and fun.

The average resident of Hawaii, tied to the Islands for the duration, would give an eyetooth for a whirl at Mainland "hot spots," which he imagines through a glamorous haze. When he gets tired of that he recalls the fun that could be had in Hawaii before the war, in the days of dancing under the stars at the Royal Hawaiian or Waialae . . . the soft lights at the Young Roof . . . and the smoky madhouse of the Rathskeller. He smiles to himself when he recalls complaints when night life ended at midnight, and wonders how he stood the pace.

Night life in Hawaii is as tame as a church picnic compared with that of the Mainland, but the fact that it exists at all is reason for shouts of rejoicing.

Help Wanted! 21,000 Jobs in Hawaii

EILEEN O'BRIEN

❖ Wanted: workers to fill twenty-one thousand jobs in Hawaii! But if mainland papers copy, please warn the women that there are several regulations that may prevent them from coming to the islands to work.

Life in Hawaii may have been simple in the old days, but it certainly is no longer. And no one is more aware of the complications brought about by wartime stress than the officials of the Honolulu Federal Civil Service office. A chat with these men brought out some interesting facts of life about men, women, and jobs in Hawaii.

Federal agencies, for instance, need fourteen thousand workers, but even if they were magically transported here by flying carpet, no one knows where they would be able to eat or sleep. Many women applicants on the mainland have to be turned down because local regulations forbid, with a few exceptions, transportation for employment in federal agencies of service men's wives and wives of a contractor's employees. The basis for this is that if women take jobs here just to be with their husbands, they will want to run back home if the husband is transferred.

These are but a few of the complications that are causing gray hair and figures before the eyes in the local civil service office. The staff has grown from five in 1940 to thirty at present, but their task is still gargantuan, as can be seen by the fact that in the first six months of 1940 they put a mere 432 people to work, whereas in the first six months of this year, they placed more than 12,000. The total number put to work through this office since the start of the war is 26,394, not including placements from the mainland at Pearl Harbor or with the U.S.E.D.

Another problem facing the civil service office is based on a malady well known to kamaainas. In the days before the war, most soldiers spent their tour of duty here complaining bitterly about Hawaii and

First published July 1943.

praying for deliverance from the "rock." The next thing kamaainas knew, they'd be out of the army and back here to make their home! This same experience has developed among war workers, who can hardly wait to go back to the mainland when their contract expires and then send heart-rending appeals to be returned to Hawaii for another hitch.

The civil service officials would rather have a man working here who has gone through this experience and knows he likes the islands than one who is still tormented with the desire to return to his home. So they have worked out a plan that is highly successful. This makes it possible for a worker, when his contract expires, to have a sixty-day furlough or "call to work card." He goes back home, sees his family, has his fill of night life, point rationing, and transportation difficulties, and if he shows up in San Francisco within sixty days, his job in the islands is waiting for him and his transportation is paid from his home town to Hawaii.

Although their job is to recruit for positions with the government, local civil service officials are aware of Hawaii's acute labor shortage in private industry and do all they can to cooperate in the crisis that has brought about the Work to Win campaign. It has been estimated that there are about seventy-five hundred jobs open in private industry, and civil service recognizes the need for essential private industries to continue functioning. In some instances they have made transfers from federal to private agencies, where individuals can contribute more to the war effort by such a transfer.

Because of this critical shortage of workers in public and private employment, the local civil service office has been scraping the bottom of the employment barrel for more than a year. This no doubt contributes to the fact that the percentage of women working in Hawaii is higher than in mainland localities. Civil service officials have emphasized since the start of the war the use of women in jobs, such as sheet metal work, truck driving, and munitions handling, that had previously been considered man's domain.

About 80 percent of civil service placements here were women right after the start of the war, but this figure has been brought down to about 50 percent because of the influx of skilled men workers who are placed through this office.

This brings out the point that many people still consider a civil service office a place to apply only for "white collar" jobs. Actually, the need is great for electricians, aircraft mechanics, ship fitters, welders, and nearly all skilled trades.

Hawaii is ahead of the mainland in labor control measures, regulating pirating of workers, etc., because under the Office of the Military Governor a successful stabilization plan has been in operation since December 1941. In fact, we have the control here that the manpower commission on the mainland would like to have. Because the federal government is the largest employer in the territory, and government wages are standard, wages have also tended to be more stable in Hawaii than on the mainland.

Most civil service employee here get 25 percent more pay than the same job pays in other parts of the country. This increase was authorized after a cost of living survey showed that living costs in Hawaii were about 40 percent higher than elsewhere.

The Civil Service, as a national institution, has been plugging along since 1883, but never until the present war did it have to do a gigantic job with the greatest speed it could muster. A terrific number of people had to be put to work—but fast—and this meant elimination of red tape and the clumsy aspects of its machinery in the past.

One method of achieving this sped-up process was to eliminate written examinations for most jobs, except in the Post Office department. The big new deal of the Civil Service, however, dates from March 16, 1942, when war service regulations went into effect. From this time on, there have been few examinations and no civil service status for new employees. There is a trial period of one year, during which an unsatisfactory employee may be dismissed with a letter stating his services are unsatisfactory. All appointments are now good for the duration of the war and not to exceed six months after it ends.

Applying for a civil service job is now almost incredibly simple. You spend a few minutes with an interviewer and fill out a single-page form on your experience. Then you take a form letter to the federal agency needing persons with your skill. There you are fingerprinted, given a physical exam, and you can be put to work the same day.

The Civil Service is the sole recruiting agency for all positions with the U.S. government, approximately 97 percent of its work now being for the army and navy. Peacetime agencies are responsible for the remainder.

The U.S. Employment Service receives current lists showing all jobs on file with the Civil Service and makes all referrals to federal agencies through the civil service interviewer stationed there full time.

It's not only nice work, but everyone seems to get it. Whereas there were only seven thousand federal employees in Hawaii in 1940, there are now sixty thousand civilians drawing their checks from Uncle Sam.

Poor Planning Now
Means Future Regret

V. N. OSSIPOFF

❖ Honolulu's acute housing shortage that has existed since before the start of the war and the recent federal authorization to construct five hundred homes here have made the subject of construction a favorite topic of conversation in Hawaii.

The war has already had a staggering influence on what may have to be referred to as "the once fair city of Honolulu." Shelters, barracks, recreation halls, and other buildings for use by the army, navy, and OCD within the city limits have altered the appearance of Honolulu to a marked degree.

Provisions of the Honolulu building code set up for the protection of health and insurance against over-congestion do not apply to construction on federal land. These regulations also, in some cases, have been suspended on private or territorial land, with the understanding that such suspension was to be effective only for the duration of the war.

A fait accompli, however, is no easy matter to undo. So it is with some alarm then that residents of Honolulu view the city changing so rapidly in character before their very eyes. The war comes first, of course, in every consideration, but planning now for the future may accomplish much toward restoring Honolulu to its former beauty after the war.

Furthermore, in the haste and desire to alleviate the housing shortage, it would be tragically shortsighted to perpetrate poor city planning for future regret.

These are matters of serious concern to the Hawaii Chapter of the American Institute of Architects, whose members are giving them much thought and discussion.

First published September 1943.

The population of the city has increased and, with private construction at a standstill, the need for additional housing became so acute that the War Production Board has released materials for construction of approximately five hundred housing units.

Because of the limited selection of material, limited cost per unit, and the high cost of both labor and material, these units will be necessarily standardized and likely to be of a lower standard than those buildings built before the war. In some instances groups of dwellings all contiguous to each other will be built.

Although the regulations of the Board of Health and the City of Honolulu building code control the design, the term here is used in its broadest sense, and no control is extant for a group of dwellings other than those regulations that apply to each dwelling individually.

The lack of such a control was felt by the architects present at a recent meeting to be undesirable. The architects have decided to favor publicly, in the interest of all present and future residents of Honolulu, the delegation of such control to some competent body of citizens, such as the City Planning Commission, for example.

The architects do not wish by any means to impede the construction program that is so badly needed at once. But they do realize that intelligent planning now will make a great deal of difference in the appearance of Honolulu and the "pursuit of happiness" here in the future.

Hotel Street, the
Service Man's Domain

❖ Hotel Street, from River to Richards, has become the service man's domain. Like the stalls of market-day Palestine, the merchants of Honolulu have taken every available inch of space to sell their wares. The doorway or nook that once went to the shoeshine boy is now a jewelry counter. In what used to be a vegetable store now flow beer and coke.

A lad in white or khaki can find a weird assortment of things to buy. A watch or a drink are right on the route. Pin-ball machines and clothing, a hair cut or a gift to mother are available on Hotel Street between River and Richards. The narrow sidewalks haven't changed but the merchandise offered has.

You can hock your watch across from the "Y," or you can get a loan on that cameo ring. They'll treat you right and even sell you a "I Love You Dear Mother o' Mine" pillow on the way out.

Your picture: taken in three minutes with a background drop of Diamond Head on real sand, posed with a happy hula girl, all done up in the best Coney Island style. One large amusement place, which makes this its first offer, has within its establishment nearly forty additional forms of amusement. A service man on a few hours of leave can find his favorite pin-ball machine, he can determine his shooting range, his baseball batting ability, his weight, his strength, and can take a shot at miniature Japs stalking through painted jungles.

Posing with a hula girl is a top attraction on Hotel Street, with a crowd of civilians and service men always present to watch the amusing proceedings. Destination of the pictures is unknown, although some are undoubtedly sent to tease the best girl at home, or shock a doting aunt. Others are kept in wallets as mementos of Hawaii.

Hotel Street has the tawdry glitter of a miniature Coney Island or

First published October 1943.

148

of Chicago's Maxwell Street, but military authorities are glad it's there. It provides wholesome fun for the lads and a place to spend their money without too much exploitation. After all, the OPA is functioning, so jewelry prices are under control.

The gaudy street is here to stay, for the duration and possibly longer, for it gives the boys a place to spend money, have fun, and buy souvenirs from Hawaii for the folks back home.

Honolulu Looks at Tomorrow

MAYOR LESTER PETRIE

❖ Honolulu, its municipal machinery geared to war and running with amazing rhythm under conditions that might well be expected to cause it to rattle and clank, operated during its second year of global conflict so as to produce public services adequate to supply the community's immediate needs and at the same time prepare for the glowing future that is plainly visible on the horizon that is Peace. War is creating a new destiny for the city it has made the focal center of its own tragic activities in the Pacific area.

The Honolulu of yesteryear—the city that rested in placid semi-isolation two thousand miles off its United States Mainland—disappeared with the first rending crash of a Jap torpedo at Pearl Harbor on December 7, 1941. In its stead has risen a war center, bristling with arms, crowded with fighting men and those who attend them.

Yet this is only a transient phase. A new Honolulu lies ahead, for that which war has begun will, because of the creations of war itself, inevitably be carried forward into the structure of the city's future life in peace.

Development of air transport will be one of the major factors in this change. The distance between Hawaii and the Pacific Coast states has become as nothing, a mere overnight hop for travelers and goods. This American Territory has become in fact, as well as in name, an integral unit of the United States. Not only this, but its geographical location, instead of tending toward isolation as it has in the past, makes Honolulu the near neighbor by air of all the Pacific countries, the natural distribution point from which to serve them, or to police them if need be.

During the year just closed, these facts have been kept in mind by the mayor and supervisors, and by the personnel who serve the public under their direction and policies. Every move toward the improve-

---

First published December 1943.

ment and expansion of existing public services, or for the development of new governmental activities, has been made with a view to its utility under future requirements.

One of the greatest obstacles overcome by the administration was a paucity of funds. Under existing laws the territorial legislature, in which Honolulu, despite its majority population, has a minority voice, controls municipal finances. Territorial and local taxes are collected through a single agency and are dispersed by legislative order. Sometimes it happens, as it did this year, that the legislators show insufficient concern for local needs and leave the municipality in poverty while the territorial treasury bulges with cash from tax revenues.

In spite of legislative disregard for the city's financial needs, the City and County managed to contrive means of getting some major developments under way and planned others to be achieved when the money is available. With Federal assistance, Honolulu acquired two new rubbish incinerators and made ready for their installation, took the preliminary steps for a master plan for a complete sewerage and sewage disposal system, and extended and improved its suburban water system.

It reorganized its rubbish and garbage collection system and its machinery for war rent control. It maintained its parks and playgrounds insofar as was possible while much of their areas is devoted to war purposes; repaired, improved, and renovated public school buildings and grounds throughout the Island of Oahu in accordance with a schedule of operations; and made alterations at the City Hall that increased its office capacity materially.

Dim-out street light and traffic signal systems were installed and maintained as soon as military regulations permitted. And special attention was devoted to white line street marking in the interests of safety, particularly for night driving, which is especially important in war.

Highway maintenance was carried on as far as materials and manpower permitted, and there was some new road and street construction. Most of the highways outside the city proper are the responsibility of the territorial government, but they present a problem that is community wide. Under the terrific pounding of war traffic, these roads, and some of the city streets that are a problem of the municipality, have deteriorated rapidly. Several of them may have to be rebuilt, and the cost will be tremendous.

Recognizing the gravity of this situation, the municipal administration invited territorial and Army and Navy authorities to a conference, at which it was agreed that a survey should be made and the problem considered jointly. By this means we hope to halt the disintegration of the highways and repair them before they are destroyed.

While all these matters were occupying the City and County administration's attention, it found time to look ahead and build for the future. Honolulu's destiny is to continue in peace what it has become in war the Hub of Pacific Affairs. It is toward this end that the city's administration is building, alert to the responsibilities and opportunities of the large and important city that will be ours when the fighting ends and the world is rebuilt.

Hawaii Rifles—Big Island Volunteer Unit

EARL CHALLENGER

Note: *The writer is a first lieutenant, inactive, Hawaii Rifles. He is now an inactive member because he is no longer living on the Big Island, having transferred his place of business to Honolulu.*

❖ The scarlet Lehua flower is the red badge of courage as well as the official insignia of the Hawaii Rifles. A profound poetic insight could have chosen no more eloquent symbol than this for the fighting men of the Volunteer regiments of the Island of Hawaii. For upon the tortured and riven black lava flows, first to split the barren rock with its roots and to grow after the lichens and ferns, is the mighty Ohia tree, whose flame-flower Lehua blossoms are indeed nature's own triumphant beacons of courage.

Only such inherent courage could have inspired humble Filipino coffee pickers and plantation workers, Hawaiian and Portuguese cowboys, gentle school teachers, men of business, sugar plantation technologists and managers, and all the rest—most of them with no previous military training whatever, many even unable to speak our language very well—to rise up to defend those same lava flows, those great mountains, those convulsed, tossed, and rubricated volcanic folds that are the Island of Hawaii.

That the enemy did not come to the Big Island in those early months of the war has robbed history of another epic, bloody but glorious, in which brave Filipino-Americans would have stood side by side with their Caucasian and Hawaiian-American brethren in a struggle ranking in ferocity with Bataan. As the Volunteer regiments of the Island of Hawaii now stand, beautifully trained soldiers, armed, closely conversant with and adept in handling all weapons, they have

First published December 1943.

only one regret. That is that the enemy has chosen, and wisely, to remain well out of their reach to date.

Anyone who has not seen the Island of Hawaii or gone around it, has no conception of the job, viewed from a military standpoint, that these simple men of radiant courage eagerly volunteered to take on to defend the place to the death, if need be, before a possible invader.

Before they could get arms, Filipino Volunteers hammered out home-made bolos, and fearful weapons they were. The first unofficial but fervent order issued in our newly organized company in Kona was to go home and make them.

Lacking plantation machine shops and forges in Kona, Filipinos who worked all day long perforce sat up nights hammering and filing out their bolos over wood fires in their blacked-out, poorly ventilated shacks. Fresh, unsalted Hereford bull hides were obtained, out of which scabbards (*sacuban,* in Visayan) were tailor-made for each knife and sewn with rawhide thongs. The red Hereford hair was left on them. These bolos were the first weapons, forged by the men themselves. There were similar primitive beginnings elsewhere.

If the enemy had come at that time, there is no doubt but that every one of these men would have advanced to the beach heads, perhaps to die for the American Flag, but to leave such a whittling of Nipponese weasands as would have carved a goodly niche in history.

The Volunteers bought their own khaki cloth to have uniforms made (as have other islands' units). In Kona, the school-teacher wife of an officer opened her school room on a Sunday, cut the cloth from bolts, and acted as quartermaster. Each Filipino would run in and get his cloth while the rest sweated and drilled on the parade ground. When American soldiers came to train them, they were amazed by the loyal, fervent kind of willingness that animated these Volunteers. And they trained them splendidly.

On the subject of bolos. . . . To our company in Kona came the enviable honor and privilege of presenting a bolo to a U.S. Army General, Commanding. Pancho, now our first sergeant, always our best bolo maker "armorer," was assigned to the job by the writer.

Pancho made a beauty of a knife, the kind of deadly beauty to make the onlooker's viscera tighten and ache when it was unsheathed. But Pancho was not content. For his General, only the best would do. So he asked, as a special honor, that he be permitted to poison the blade, as his father in the Philippines had taught him, handing on a tradition generations old.

He called it *subo* in Visayan. There were two kinds, impregnated in the blade. One would make a man awfully sick, but the man would live if the blade didn't kill him. The other form of *subo* would kill the victim in any case, but after several days of unspeakable anguish, from even a scratch.

With delicate tact, Pancho was finally dissuaded from the project by an explanation readily understandable to him. This was that the great American General would treasure the knife, take it home after the wars, hang it on his wall in a place of honor or put it in a glass case. There, possibly, some lovely lady would see the bolo and inevitably cut herself with it. . . . "You know how women are, Pancho, they just can't let these things alone." He understood, and a warrior's pride was intact. Our General, if he reads this, will no doubt appreciate this added information regarding the bolo our Visayans gave him with love and devotion.

Today, the Volunteers of the Island of Hawaii, wearing their Lehua flower emblem, stand ready and armed, along with the Volunteer contingents of all the islands, ready to meet any foe and prove themselves formidable fighters. The Filipinos still have their bolos and know how to use them, as many a wide-eyed U.S. Army man has witnessed in their exhibitions of their own kind of fighting.

It was not for nothing that the cavalry platoon, led by Platoon Sgt. Kaulu Pohaku, under Lt. Col. of Hawaii Rifles Ronald K. von Holt, and organized at Kahua Ranch, called themselves the "Quick Maki Men" (die quick men). Those fearless cowboys and horsemen, knowing the terrain, realizing the open invitation to possible enemy attack along Hawaii's lengthy and meandering coastlines, simply embodied prescient insight in a phrase.

They literally came on the run to volunteer. They formed ranks barehanded and without arms and training, but from the first they were ready to fight. And they would have fought with bare hands, even before those of the Filipinos who had had time to make bolos. Training they received later, much of it through interpreters in the Filipino dialects. Regular soldiers were few at the beginning. Arms came as soon as they could. And the long convoys of American troops, a never-to-be-forgotten joyous sight on that island, came as soon as they could.

But even before they knew how, or with what, the Filipinos and the rest were ready to fight.

First to conceive of the Hawaii Rifles as an organized civilian-militia was J. Scott B. Pratt, manager of Kohala Sugar Company, now Colonel and a Regimental Commander, who worked with Maj. Lester W. Bryan, U.S. Army Hawaii District Intelligence Officer and present Hawaii Rifles instructor and inspector. They both took the idea to Lt. Col. V. C. Burton, then Commanding Officer of the Hawaii District, with the result that the organization became a fact. To these men, and to Brig. Gen. Herbert T. Gibson, U.S. Army; and to Hawaii Rifles Col. A. T. Spalding and other leaders, the men of the Hawaii Rifles feel a deep debt of gratitude.

Invasion by Haoles at Niihau

LaSELLE GILMAN

❖ Mysterious Niihau may still be isolated, remote from a world at war, and jealously guarded against the encroachments of a decadent civilization, but it is Hawaii's hermit island no longer.

The war—and the Army—have revolutionized Niihau. A curious transition has taken place on this tiny little isle lying twenty miles off the rugged coast of Kauai. The modern world of jeeps, radios, movies, electric lights, and bold-eyed strangers in uniform has invaded that legendary baronial estate with its 130 inhabitants.

Niihau, until the Japanese attack on Pearl Harbor, was a quiet, lonely chunk of coral and volcanic rock, virtually unknown even to Hawaii residents, who heard vague, curious tales about it from time to time.

But when a lost Japanese pilot who was forced down there after the Pearl Harbor blitz terrorized the bewildered population for nearly a week, and was finally killed by a giant Hawaiian, Niihau made headlines around the world—a one-day wonder story.

Niihau is about twenty miles long, about six wide, rises to some thirteen hundred feet at the highest point, and boasts seventy-two square miles, mostly devoted to a large private cattle and sheep ranch. Around the primitive Hawaiian homes roam pigs and poultry, and the isle abounds in ducks, plover, curlew, peafowl, pheasants, quail, partridges, and mynahs.

The island was owned until recently by Aubrey Robinson, who died a few years ago at the age of eighty-two, leaving an estate appraised at nearly $3.5 million. His widow still lives on the Kauai coast opposite Niihau, and the Robinson interests are now directed by the sons: Sinclair, Selwyn, Lester, and Aylmer.

First published December 1943.

The manner of life at Niihau has not changed for fifty to seventy-five years, and the horse-and-buggy days prevail, the changes of the outside world ignored. The residents are pure Hawaiians; the women make fine lauhala matting and shell leis and the men are cowboys. The only haole on the island for years was John Renne, the ranch foreman.

Nothing on Niihau was ever modernized before December Seventh. Many of the people were born and died on the island without ever leaving it. All were very religious. The Hawaiian teacher of the little four-grade schoolhouse was also the preacher. The Robinsons instituted prohibition seventy-five years ago and Niihau was teetotal.

Neither was tobacco allowed, nor radios, phonographs, movies, automobiles, hard-paved roads, stores, markets, electricity, factories, nor jails (those who committed misdemeanors were deported). Dogs and cats were kapu, as were uninvited visitors.

The excitement over the enemy Jap and his final capture by Benjamin Kanahele and his husky wife had scarcely died down when the real revolution on Niihau began.

The Army had never been welcome on Niihau, but welcome or not, it promptly moved in and stayed there from that day on. And the Navy called when it pleased and kept a close guard on the shores. The Army likewise quietly moved into the previously kapu Robinson estate at Makaweli. They did a lot of defense work similar to that rushed everywhere in Hawaii, and they garrisoned troops on Niihau, turning a deaf ear to any objection that might be raised.

With the troops came the Twentieth Century: radios, movies, beer canteens, dogs, cats, tobacco, jeeps, trucks, post exchanges, electric lights, refrigerators, guns, and ammunition. There also came strange haole soldiers who spoke strange jargons to Niihau ears, and whose manners and customs were even more strange. They didn't all go to church, and they sometimes used profanity, and they kidded the shy young Niihau girls openly, and told the wide-eyed boys tall stories about the outside world—particularly about distant parts of the fabulous Mainland. They didn't know the meaning of the word "kapu," but they could show the inhabitants exciting moving pictures and let them listen to jam sessions on the radio.

Later, as result of some negotiations, most of the haole soldiers were withdrawn and replaced by troops of Hawaiian blood, but the change had been made and the innovations remained. Niihau would never be the same again. Kauai residents watched these developments with amusement and interest; some thought it was a good thing, some were a little sad.

Niihau is 100 percent in the war effort today, raising beef for the Army and the Hawaiian markets. And the traffic between the forbidden isle and the Kauai coast is relatively heavy. Though you've still got to be a Somebody with pretty urgent business there to get an invitation.

The Year in Retrospect

❖ Compared with the revolutionary changes that turned Hawaii topsy-turvy the year before, the past year has been a relatively uneventful one in Hawaii. Although still living under more controls than exist anywhere else in the country, the people of the Islands have experienced gradual lifting of many restrictions so that life seems almost luxurious by contrast with the preceding year. Electrifying knowledge that they are on the threshold of the forthcoming mighty offensive in the Pacific, however, kept Islanders on the alert and hard at work, with little time or opportunity for play.

On the first of January this year, Gen. Delos C. Emmons, then military governor of the Territory, said, "Hawaii, safe today under protecting guns of one of the greatest fortresses on earth against any invasion the Japanese currently may be able to organize, is being steadily strengthened against a possible climactic battle within the next few years."

Guadalcanal and New Guinea were not yet conquered but had been turned into "Bataans" for the hard-pressed Japs. Wake had been raided in a hit-and-run manner a week before, but the slow gains in the Pacific were almost infinitesimal on the map. The Solomons invasion was described as a miniature preview of what is to come, but the few toeholds of the "defensive offensive" were like "gnawing on the toenail of a colossus."

Early in January the *New York World Telegram* wrote, "Since the Pearl Harbor attack, Oahu has lived a life of warfare to an extent that has befallen no place on our mainland. . . . The *Paradise of the Pacific* has had to change in a greater degree than any of us at home can fully visualize from the carefree manners of peacetime to the grim-visaged manners of war. . . . If we lost Oahu we might lose the war to Japan."

This editorial was in connection with the controversy over repeal of martial law and restoration of civil rights, a matter that was the

First published December 1943.

160

subject of wide interest and discussion both here and on the mainland until the compromise between civil and military authorities was reached and put into effect in March.

Meanwhile, in January it was announced that movies may stay open until 9:30 and stores and business offices until ten, subject to stringent dim-out regulations. . . . An experiment in blackout traffic lights was termed a failure. . . . Artie Shaw was playing at the Breakers. . . . Joe E. Brown made a surprise appearance at Tripler hospital en route to a tour of the South Pacific bases. . . . There was a black market in refrigerators. . . . The Junior Chamber had launched its "Serve in Silence" campaign. . . . Sale of sliced bread was banned, only to be announced later that the ban did not apply in Hawaii.

January brought Hawaii a flood that was a "military secret" for several days, with a fourteen-inch rainfall in seventy-two hours. . . . The Navy announced the loss of the *Hornet,* the *Northampton, Juneau, Atlanta,* and six destroyers . . . and the first air raid alarm in ten months shrieked in the middle of the night. Chlorination of water was begun . . . smoking was permitted in the blackout (except in the case of air raid alarms), and the plan to accept volunteers of Japanese ancestry for military duty was announced.

During this period and for the months that have followed until the present, there was much talk and little action on many problems that still remain to be settled. Among these are: juvenile delinquency, a new juvenile detention home, the rat scourge, a downtown comfort station, housing, shortage of fish and poi, the problem of shoeshine boys, and the traffic snarl.

In February shipments of coffee, unrationed in Hawaii, were banned to the mainland . . . banks made an appeal to penny hoarders because of an acute shortage of coppers. . . . Senator Sanji Abe, who had been in custodial detention since the September before, resigned from the legislature . . . a butter shortage developed, and the Waialae Golf Club was taken over by the Army as a recreation center. A sharp rise in psychiatric problems was noted by the Hawaii Medical Association. . . . Ickes praised the Island population for its contribution to the war effort . . . and plans were under way for a six-lane highway to Pearl Harbor to overcome a dangerous bottleneck.

The twenty-second legislature convened on February 17, in a ceremony colorful with leis, island music, and other Hawaiian traditions. The momentous session approved Hawaii's largest budget to date and functioned with a minimum of friction. Also in February, Rabaul, Sala-maua, and Koepang were pasted by allied planes, the Japanese withdrew from Guadalcanal. . . . Secretary of the Navy Frank Knox visited Hawaii. . . . Liquor was banned from officers' clubs on army posts . . . and five hundred dim-out lights for main highways were approved by military authorities.

The month of March brought "restoration day" to Hawaii, when martial law was partially lifted by restoring certain functions to civil authorities, marking an end of fifteen months of absolute military rule. The changeover made little difference to the average civilian, although the principles involved were of history-making significance.

During this month the manpower commission "froze" workers of essential industries to their jobs . . . black market offenders in the fields of jewelry, drugs, dairy products, and groceries were given heavy fines . . . the Army released information on its training courses in ranger-commando jungle tactics . . . a crowd of twenty thousand witnessed a ceremony honoring twenty-six hundred AJA volunteers . . . and allied invasion of Japan by the end of 1945 was predicted by Frank H. Bartholomew, United Press vice-president.

Further modification of the blackout took place in April, when it was announced that one dim-out bulb would be permitted for every hundred square feet of floor space, instead of the two hundred formerly allowed. . . . News that Brig. Gen. Thomas H. Green, executive to the military governor since the war began, would be detached from Hawaii was received regretfully by Island residents. As judge advocate of the Hawaiian department, he had prepared detailed plans for the situation that developed on December Seventh and the military regulations that were immediately put into effect.

The OPA in April reared its authority and announced a "simplified revised plan to control food prices on Oahu at both wholesale and retail levels." It also announced that gasoline rationing, mainland style, would be put into effect. This was done in spite of protests from the press that advocated retention of the existing rationing method. The new system was instituted in the various islands in succession, starting with Kauai, and reaching Oahu October first.

Eighty tons of bombs, a mere pittance compared with recent developments, were dropped on Rabaul, and a raid on Nauru left phosphate works and airdrome areas gutted and bomb scarred. . . . And a newspaper headline stated, "Pacific front lull appears to be ended." . . . The

Local guardsmen were stationed at key buildings throughout Honolulu. Sand-filled sugar sacks restricted entry to those who worked there or were on official business.

Trenches were dug across school lawns in a zigzag pattern as protection against wholesale death from strafers until permanent bomb shelters could be built.

Organized under fire and activated two hours after the attack, Hawaii Territorial Guard was on duty at vital points by nightfall.

So often did Army tanks, large guns, and other mechanized equipment rumble through Honolulu's streets that special traffic rules were passed to ensure their rapid deployment.

Island beaches provided an ideal training ground for the military.

Flower leis became scarce as lei makers turned their talents to weaving camouflage netting for the military.

Many of Hawaii's businessmen joined the Honolulu Businessmen's Military Training Corps (BMTC) and were immediately assigned to strategic locations to protect the civilian population.

The Hawaii Territorial Guard was another civilian group activated by the military in Hawaii.

The entire Honolulu waterfront was fenced off and guarded during the war.

legislature aired conditions at Kamehameha schools in an investigation of the Bishop Estate's trusteeship over these institutions, with a result that this fall a new elementary department was opened with 320 pupils of Hawaiian or part-Hawaiian blood enrolled at the schools. . . . Halekai, a new club for service officers, was opened in the renovated home of the late Judge James Steiner at Waikiki . . . and Maluhia, described as the finest enlisted men's club in the world, was opened at Fort De Russy.

May Day is Lei Day in Hawaii, but it was also Bond Day this year. . . . Early in the month Governor Stainback announced the opening of a Work to Win campaign, "to enlist every able-bodied man and woman in Hawaii in war-useful work." . . . The Army conducted elaborate war maneuvers on Oahu. . . . Harold Rice made headlines by quitting the Republican Party and joining the Democrats . . . the new "dime-like" pennies appeared . . . and Hawaii became a pioneer by establishing a pay-as-you-go tax plan, on a 2 percent withholding basis.

Three new traffic lanes were completed on the Pearl Harbor highway, breaking a strategic bottleneck . . . police control was taken over by the Governor as the result of legislative action. . . . Hawaii was declared a critical labor area by Washington authorities . . . and the Washington office of the Equal Rights Commission was closed, due to a lack of appropriation of funds by the legislature. Fun-starved civilian workers were cheered by the announcement that liquor stores must stay open until 6:30 and may remain open until 7:30. This was followed soon by a regulation requiring bars to remain open six hours between noon and 7 P.M., making possible an hour or two of conviviality after working hours.

News of a change of command in the Hawaiian department was another highlight of the month of May, with the aloha of the people in Hawaii whom he had governed with consideration and skill during black and difficult days, General Emmons left for another command. He was relieved by Maj. Gen. Robert C. Richardson, Jr., who has also won respect from civilian as well as the military population. . . . The month of May ended with solemn and appropriate services at Pearl Harbor and elsewhere for the dead heroes of The Seventh and other battles.

Kamehameha Day in June was not observed as a gala holiday as it was in the past, but was noteworthy chiefly for the bond drive conducted by the Hawaiian Civic Club. June brought the end of a school year, with practically every student old enough to do so taking some sort of employment to relieve Hawaii's crucial manpower shortage. Also in June the OPA threatened action on rent gouging . . . a flu epidemic of medium proportions took place. . . . Hawaii had its eighth draftee induction, while about 80 percent of its 140,000 registrants remained deferred due chiefly to the manpower shortage . . . and the transportation jam of "stranded Hawaiians" on the coast became increasingly serious.

A new program of controlled lighting, which was put into effect in July, brought relief to Island residents and did much to increase morale. Under the new system, lights may be left on until 10 P.M., with windows open unless they face the sea. . . . The Fourth of July was another holiday notable chiefly for its bond drive and an elaborate demonstration at the stadium of the work of OCD wardens. Also in July the HRT "slowdown" strike took place, one of the few labor disturbances to have developed in Hawaii since the start of the war.

Early in August an epidemic of dengue fever developed, which resulted in the loss to Hawaii's work pool of many essential manhours. From August 9 until September 13, service men were forbidden to enter the Waikiki district, an area heavily infested by the fever-laden mosquitoes. Army authorities joined forces with local health officials in a vigorous campaign of public education and spraying of infested areas, thus preventing the epidemic from attaining catastrophic proportions.

Figures were released during this period that showed Hawaii's bank assets to be up 49 percent over the preceding year and gross income for business in the Islands to be up 41 percent during the first six months over the same period a year before. . . . Lt. Lanny Ross arrived on his way to a tour of the "jungle circuit" of the South Pacific . . . a visit was made by Undersecretary of War Robert P. Patterson . . . and Mayor Petrie returned from an official visit to Washington. . . . The Hawaii edition of *Time* was launched . . . and the Catholic cathedral celebrated its 100th anniversary . . . and Kiska was retaken.

Meanwhile the housing situation remained as desperate as ever in spite of much talk and strong protests in the local press. Finally, in August, construction of six hundred homes was authorized by the National Housing Agency, the Navy announced it would make available five hundred homes by moving officers into barracks, and later the first of a group of houses was built under Title VI of the National

Housing Act, with approved mortgages by the FHA. The uproar over housing during the year included a strongly protested threat by the OPA to take over rent control, accusations of "rent gouging" on the part of landlords, senate hearings, enforced registration of landlords, and an amended rent control ordinance by the board of supervisors. In August Robert R. Spencer was selected to supervise registration of landlords, and a month later he was appointed chief administrator of rent control.

The fall season began with the return to school of 83,018 pupils in the Territory and the announcement that the plan for student work in sugar and pineapple fields one day in every two weeks would be adopted by public and private schools. . . . The ban on "re-caps" for passenger cars was lifted. . . . Christmas shopping for service men was urged . . . gang fights and hoodlumism became a problem . . . brighter lights for auto headlights were authorized . . . the OCD conducted maneuvers . . . Mrs. Eleanor Roosevelt and the "flying senators" visited Hawaii . . . Theo. H. Davies had labor trouble . . . and the fall of Italy was greeted coolly by Island residents, who were aware that the hardest part of the fight was still ahead.

With the violent attacks on Jap-held Marcus and Wake islands, a conference in Honolulu between Admirals King, Halsey, and Nimitz, and the suspense in the air they felt rather than saw, residents of the Islands began to feel that the "big push" in the Pacific would soon begin.

They felt it, too, because the Navy announced that civilian passage to Hawaii from the West Coast was indefinitely postponed and because they were told to tighten their belts and prepare for a reduction in food shipments from the Mainland. With this came a request for voluntary reduction of food consumption, to prevent the necessity of dreaded point rationing as yet not instituted in the Islands. Shipments of butter from the Mainland were to be reduced 20 percent, evaporated milk 15 percent, and canned fruits and vegetables 33 percent.

A visit by an enemy plane was accepted without hysterics, and the people of the Islands felt themselves ready to meet any eventuality the coming months might bring.

1944

On January 31, U.S. forces invaded the Marshall Islands, and after three weeks of fighting that island group was under U.S. control. On February 3, U.S. warships shelled the Kurile Islands in Northern Japan. On April 22, the Allies invaded New Guinea. On August 10, Guam was retaken.

In May, blackout restrictions were finally lifted, but practice exercises would be conducted until the end of the war.

In June, ten civilians and four soldiers were killed and fifteen civilians injured when two Army planes collided and crashed in Kalihi-kai.

President Roosevelt arrived in Honolulu for a military strategy conference with Gen. Douglas MacArthur and Admirals Nimitz and Leahy on July 21. FDR departed on the 29th.

In September, houses of prostitution were ordered closed.

On October 20, U.S. forces landed on Leyte Island in the Philippines. The Japanese sent a major naval force to the area, and in the ensuing Battle of Leyte Gulf the Japanese lost four carriers, three battleships, and ten cruisers. Just hours before the naval victory, President Roosevelt ordered martial law terminated and restored *habeas corpus*.

The 1944 election campaign turned nasty. At the center of controversy was Democratic National Committeewoman Alice Kamokila Campbell. A wealthy woman who supported martial law and Hawaiian nationalism, she represented Moloka'i in the senate. During the campaign she advocated legalization of prostitution and accused AJAs of bloc voting. And she further irritated her own Democratic party when she backed the candidacy of a Republican woman for the territorial senate. Above all else, she was against statehood.

Finishing School of the South Pacific Combat Soldier

LT. GORDON A. KRAMER

❖ "Guts at both ends of the bayonet," the traditional motto of "Wild Bill" echoes and re-echoes itself throughout the huge jungle valleys in Hawaii that Lt. Col. William Crowell Saffarrans has picked for his school. Ever the practical, never the spectacular, "Wild Bill" Saffarrans has inaugurated the most astounding "bill of goods" ever to be delivered into a general's lap.

Innocently placed by the side of one of Oahu's scenic highways stands the headquarters and camp sites of the Unit Jungle Training Camp. It reveals little of the explosive quality of training going on in the nearby valleys. From early morning to late at night, steady streams of trucks take eager soldiers in conveyor belt rhythm to the humming beehives of activity. The incessant roar of dynamite, the blasts of bangalores, and the hiss and splatter of heavy machine-gun fire pace the individual soldier through his classes against a background of intricate yet intriguing jungle realms.

General Richardson ordered "Wild Bill" to Oahu from his Second Army Ranger's School at Camp Forrest, Tenn. This former Georgetown University football star, coach of the champion teams of the Ninth Infantry in Texas and the infantry in the Hawaiian Islands, is a trainer of men.

Clad in his characteristic coveralls, seemingly in at least a half dozen places at one time in his dwarfed jeep, "Wild Bill" greets everyone on the run with a wave of his arm and a hearty "Hiya."

"To h—— with the show and spectacular," says this rugged individual, "you can't win battles with beautiful displays. The training of the soldier as an integral part of his unit has but one aim: victory on the field of battle. A show for anyone takes up time. It's out."

First published January 1944.

172

His next spot he hoped was China. General Richardson had other ideas. Since the time he hopped from the bomber that brought him from the mainland and reported to the General, he has been on the go. Plans were drawn up. He was taken to an isolated valley, "and," prompted the General, "here's what we want." In exactly eleven days, this human dynamo had ready an entire curriculum with all the trimmings, living quarters, and administration areas for fourteen hundred men . . . twenty-eight hundred in four weeks . . . forty-two hundred in six weeks. All this while the camp roared with the activity of its first classes.

The post was honored the other day with the presence of General Richardson himself, who was well pleased with the accomplishments of the school. He interrupted several classes to address them briefly: "The importance of the training of squads and platoons and their leaders reaches gigantic proportions in jungle warfare. You are not being let down. My purpose of bringing the commandant of your school to you has been for the explicit purpose of fitting the individual soldier with as much concrete knowledge of the work he is about to be doing as is possible."

The men themselves are enthusiastic. It is training they have been looking for. When you are able to see them in the dense jungles at work, you will readily recognize the meaning of "practical work." Everyone is trained, no one overlooked. Officers and men alike, regardless of grade or branch, complete the courses as infantrymen with fatigues, rifle, and bayonet as their uniform.

Trained instructors put them through their paces. Time is devoted to the more tame subjects as well as the rough. The men must learn new and timely physical exercises to train and coordinate their muscles and move about on short quick marches to improve their wind and endurance. They enter into direct physical hand-to-hand combat and learn to master the art of dirty fighting at its height.

Fundamentals and advanced work in construction and passage of wire entanglements tears and rips the uniform and the flesh beneath. Bangalore torpedoes rock the ground as the men learn to maneuver and fuse these rod-like destructive weapons. Fifty-caliber tracers whine above their heads as they crawl through the mazes of barbed wire. Dynamite is placed in every man's hands. He fuses and detonates it as he hears lectures and watches demonstrations of destruction. He learns how to split steel and crush concrete with TNT. He works with booby traps and searches warily for their presence. Takes his injuries with a grin and pushes forward to his next assignment.

"We do not train a selected few," says "Wild Bill," the commandant of this efficient and effective organization, "and expect them in return to impart their learnings to their units at a future date in areas entirely unsuited to such training. The individual, the soldier, is taught the finer arts of jungle fighting. Squads and platoons are broken down and small groups act together; the leaders are taught their responsibilities and work out their problems under trained watchful eyes and careful critique."

Patrol work and the art of concealment and ambush hit the spotlight in the course. Men work in the jungle both night and day, learning to feel their way cautiously along. They set ambushes and trap one another. They are corrected in their errors.

A village, such as the Japanese have been known to inhabit, is approached scientifically and eliminated in the same manner. Tojo dummies poke their heads and bodies obtrusively from doors and windows and race on wires from house to house. Tommy guns spit their deadly missiles, bayonets strike at momentary targets, land mines shatter the ground as well as the nerves and add to the confusion with their ear-splitting, mud-splashing explosions. Rifles pound furiously as squads take turns in mopping up this enemy area while the remainder of the class follows behind the instructor, being critiqued on the spot in what they are soon to participate. It was with pleasure that the commandant assigned a special crew to reconstruct and rebuild these mutilated Jap counterparts that the over-enthusiastic students rip, tear, butt, and shoot to shreds hourly. Casualties are expected and do happen, but not too frequently. Competent crews with waiting ambulances stand by at all times. A surgeon and his staff are ready for any and all accidents.

The men are all taught to shoot from the hip with any type of weapon and surprise themselves with their accuracy at shooting at sound and quick-appearing targets. They learn the technique of crossing seemingly impassable streams, intact and dry and able to carry the battle to the enemy on the opposite side, all the while under fire. They are taught how to storm and conquer typical Japanese pill boxes that hold them off with aggravating fire from hidden machine-gun positions.

Toward the end of the week, the men, fatigued, but willing, are put through a course adequately named "Combat Reaction Proficiency." The instructor, under the careful guidance of "Wild Bill" by his own tongue, stays awake nights to think up the impossible and extreme in taunting his students to desperation. Following the narrow jungle trail, they meet with obstacles dreamed up by this "Svengali" of the school. Booby traps explode, dummies fall on the backs of the passers-by, pits of mud yawn unexpectedly at their feet, and streams are crossed on wobbly wire foot bridges amid the din and explosion of earth and water from controlled mines that almost invariably throw the crosser to the sticky water below. The men continue on. They are being graded. Their reactions to situations and their reflexes are being checked. Dummies fire at them from concealed positions in trees and lunge at them to draw bayonet strokes on the path. At the end the men are tired but pleased. Their laughing, panting attitude shows its results.

The organization, production-line speed, and efficiency that "Wild Bill" Saffarrans has placed the Unit Jungle Training Camp on a "paying basis" in such a short time is amazing. The combat teams that enter its portals of learning each week leave after seven days, tired but satisfied. Satisfied down to the last buck private who realizes he has at last gone through a course of training that will fit him individually as an indispensable part of his squad, his platoon, and his unit.

Combat team commanders are high in their praise of the training at the school, and these men are critical, very critical, of the training their men receive. They usually voice but one regret: "We're only sorry something like this hasn't been available to us in the past. It is invaluable training."

In this way has Lt. Col. William C. Saffarrans made the American soldier more capable in the exercise of his duties with the "finishing school of the South Pacific combat soldier."

Hawaiian Economy, Present and Future

DR. RUBY T. NORRIS,
SENIOR ECONOMIST,
OFFICE OF PRICE ADMINISTRATION

Note: *The following article represents the personal views of the writer and is not an official release from the Office of Price Administration.*

❖ The war is effecting many and sweeping changes in the economy of the Islands. The basic production of Hawaii—cane and pines—is being carried on under terrific strain. The Islands have been transformed into a fortress. The new airports and defense projects have commandeered much excellent land; and the labor supply has drifted away into the armed forces, defense work, and the highly lucrative service trades.

The processes of importation, by which the Islands obtain the vast bulk of the consumption goods, are carried on under abnormal and trying circumstances. Old established firms find their quotas cut by their customary suppliers, and new firms are having to buy under very disadvantageous terms from far-flung sources. Invoices are high and differ widely from shipment to shipment. Goods come in, poorly selected for export, badly wrapped, handled in the boats by inexperienced help, crowded, and frequently damaged. For this chaotic buying and shipping, the consumer pays and pays and pays and cries for more. The market is so "dry" that anything that can be brought in, broadly speaking, will sell. "The lid is off." Before the war a buyer would think twice before snapping up a high-cost lot of merchandise, as he would know it would have to sell in competition with properly bought, well-known brands. Now, if he can get it, he can sell it, and at a profit.

First published March 1944.

Hence there have arisen many new ventures. The Islands are alive with new, small, manufacturing establishments in such lines as gifts, tropical novelties, and candies. Many use family labor. Equipment is pieced together with "Yankee ingenuity" taking the place of priorities. Sources of supply are high cost, perforce, in many cases. For example, many hand blocking establishments have bought cloth at retail. In almost all lines of trade, the old and large concerns are doing a smaller percent of the total business in their line, not because they are not doing more business, but because they cannot keep pace with the upsurge of the new and small. The big concern has an eye to its reputation and to the future and is less likely to buy from the high-cost mainland supply sources. Overhead is large and fixed and is not being expanded to meet what is obviously an abnormal demand. Hence, the big concern doubles its volume—but does not treble it, and the dozens of small new jobbers and manufacturers continue to rush into business.

The service trades, of course, are even more prosperous than Island manufacture. The Islands are the hosts to the fleet and the Pacific army. New concerns in entertainment and restaurant fields spring up overnight and cannot begin to meet the demand. It will be worse (or better from a business angle) when the war in Europe ends and the full attention of the armed forces is turned to the Pacific.

This, in a nutshell, is the picture of the current economy of the Hawaiian Islands as it appears to one observer. What of the future?

In the future, the primary forecast is that there will be a permanent and large population increase. Several million potential residents have had the Islands exhibited to them, at government expense! Hawaii has never had a press agent to compare with Uncle Sam. Thousands will carry back to the mainland . . . tales of the spectacular mountains, the gorgeous flowers, the active year-round sport life of the Islands. It is true that these features are somewhat obscured for many by a temporary shortage of women and the crowded conditions of wartime living. However, many a mainland lad will take his honeymoon in the Islands, will return for his vacations, will return again to retire. Others will simply return—permanently. If this forecast be correct, then certain other results will necessarily follow.

After the war, the economy of the Islands will be less focused on cane and pines than was the pre-war economy. The latter will always be important—as a primary source of cash income. Pineapple, particularly, is likely to see an important expansion. Much of the pineapple pack has been commandeered during the war by the U.S. Government for feeding the armed forces. Many citizens, especially from the low-income states, have never tasted a pineapple before. Consequently, one can predict an increasing demand for this product when conditions return to normalcy. Sugar here will fare as well as the mainland sugar industry, in all probability. The political strength of the beet and cane sugar states will probably protect the interests of the sugar producers adequately.

Even though the two segments of American sugar producers are in competition, they will act together in opposing any outside encroachments on their market. The industry is more mature than pineapple, more of the earth's surface is adapted to sugar production than it is to pineapple, and the best land for this purpose is already under cultivation and has been for some time. No great expansion in sugar cultivation is therefore to be expected in the Islands.

Importation of mainland products will continue on an ever increasing scale after the war. The population of the Islands will be larger—and incomes per capita will be larger. Normally the Islander is a very large importer. For example, in 1940 the per capita trade of the Territory was about ten times the per capita trade of continental United States. In addition, after the war has been won, the Islands will be the point of dispersion for the American export trade to the entire Pacific area. China will need plumbing, steel, and concrete with which to rebuild her cities and industrialize her plants. American capital will be active in the Philippines, the Dutch and British East Indies, Australia, and Japan in all probability, whether or not we retain any political interest in these areas. American industrial equipment will unquestionably emerge preeminent from this war, which it did so much to win. The prestige of American products has never been higher. In the expansion of the Asiatic export trade, already rapidly increasing in recent decades, the Hawaiian Islands will naturally be the funneling point for the Pacific area.

Local manufacture will be very considerably affected by the return to normalcy of the mainland economy. Many lines have sprung up under the protection of the shipping space shortage, and they will not be able to survive the normal competition of effective mass production methods. Some of the methods that have perforce been employed here during the war have been extremely primitive. In some lines, the

Island manufacture can import and effectively utilize the modern machinery available to the mainland manufacturer, and this will undoubtedly be done in many cases. In many other lines, however, the small size of this market and paucity of raw materials will make competition permanently disadvantageous in comparison with the mainland. That many local producers realize this fact is attested to by their frank statements to OPA in the estimate of their overhead costs. Many an Island concern has been amortizing his plant during the war period with no serious expectation of continuing in business thereafter.

The future of local manufacture will lie, this observer thinks, in the following lines: perishables such as bakery products; heavy items such as concrete; and commodities made from local raw materials, such as canec and handicraft products. It is in the last field that the great undeveloped potentialities for income lie. The Islands abound in talent, and materials for handicraft products, thus far, are only partially exploited.

Modern interior decoration, now largely confined to plain weaves such as broadloom for rugs, would welcome with enthusiasm the lauhala rugs so common in Island homes. Many delightful furniture designs are found here that are not available in the mainland. Salad bowls and trays of koa, lauhala table mats, purses and waste baskets, jewelry of local design, and hand painted objects could enjoy a tremendous expansion if properly marketed. The mainland—superior in mass production of standardized items—will never effectively compete in these lines. Furthermore, it is evident that many elements of the population would take a keen relish in participating in the manufacture of such products. It seems to the writer that both as manufacturer and assembler, and possibly finisher of south Pacific Island furniture and handicrafts products, an important export industry could be developed here.

The same possibilities for innovation exist in agricultural novelties. The palate of the newcomer is delighted with the papaya, the mango, and the guava, to name only a few. Properly selected and ripened, the papaya alone could become a major challenger to the grapefruit and the melon in the mainland breakfast diet. The market for tropical nuts such as the Macadamia and the Lichee nuts could be greatly expanded.

The service trades, if the population forecast given above holds good, will remain in an expanded condition. As a great tourist center, vacation land, and retirement area, and with a far greater permanent population, the Islands will require more theaters, more restaurants, and more service trades of all kinds.

These are the outlines of the future economy of Hawaii as they appear to this observer. It is a bright future, primarily because Hawaii is a delightful place.

Capital of the Pacific

The overall part Hawaii will play in the post-war world will be determined at conference tables in Washington, London, Moscow, and Chungking. But we can begin to plan now against the day when, possibly, Hawaii will be the capital of the American Pacific area.

The knowledge available in Hawaii of tropical agriculture, of race relations, of world trade, of development and exploitation according to American standards surpasses that to be found anywhere in the Americas and should be utilized to the full. Hawaii has an outstanding record for meeting a great variety of problems and for solving them in an American way. The pattern, suitably cleared of mistakes and defects, should provide the working basis for this new estate.

In other words, we must be prepared to accept international agreements, even though they affect our prewar agricultural economy, and we must be prepared to recognize our new position in the Pacific, even though it means severe competition and adjustment. In addition, let us hope that conflicts between racial, social, and economic factions within our own society can be faced and solved to the greater benefit of all.

In Hawaii's probable future status as the political, social, and financial capital of the Pacific, we may anticipate a large permanent army and navy personnel, a great influx of mainlanders and mainland capital, schools and a university of the highest standards, tourists attracted by greatly improved recreational facilities, and great changes in our agriculture. —From an article by Dr. J. H. Beaumont, Director, Hawaii Agricultural Experiment Station, in *Hawaii Farm and Home*.

A Yank's-Eye View of Honolulu

CPL. BILL REED

❖ The war hasn't changed the people of Honolulu a bit. They are still as hopelessly sentimental, as wildly romantic, and as childishly imaginative as they were in the days before the blitz. When the Japs blasted their ivory tower with death-dealing bombs and machine-gun bullets, they were stunned into realism for only a moment. On December 8, 1941, Honolulu citizens were just as sentimental as they were on December 6. The only difference was the change in the object of their affection.

Sentimentality is usually a very funny trait. It is what makes women weep at the movies, men blow their noses at weddings, and Brooklyn baseball fans throw pop bottles. But sometimes sentimentality rises above its mush level and assumes heroic proportions. That is what it did during that frenzied December two years ago, when the easy-going, pleasure-loving citizens of Honolulu set about the harsh business of war.

The lush, balmy pre-war days in this tourist-camp community fully justified the dream-like existence of its inhabitants. They lived in a world of music, flowers, and gay, colorful holidays. It was the world of Johnny Noble and his island songs—a world of hula girls and beach boys and lei-sellers. Everything in this world was soft and luxuriant. Nowhere was there a better example of what Hitler and Tojo serenely believed were "decadent democracies."

When war came, Honolulu was the only American city that lived in constant fear of immediate enemy invasion. Its dwellings were the only American homes to come face to face with Axis terror. Overnight, Honolulu was changed from a community that was smug in its security to one in which the people expected devastating punishment from Jap bombers, ships, and submarines.

First published April 1944.

Overnight, the people's absurd sentimentality about their beloved island "paradise" became the most potent weapon against the Japs in their proposed conquest of the Pacific.

It was only a few hours after Pearl Harbor was attacked that Joseph P. Poindexter, civilian governor of the Territory of Hawaii, declared that an emergency existed, and the military governor assumed command. Martial law was immediately put into effect, and there were regulations on the sale of food, gasoline rationing, and discontinuation of the publication of certain periodicals, particularly those that were believed to be pro-Japanese. The most rigid blackout in the world was enforced from sunset to sunrise, and there was a curfew after 1800. . . . The people accepted the severe regulations imposed by the military government with the same mad enthusiasm that they had received Johnny Noble's latest song, Winona Love's newest hula, and the monthly issue of the *Paradise of the Pacific*.

Today, more than two years after the blitz, wartime Honolulu is fantastic. It is a city of a thousand subdued conflicts—between the "kamaainas" and the "malihinis," between servicemen and civilians, between the many races that form blurry dividing lines among the social classes. The old resident kamaainas, who knew only the moneyed, partying whites that came from the Mainland to winter at Waikiki, resent the boisterous, rude malihinis who have come to shops at Pearl Harbor or to construction jobs at Hickam. And the malihinis accuse the kamaainas of selfishness, coldness, and indifference because the facilities for hospitality and amusement are taxed beyond capacity. Some of the civilians object to servicemen who fill the bars and hotels when they are in town on pass, and some servicemen wonder that civilians should begrudge them eight hours of freedom each week. . . .

It is more pleasant to live in Honolulu now than it was just after the blitz. Early in March 1943, the Army relinquished a large part of its territorial control to the civil government. It was a sentimental day for the sentimental Honoluluans, and the "restoration" ceremonies were conducted in the throne room of the Iolani Palace. The room was filled with smiling people wearing leis, and the string section of the Royal Hawaiian Band played "Song of the Islands."

The Iolani Palace grounds, now mushroomed with small wooden buildings housing many new offices of the wartime government, are no longer so rigidly guarded, and many of the important business buildings have members of the Business Men's Training Corps for sentries instead of soldiers and marines. The Royal Hawaiian Hotel is a recreation spot for servicemen, and the entire Waikiki district is teeming with soldiers, sailors, marines, and defense workers. . . .

Honolulu is a fabulous, unbelievable city . . . where a strange, mysterious woman, clad in a tight sweater and bellbottomed slacks materialized from nowhere to give a dinner for 150 servicemen . . . where each Sunday afternoon an earnest group of Filipino parishioners holds revival meetings in the middle of Maunakea Street's pool rooms and chow houses . . . where the Hawaii Tourist Bureau still receives letters from people on the Mainland requesting information about vacationing in the islands . . . where men have gone to sleep in barber chairs and awakened to find they had been charged as much as twelve dollars for "the works" . . . where a statue of Kamehameha, the Mighty Warrior, still looks down on a brood of the most sentimental people ever created by the good, gray gods. —*From* Yank, *the Army Weekly.*

Hawaii's Debt on Army Day

❖ In observing Army Day, Hawaii owes a special debt of gratitude to the Americans of Japanese ancestry fighting gallantly in Europe, not only for their share in fighting the war, but because they have become symbols throughout the world that Americanism is not a matter of "race, color, or creed."

Although the AJAs themselves would prefer not to be singled out because of their racial background, most of them are aware that theirs is an opportunity to prove once and for all their loyalty to the American way of life. Those who return to Hawaii will be entitled to all the honor and respect a country can pay to its fighting men in uniform.

The following are excerpts from AJA soldiers' letters on the Mainland and on the fighting front in Italy:

"Surely the boys are putting up a courageous fight, but we do not go into battle with 'smiling faces' as the papers say. War isn't like that. Everyone is tense and alert before going into a battle, wondering, worrying, when and where the enemy will start shooting first. . . . It rains almost every day here in Italy. We sleep in foxholes with more than three inches of water, wet blankets, wet socks, and damp clothes. When this war is over and when I get home, I am going to buy myself the best bed in Honolulu with a 'beauty sleep' mattress. . . . The enemy has thrown everything it has against us—artillery, mortars, multi-barreled 'screaming meemies,' machine guns, machine pistols, rifles, grenades, mines, booby traps, and aerial bombing and shelling. I'm one of the lucky ones who haven't been scratched. . . ."

"What bothers me now is whether the homefolk will not fail us in the long run? . . . People (of Japanese extraction) in Hawaii cannot fail the understanding and trust that a few of those high officials hold for them, and they should thank their lucky stars that they have such men of broad vision in control. If they do not realize that they will be the focus of attention more and more as the war swings to the Pacific,

First published April 1944.

184

and do not take active steps to alleviate or improve such an enviable position, then they certainly will have lost a home-front war just as certain as we will emerge victorious in our share of the war. If the American Japanese in Hawaii are still 'on the spot' even after their AJ soldiers come marching home, then the people themselves at home are to be blamed. If, during the course of this war, they have not won and earned for themselves a more secure and trusted status in the community, then we, who have left everything so dear to us in Hawaii, are fighting a losing battle as far as the home-front Hawaii is concerned. I wonder if the people back home really know how dearly and nostalgically we think of our homeland and how fervent our hopes of returning there to pick up our normal peaceful and trusted lives again."

"You can tell the homefolks that if they fail their part and shun their responsibility back there, then we might as well forget about Hawaii and settle in Africa, Burma, the Solomons, or wherever we may be when the war ends, because Hawaii would not be worth living in then."

❖ In touching ceremonies last month, Purple Heart Awards were presented to the next of kin of fifty-eight American soldiers from Hawaii, members of the 100th Infantry Battalion, who died fighting in Europe. The presentations were made by Col. Kendall J. Fielder, assistant chief of staff for military intelligence, for Lt. Gen. Robert C. Richardson, commanding general of the Pacific area. Said Colonel Fielder, "The War Department through General Richardson wants you to accept this medal as a token of recognition of your soldier's complete devotion to duty and as a symbol of sincere sympathy with you in your bereavement and of our pride in your boy's valor." Said a widow of one of the men on behalf of the bereaved relatives, "We know that their sacrifice has not been in vain. It is up to us who remain to carry on."

Honolulu . . . Island Boomtown

❖ Astronomical figures on money spending are no novelty these days, but the staggering amount of money that has been circulating in Honolulu since the start of the war is probably unequaled in any area of the same geographical limitations and civilian population.

Since the start of the war, for instance, the amount of money spent in retailing has increased $22 million, or more than 75 percent. The amount spent on amusements is up $5 million, or 80 percent; bank deposits have soared $120 million, or 75 percent. Postal receipts have increased 300 percent since the start of the war.

Fourteen million dollars were spent on liquor in 1943, compared with less than $10 million in 1941, when there was no liquor rationing and bars were opening from early morning until midnight. Five million of this sizable amount of money was spent on locally manufactured liquor and $4.5 million on locally manufactured beer. This output represents the amount spent at bars and on the approximately one hundred thousand liquor permits held by civilians, and does not take into consideration the amounts spent for the pauses that refresh at officers' clubs, post exchanges, and ship service stores, a sum that staggers the imagination even to guess.

Stock and bond transactions have increased 70 percent since 1941, and real estate 60 percent. Taxis have had an increase of 150 percent in the number of passengers and 50 percent in gross receipts. On tattooing alone, more than half a million dollars were spent last year.

That local civilians are not letting these hundreds of millions of dollars float through the air apathetically is shown by the fact that more than 8,000 new businesses were established during the first two years of the war, and 628 new businesses during January 1944 alone. Some of these, of course, were new businesses in name only, representing a change of ownership, incorporation, or disincorporation, but thousands of them are entirely new forms of money-making. Many of the

---

First published May 1944.

businesses are relatively unimpressive, such as moveable lunch wagons or hot dog stands, while others are of gigantic proportions, such as huge recreation centers, curio manufacturing, and candy making.

A large portion of these new ventures are carried on in private homes, with papa, mamma, and all the children pitching in to make hula dolls, paper bags for potato chips, or some novelty that will attract the money burning holes in the pockets of service men and war workers. Much inventiveness has been used to convert secondhand machinery and parts into miniature home factories for turning out everything from popcorn to poker chips.

The total gross income for Oahu alone rose from approximately $517 million in 1941, to $784 million in 1943, on the basis of business transacted.

Of the billions that have been handed out in payrolls to civilians and service personnel, much has been salted away for future reference. Sale of stocks and bonds since before the war rose $3.5 million, or 70 percent, and real estate had a $17 million, or 60 percent, increase. But in war bond purchases, the people of Hawaii really took the rag off'n the bush.

Averaging a purchase of $4 million a month in Series E bonds alone, the people here have led all states and territories in per capita purchases of E, F, and G series since May 1941, when the sale of bonds started.

This Midas-like flow of money in Honolulu has produced effects that may be viewed both with alarm and satisfaction. Many of the downtown streets have acquired a honky-tonk atmosphere that is approaching an all-time high in tawdriness, but it is more than tolerated for the small amount of fun it offers bored and lonely service men.

The divorce rate is almost three times as high here as it is on the mainland, the figures being approximately 2.9 divorces for each six marriages in Hawaii, compared with approximately one divorce for six marriages on the mainland. Incidentally, haoles lead by far in the racial breakdown of divorce figures, 625 haoles having been granted divorces in 1943, compared with 283 Hawaiians and part-Hawaiians, 148 Filipinos, 125 Japanese, and 80 Chinese.

There has been no abnormal increase in juvenile delinquency, contrary to trends as reported from mainland statistics, according to the report of the crime prevention bureau. During the first two war years, there were fewer arrests among juveniles than for any year in the preceding ten for "part one" offenses, such as murder, rape, robbery, and auto theft. There were, however, a considerable number of arrests for offenses such as forgery, prostitution, liquor law violations, gambling, and vagrancy.

Arrests for the two full war years of 1942 and 1943 were actually seventy-eight less in number than for the preceding two years. A significant trend, however, is shown by the fact that there was a 45 percent increase in persons charged for sex offenses for 1943 over 1942 and by the alarming increase of the number of girls arrested compared with the number of boys. Arrests of boys declined 11 percent and arrests of girls increased 97 percent during the two war years, compared with the previous two years. In normal years arrests of boys outnumber those of girls seven or eight to one.

The abnormal ratio of men to women in Hawaii and the fact that many working mothers no longer maintain proper oversight of their daughters are undoubtedly factors in the increase of arrests among girls and the rise in the number of sex offenses.

A breakdown of the liquor situation brings to light several interesting points. The islands produced in 1943 about 158,000 cases of hard liquor, for which the consumers paid approximately $5 million. Local industry also produced last year 1.5 million cases of beer, for which about $4 million was paid. The spirits and brew were turned out in five rectifying plants, three of which are new since the start of the war, and two breweries.

In 1941 there were 525 permits issued for the selling of retail liquor. After the war no alien has been permitted to sell liquor, so the number of licenses dropped to 302 in 1942 and 323 last year. During the year before the war, a total sale of nearly $10 million was divided among the 525 permit holders, whereas in the following year more than $10 million worth of business went to only 302 establishments, and last year $14 million went to 323 license holders.

Consumption of so much liquor during the two war years is interesting when one takes into consideration the fact that during that time bars were open from only two to five hours, instead of fifteen, and liquor was rationed to one quart or one case of beer per week to each individual, instead of unlimited quantities. Consumption of soft drinks, just for the record, has increased more than 200 percent since The Seventh.

As for amusements, motion pictures account for nearly $5 million of the $11 million shelled out. Football and baseball took in $190,000, and admissions for wrestling, skating, and boxing account for $450,000. The remaining $5 million that is accounted for by the tax office is represented by such forms of income as pin ball machines, juke boxes, pool halls, amusement centers, and the receipts of licensed "entertainers," or prostitutes, of which there are approximately 260 registered with the police.

The church picture is a bright one, all churches reporting an increased attendance (except in Oriental branches) of from 100 to 200 percent. The increased attendance is attributed both to wartime spiritual fervor among civilians and to the large numbers of service men in the pews. Many churches have wiped out their financial indebtedness, have increased their staffs, and have been able to make substantial contributions to various forms of good works. Most churches have funds and plans for expansions when materials become available.

Increased attendance at such institutions as the Library of Hawaii and the Honolulu Academy of Arts are other satisfying by-products of Honolulu's boomtown increase of pace.

Incidental addenda: There were 288 restaurants here in 1939, and there are now 630, but it's still practically impossible to get a meal without standing in line. . . . Businessmen say, "We can sell anything. It's just a matter of getting it to sell." . . . In 1940 the Honolulu Rapid Transit had a daily average of 86,281 passengers, and in 1943 the daily average was 232,000! . . . Of the approximately three hundred women lei sellers engaged in business before the war, nearly 95 percent are engaged in camouflage work for military authorities. . . . All this milling about and exchanging of billions of dollars has taken place in a city of only eighty-two square miles, with a civilian population of somewhat more than two hundred thousand. (Population figures have been banned since the start of the war, and the number of military personnel is obviously restricted information.)

Frank Comments by a Feminine Legislator

KAMOKILA CAMPBELL,

DEMOCRATIC SENATOR OF MOLOKAI
AND NATIONAL COMMITTEE-WOMAN

❖ As an American with the soul of an Hawaiian, living in the midst of a polyglot community, I shall think aloud so that the holders of Hawaii's destiny may hear.

When two grand old political parties, like the Republican and Democratic parties of Hawaii, permit their representation of our government to develop into a poker game, with cards stacked against personalities and chips on shoulders, responsible leaders of this community should take a definite stand for rebuilding the parties along American ideals.

Our present civil service laws appear contradictory to American principles when they deprive a man of his rights to participate openly in the affairs of his government. Both parties could stand new blood, and Hawaii calls to its youth for the protection of her future generations. If civil service laws interfere with the interests of our youth in political affairs, then let us change the laws.

The Japanese element in Hawaii is giving us something to think about, making us wonder sometimes, like Alice in Wonderland. I have been wondering whether in pressing the issue of immediate statehood for Hawaii we would not be diving into waters far beyond our depth. When we first thought of statehood, there was no racial prejudice, no alien enemies, no suspicion. Today Hawaii speaks for herself under many strained conditions. Until the necessary protective adjustments are made by our American leaders, Hawaii should rest on her past laurels of self-government. I would consider it a form of treason to sell

First published June 1944.

out my Hawaii for a vote in Congress under the conditions of war and local chaos that exist in the Territory today.

If we are someday to become the forty-ninth star on the flag of our country, then let it be as brilliant in traditional background of Americanism as all the other forty-eight states in the nation's banner. After this war, what are we to have in this Territory—a Japanese-America by force of numbers, or an American-Hawaii by adoption of intrinsically American principles?

Which is to awaken first in our beautiful Hawaii, Capital or Labor? Labor in the past, as immigrants and ignoramuses, was satisfied with the crumbs that fell from the master's table. Today, Labor, as university graduates with leaders of the same caliber, demands ceiling prices on the crumbs before they fall.

In Hawaii, when construction or industry men talk about their labor problems, two subjects leap to the fore—shortage of skilled workmen and seasonal employment. It is not only the ownership of construction and industry that pays for the seasonal character of business; it's employees and the public that also pay.

"Ownership" pays through being unable to secure for brief and interrupted periods of employment the higher quality of labor that would be attracted to steady and lasting positions. It pays in labor turnover and in labor discontent, both of them reflected in overhead. The "Workmen" sign on when and where they can find jobs, hold these jobs until completed, after which the cycle of searching for another job begins once again. No matter how capable a man is, positions are not always available. The "Public's" loss is in the necessity of supporting the unemployed and in the higher prices imposed by the contractor's higher cost of performance, which in their turn trace back to seasonalism.

There are many men in Hawaii's war work today who are members of various Mainland and local unions and who feel that strikes should be outlawed for the duration. Members of these unions are just as patriotic as the best of us and they do not want to let our fighting men down, but they are sometimes misled by arrogant, power-mad leaders who force sit-downs and walkouts on deliberately erroneous issues, which the average working man has neither the time nor the circumstances to investigate.

I believe that a better understanding between capital and labor could be effected through giving American workers more incentive, more free enterprise, and more initiative. I feel that the profit motive should be held out to them, making the individual feel he is directly working for the welfare of the whole nation and is not being exploited for the sole profit of the management and stockholders.

We know that there are two types of labor leadership—militant and administrative, and that industry today can help immeasurably in determining the type of labor leadership we are to have in Hawaii. If employers are going to fight labor, then labor will provide militant leadership. If on the other hand, the employers are cooperative, then administrative leadership will be furnished and provide the type of cooperation that is most desirable.

With no reflections upon federal court decisions, community emotions, civil and military government administration, racial prejudice, or "feudal Hawaii" sentiments, but purely from the standpoint of one deeply interested in Hawaii's present and future security, I speak on the subject of martial law and provost courts. I am 100 percent for martial law and the provost courts in Hawaii for the duration of this war.

Not until Adm. Chester W. Nimitz and General Richardson appeared in person to testify in the habeas corpus hearing of Lloyd C. Duncan did I appreciate the tremendous responsibilities imposed on both these experienced leaders. Although Admiral Nimitz did not testify at length as did General Richardson, his dignified silence told much.

The essence of General Richardson's testimony was just this—that from a military point of view this group of islands is the keynote of the defense of the western coast of our country, being the apex of a bastion formed with Alaska and the Panama Canal. Therefore, the security of this area is paramount to the strategic success of our army and navy and also for the defense of our country. Should it be penetrated at any time, we would suffer, both tactically and materially, and there would be a serious interference with the prosecution of the war.

He specifically stated that under his directive of the war department, he had been assigned to command all the ground and air troops of the army of the Central Pacific Area. And, in addition to that, he was to execute and supervise any operations that may be assigned to him by the Commander-in-Chief of the Pacific Ocean Areas, Admiral Nimitz.

In order to enable him to carry out his responsibilities, to achieve security, which is the only reason for the existing modified form of martial law, he had been required to publish certain regulations, and that in order to enforce these, he must have some form of court.

"Have you no confidence in the provost courts?" the General asked. "Remember the judges are American just like you, only they wear khaki. Most of them were outstanding jurists before they entered the army, and when the war is over they will doff their khaki and return to civil life.

"I could well understand the layman's feeling if there were any abuses in the provost courts. On the contrary, they have exercised the utmost care to insure justice. I am positive that in this community there are many potentially disloyal Japanese; we are constantly picking them up. We have never had an instance of a Japanese impugning the loyalty of one of their own blood. Therefore we have a right to be suspicious.

"These thousands and thousands of boys in the services are entitled to security. The fleet is entitled to security. I would remind you that eternal vigilance is the price of liberty, and I know that the people on the Mainland would never stand for another Pearl Harbor."

Many civilians feel as I do, but do not dare to express themselves. Martial law as it exists today is most essential for the security of Hawaii. Let us who believe in real democracy stand by our military leaders.

Should Service Men "Date" Oriental Girls?

DOROTHY JIM AND TAKIKO TAKIGUCHI

❖ An interesting outgrowth of the war in Hawaii is the problem of social relations between civilians and service men. The influx of these mainland soldiers has created a sociological problem that no doubt will play a large part in shaping our social and cultural life in after years.

Hawaii's population is so diverse in character and culture that, on the surface, the addition of another social group will not affect its basic nature too seriously. However, these men are not merely another cultural group immigrating to the islands for the purpose of becoming someday a permanent element in the population. They are not arriving as many of our ancestors did—to work in the plantations, and thus become integral members of the island community. Except in a few cases, a large majority of these men of our armed forces have only a transitory interest in Hawaii and its people. Their very existence in the services necessitates such an attitude.

Interracial dating is an important phase of the social relations between the civilian and the service man. To gather data on this very real and pressing social problem, questionnaires were sent out to individuals from various occupational groups, including University of Hawaii students and professors, social workers and school teachers, service men, war workers, housewives, and four members of the Varsity Victory Volunteers. Those questioned were fairly evenly divided between haoles and Japanese, males and females.

"What do you think of Orientals dating service men?" was the first question asked, the question being one of increasing concern and significance since the war. Dating between service men and Orientals occurred prior to the outbreak of war, but it was a relatively minor problem. The operation of strict family controls, the fear of "talk" and of

First published July 1944.

194

being categorized as "soldier meat," the loss of social status—these factors all served to discourage dating between Orientals and service men.

But today the attitude of many has taken a decided turn and reflects a definite trend toward a greater acceptance and approval of such dating. The survey revealed that about 72 percent of the individuals expressed approval, 22 percent disapproval, and 6 percent no specific opinion. Only one group, the haole female college students, showed disapproval of the relationship as a group opinion.

It is not surprising that many of the Oriental girls should find the newly acquired freedom of contact with the mainland haole boy both stimulating and profitable. Accustomed to playing a subordinate role in the family and society, the Oriental girl finds herself suddenly placed on a pedestal by the gallant American youth in search of feminine companionship. Consequently, she finds these men very attractive. On the other hand, the Oriental girl inflates his ego by modestly submitting to his every wish, without too much questioning. This has led many individuals to believe that the Oriental girls are too easily "snowed under" by the service men.

The different moral background of the two groups has made appropriate conduct difficult to define. What is embarrassing to the Orientals may be regarded only as commonplace and insignificant to the Occidentals.

❖ The service man is accustomed to free and informal association with adolescent girls, and the local Oriental girl frequently is quite inexperienced in dealing with the romantic overtures of the mainlanders. This situation naturally leads to exploitation of the local girls under certain circumstances.

Dating for fun, present in the pre-war friendships of Oriental girls, is now in part supplanted by dating as a morale-building and patriotic gesture, which has assumed a new significance for the Oriental girls since their friends and relatives joined the service.

Some approved of the relationship because of the sociological importance of the intermingling of races. They stated that it was only through social interaction that the two ethnic groups will come to know and understand each other, thus helping to overcome racial prejudices and misunderstandings.

Hawaii is faced with an acute sex disproportion and a dearth of haole women. A considerable number of those questioned recognized that the normal, natural craving for feminine companionship would under these circumstances lead to the service men dating Oriental girls. It is both human and natural, so why interfere?

"Is it better to date in groups or alone?" was another question asked. As expected, a greater number (64 percent) favored group dating over the single dates. Avoiding social disapproval and gossip and "keeping the best front forward" were common reasons stated, especially by those sensitive to local family traditions. On the other hand, 23 percent replied that either type of dating was all right while 13 percent favored single dates.

"What chance of happiness has a girl who marries a service man?" was a question that brought many interesting comments.

Service men stationed on the islands prior to the war have married local Oriental girls, and these legally recognized marriages have met with no adverse public opinion, although individuals and groups privately oppose such a procedure.

The advent of war has greatly complicated the picture because such marriages are not only interracial but are also war marriages. That many young couples are caught in the fever of wartime marriages with an "eat, drink, and be merry for tomorrow you die" philosophy was noted. The tensions and uncertainties of wartime living and restrictions are conducive to a let-down of moral standards.

That there is little chance for happiness in such marriages was the opinion of 78 percent among all the groups, the most important obstacle being the differences in race and culture of the man and girl.

Nearly one-fifth of those questioned, however, ventured the opinion that an Oriental girl who marries a service man has just as much chance of happiness as any other couple, the most important factors being the character and personality of the parties concerned and the devotion with which marriage is entered. Attendant factors, such as racial-cultural differences and social and family disapproval, were rated secondary in importance.

"Do you think service men have marriage in mind when dating these girls?" brought a high degree of similarity in the answers. One person out of sixty-seven believed that service men have marriage in mind when dating girls. A desire of service men for feminine companionship to combat loneliness and the ultra-masculine atmosphere of their routine lives was believed to be their motive in dating Oriental girls, with marriage a remote or impossible consideration.

That serious and numerous problems may result in an Oriental girl–service man marriage was recognized by most of the individuals questioned. Ninety percent agreed that the families of the girls might be seriously affected and that the extent of disruption in the family may range from mere disapproval to the disowning of the girl by the family.

"Will the service man take his Oriental wife back home with him to the mainland?" brought answers that were nearly three-fourths in the negative. The insurmountable social barriers that must be encountered by an Oriental wife on the mainland were emphasized again and again. Factors such as small-town talk, community pressure, and social ostracism must be faced realistically, the quizees agreed. That Hawaii's mores of racial equality are not operative on the mainland is another inescapable fact.

A realistic and tragic picture of what may happen to the Oriental wife and the haole husband on the mainland was drawn by a mainland haole defense worker. He said, in part, "He will be cut off from life that he knew in pre-war days. His economic life will also be seriously affected, and there will come a time when he will blame her for all of his woes, even though he may have begged her to marry him." A few of the service men who answered the questionnaires were more optimistic, but their opinions cannot be regarded as reflecting the attitudes of the mass of service men in Hawaii.

"What chance is there that these men will continue to regard their war brides as their wives?" In answer to this question, more than half of the individuals expressed the opinion that there is very small chance that these men will continue to regard their war brides as their wives. That the men, protected by the service, will leave and forget their Oriental wives was a common observation.

About one-fifth of those questioned, however, believed that the men will continue to be faithful to their war brides after the war. Nearly 25 percent replied that no definite answers can be given because factors such as the strength of acquaintance, the character of the individuals concerned, and the basis for marriage must be taken into consideration.

Note: *This article is a condensation of "Attitudes on Dating of Oriental Girls with Service Men," from* Social Process in Hawaii, *a booklet recently published by the Sociology Club of the University of Hawaii.*

War Workers as a Social Group

CORY WILSON

❖ Early in 1941 Honolulu opened its gates and started running another social group through its already strained digestive system. To this city, still struggling to assimilate such racial, cultural, and social groups as the Chinese, Japanese, Koreans, Filipinos, Portuguese, Puerto Ricans, Caucasians, Hawaiians, plantation workers, and the Army and Navy, another group known as mainland defense workers had to be added.

This group was designated "defense workers" before December 7, and in spite of efforts to change the appellation to "war workers," or many other variations, they are still known as defense workers and likely will be after the war is over.

As a social group, defense workers compare more nearly with the Army and Navy in their relation to the rest of the population than with any other of Honolulu's varied groups. To the other social groups, Honolulu is home, but to the Army, Navy, and defense workers it is merely a place of sojourn for a year or two, to serve out a contract or enlistment, and then to leave, adding this to past experience. This factor and the attitude necessarily arising from it have a great deal to do with the relation of these three groups to the remainder of the population.

At the outset it would be well to consider the types of men who make up the defense group from the mainland. First of all these men tend to be rather young. Most are in the age bracket of twenty to forty, because a man with several children isn't as likely to accept a job in the more remote corners of the world as a man with no dependents. However, there are a surprising number of men who have left rather large families on the mainland to work in Honolulu.

If asked why they came, the men give varied reasons, but all agree that one was a curiosity about the islands. For young and old alike, the romantic lure of the islands, caused by years of successful adver-

---

First published August 1944.

tising, is the underlying reason for their coming. In addition there are other reasons, such as: an opportunity to make more money than ever before, poor adjustment socially or in the job at home, desire to escape compulsory military service, a chance to make a little industrial training go a long way because of the excess of demand over supply in industrial manpower in Honolulu, and, not to be overlooked, the natural call of a congenial climate.

Most of the older men with families came because they thought it possible to maintain themselves here, and their families on the mainland, and still be financially ahead. A few came because of a desire to escape an unpleasant home. Most of these married men who came before the war had expected to be followed shortly by their families. Sudden outbreak of war kept these families from being reunited.

Since the war began, the men who have come, both young and old, have come mainly because of patriotic compulsion. Thousands have transferred from mainland Navy yards to the Pearl Harbor yard with something of a crusading spirit to help repair the damage done at Pearl Harbor.

There is no reason to believe that these men represent anything but the average mainland industrial and construction worker, except perhaps that they are the more adventurous of the lot. What they represent on the mainland has nothing to do with the way they are regarded in the islands. In Honolulu they are having to answer to a new set of standards.

Self-disillusionment is one of the first processes the newly arrived defense worker has to go through in Honolulu. He may be either the product of a small community where he is well known and considered a man about town, or else he came from a city like Brooklyn, Chicago, or New York and feels that gives him the natural right to make light of smaller cities.

The primary lesson this fellow has to learn is that he is no longer a glamour boy. In Hawaii, that is reserved for the air corps and beach boys. The second thing to learn is that no matter how clever or how handsome he was at home, there are a thousand defense workers, two thousand sailors, and three thousand soldiers just a little more clever and handsome. The next important lesson is that no one in Honolulu especially cares to hear about what a great personality he was at home, or how high the building, how deep the snow, how long the trains, or how late the night clubs. As a result of these lessons this fellow may lose his former attitude, take on a persecution complex, and go around with a chip on his shoulder, critical, discontented, and maladjusted.

If the average Honoluluan was asked to characterize a typical mainland defense worker, the characterization would probably go something like this: "When you meet him on the bus, if he's going to or from work, he is usually dressed in dirty work clothes and wearing a badge.... Otherwise he is probably wearing either a faded polo shirt or a purple spangled aloha shirt. Defense workers have almost taken these shirts away from the local men, but if they knew how poorly they wear them, they would hasten to give them back.

"He looks at other racial groups with a condescending air. If there is any liquor in town, he is drinking. If he can find any girl with correspondingly low morals, he is probably 'shacked up' (the crude term used throughout the islands for common law marriage). He is making a wheelbarrow load full of money...."

This characterization, while it is obviously unfair and can be applied to only a small percentage of the group, has nevertheless been earned for the entire group by its minority. This city, which has been host to the Pacific fleet for twenty or thirty years, and is beginning more and more to feel like a suburb of Schofield Barracks, has little time and sympathy to waste on men who have no other civic interest than that of having the bus service improved, territorial income taxes abolished, and the housing situation relieved.

The defense workers who arrived in Honolulu for the most part lived in the naval cantonment or in barracks provided at Red Hill, Wheeler Field, or wherever the project was located. But more and more there was a tendency to disperse over the city. First the downtown hotels were patronized. Then the districts up and down the main streets of King and Beretania were patronized. Gradually workers moved into outlying middle class districts of Kalihi, Kaimuki, and Kapahulu. The big movement, however, started for Waikiki.

Now that tourists could no longer patronize the hotels and apartment houses of famed Waikiki, the defense workers were about the only ones remaining with enough money to afford them. Most of those who have moved to Waikiki are the younger men who want to take advantage of the beach, the bars, and the bowling alley. These are the smart set of the defense workers. It is chiefly they who wear the multicolored aloha shirts with tails flapping in the breeze, and it is they who have the reputation for pitching endless numbers of wild parties.

One of the most socially significant things about the adjustment of the defense group in Hawaii is their relation with other races, mainly the Polynesians, Orientals, and Filipinos. As can be expected, these men from the mainland come with mainland attitudes toward these racial groups. To those from the west coast, Orientals were not an uncommon sight, but the sight that was uncommon was inter-racial association. Each newcomer underwent the same shock. They all came to the conclusion that Honolulu was indeed unique in that respect.

But time and a dearth of Caucasian women made their changes, and most of these men changed more quickly than they had ever thought possible. The first clue that a change was taking place was when the defense workers began to note distinction in beauty among the Hawaiian or Oriental girls and to discover that some of them are prettier than others. From there on, the change was rapid. Most of these young men were surprised at the freedom of some of these girls from inhibitions. Many of them seemed more like the girls back home than the usually badly spoiled Caucasian girls remaining on the island.

The defense worker received the jolt of his life when he found that the other races had turned the tables on him and were eyeing him appraisingly, were calculating his probable social status, and were often "looking down their noses" at him when he moved into their community. To some of the more poorly educated girls of other races, it might seem an aid to prestige to be seen with Caucasian boys, but to the elite and educated, this is considered an open announcement that they cannot attract boys of their own race.

Many of the educated girls of Oriental ancestry, however, do associate with Caucasian boys simply for the thrill of over-stepping social taboos. Most educated island girls of other races object to close association with defense workers, not because they harbor racial prejudice against Caucasians, but because the intentions of these men are generally held to be not too honorable.

A great part of the female population of Honolulu, however, is not highly educated and is not worried a great deal about social taboos. This is the element that figures prominently with defense workers in establishing a new pattern of life in Honolulu. As has been mentioned before, most of these men feel that they are here for only a short while and are on something like a vacation, a camping trip, or a spree. Their mothers and Aunt Marys not being here to give a disapproving frown, they "let themselves go" and give their morals a holiday. However, some of them express surprise at the ease with which some of the island women can accommodate themselves to such a "morality of convenience."

Some of these men will marry and become citizens of the community, continuing to live here after the war is over. Some will send to the mainland for their wives and sweethearts and spend the remainder of the lives in the islands, but the majority will return to the mainland at the first opportunity offered. This is only natural because their wives or prospective wives are there.

The men do a great deal of complaining about petty things. They complain if they have to work long hours for weeks on end without a day of rest, but rebel if forced to take off one day in eight. If work is piled on them, they complain; if it is slack, they cry out and want to return to the mainland where they are really needed. They complain about the pep posters on defense projects and about the liquor shortage.

But those who have lived and worked with these men know that these are only surface problems. They know that an underlying cause of the discontent is the absence of the wives and children or of feminine companionship. In short, they are lonely. There is no apparent way to relieve this discontent, but if there were, the petty grievances would doubtlessly disappear by the hundreds.

The favorite topic of conversation among defense workers is anything relative to the mainland. Instead of the traditional "hello" or "how are you," they'll say, "When are you going back to the mainland?" If two defense workers talk together for more than five minutes, the conversation will drift around to: "How would you like to be on the mainland for just one night?", "Well, tonight is Saturday night, so if we were home we'd just be getting ready to . . .", and so it goes on incessantly.

Many of these men will of necessity be in Hawaii, particularly Honolulu and Oahu, for the duration of the war. Their adjustment will improve as time goes on, but never to the point that they will cease to stand out as another of Hawaii's many social groups.

Note: *This article was condensed from* Social Process in Hawaii, *published by the Sociology Club of the University of Hawaii. A footnote states that the author makes no pretense of exhausting the subject material.*

Honolulu Civic Center: An Analysis

HART WOOD

❖ The present Civic Center is a bit of Honolulu and Hawaii that is picturesque, beautiful, and distinctive. It is characteristic of old Honolulu. It is something that none of us would want to see abolished. The buildings of which our Civic Center is composed are Federal, Territorial, and Municipal in function: i.e., Iolani Palace, Judiciary Building, City Hall, Post Office, Territorial Office, Board of Health, Library of Hawaii, Tax Office Building, and the Archives Building. Most, if not all of these, are urgently in need of space to accommodate their rapidly expanding functions.

This naturally leads to the question of the location of these buildings, i.e., the Civic Center, or more properly in this case—the Administrative Center. We have a good Civic Center, why not keep it? The answer to this question involves several factors. Let us consider briefly what they are.

First, as we have observed, it was built for a city much smaller than Honolulu now is; less than one-twentieth the present size. When Iolani Palace was built, the population of Honolulu was fourteen thousand and of Oahu twenty thousand.

Second, much of the property needed for expansion is occupied under private or semi-private ownership; i.e., Hawaiian Electric, Y.W.C.A., Army and Navy Y.M.C.A., and Kawaiahao Church.

Third, in addition, several of the public buildings that occupy key positions are so located as to block, or at least seriously interfere with, any orderly expansion. Obviously, they were placed without any idea that the Civic Center would ever have to serve a city of nearly one-third of a million population. Realizing the need for constructive thought on this matter, some six years ago, a competition for a plan for a new civic center was held under the joint sponsorship of the City Planning Commission and the Territorial Planning Board.

First published September 1944.

The first public building to be erected thereafter was the addition to the Judiciary Building, and this was done in total disregard of the Prize Winning Design, and, as a result, the Prize Winning Design was subsequently abandoned.

Following this, the Territorial Planning Board developed a "Suggested Plan," which was published in the Territorial Planning Board's Publication No. 10 (The Report on the Legislative-Executive Quarters). This plan was designated "Suggested" because it was felt that the problem required more time to study than the Board had been able to give it.

So the matter rested until this year when the Governor, under the Defense Act, created the Postwar Planning Division of the Department of Public Works, among whose duties is that of furnishing surveys, reports, estimates, etc., for the guidance of the Legislature in providing appropriations and priorities for public works projects, including housing accommodations for the legislative-executive quarters and other territorial agencies.

Starting with the Territorial Planning Board's "Suggested Plan," it soon became still further evident that more study should be given to this matter for the following reasons:

1. The site assigned to the Legislative-Executive Building in this scheme (Schumann Block) is too small. Furthermore, it is off-center and occupies a subordinate position in the scheme. Obviously it is an unsuitable site and was so recognized by the Territorial Planning Board when the scheme was under consideration, and this was the principal reason (though not the only reason) for withholding approval.

2. The Armory Block was also considered as a site for this building, but although it could be made to serve, it is likewise too small and is also off-center and kapakahi in the scheme. (So much for the mauka side.)

3. Extension toward the waterfront is blocked by existing buildings, particularly the Judiciary Building, which is considered invincible for historical and sentimental reasons.

4. In the Waikiki direction, the same holds true with regard to Kawaiahao Church, the Library of Hawaii, and the City Hall.

5. On the Ewa side are the Hawaiian Electric, Y.W.C.A., Army and Navy Y.M.C.A., and other expensive sites and buildings.

The only expansion feasible is by the acquisition of contiguous bits of property here and there available and the widening and straightening of a few of the streets involved, not thereby producing anything more than an unbalanced and incoherent result, with Iolani Palace, instead of the new Legislative-Executive Building, occupying the key position. And the principal streets are so fixed as to defy any attempt at construction adjustment such as would be required for an appropriate setting for our Territorial Government Buildings.

In short, the present Civic Center does not lend itself to the requirements for the future development of the Territorial Public Building Program, and it must be remembered that the Territorial Buildings will form a major portion of the buildings that will go to make up the Civic or Administrative Center.

What then to do? Shall we proceed to add to the present Civic Center regardless; shall we continue to try to find a solution in the present Civic Center area; or shall we look for a new site?

Shall the Territory have a separate Civic Center or Administrative Center, or shall the City and County and the Territory cooperate to develop something that will have not only the charm of old Hawaii but the dignity and beauty that rightfully belong to our chief outpost in the Pacific and the natural geographic and commercial center of the great Pacific area, leaving the present Civic Center as it is, with Iolani Palace converted into a historical repository as the center of the plan, which it now is. Plenty of land is available within convenient distance that is much less expensive and that lends itself much more readily than does the present Civic Center to the dignified, orderly, and uncongested treatment that properly belongs with an Administrative Center of a community of the size and importance of Honolulu and Hawaii.

It is desirable that as many citizens as possible be informed of the problem, toward the end that suggestions and criticisms be evoked and the best possible solution be thereby achieved.

The decision will be made by the Legislature. They should have behind them in this very important matter an intelligent and informed public opinion. In this way we may arrive at what is best for all concerned.

The Pearl Harbor Memorial

MRS. VERNA CLARK

❖ The Pearl Harbor Memorial Trust is an eleemosynary corporation chartered by the Governor of the Territory of Hawaii. The objects and purpose of the corporation are "to acquire land for, build and maintain a suitable memorial dedicated to the men who fought in the battles of the Pacific, to be known as the PEARL HARBOR MEMORIAL and to solicit the donation of funds and property to the corporation for the said objects and purposes." The charter is a perpetual one.

The financial affairs and the custody, management, maintenance, investment, expenditure, and disposition of moneys and property of the corporation is governed by a board of nine active trustees who are elected by the members of the corporation.

The members of the organization are of three general classes: honorary, regular, and associate. The honorary members are the President of the United States, the Secretary of War, the Secretary of the Navy, the Governor of Hawaii, the Commanding General of the United States Army Forces in the Central Pacific Area, the Commandant of the Fourteenth Naval District, the Commanding General of the Marine Forces of the Fourteenth Naval District, and the Commanding General of the United States Army Air Forces in Hawaii.

The regular members consist of two groups: First, Charter Members and those who shall be duly elected, each having one vote. Associate Members shall be nonresidents of the Territory of Hawaii who shall, by their position, prominence, or accomplishments, be regarded as desirable and worthy of membership in this organization and shall be elected as such.

About the first of May 1942, the Commandant of the Fourteenth Naval District requested the women of the various national patriotic organizations in Hawaii to decorate graves, and conduct services on

First published October 1944.

206

Memorial Day, for the Pacific War Dead. The women then formed the Women's National Patriotic Organization, and they were so successful that they were asked to repeat the work in 1943 and again in 1944. Preceding the Memorial Day service, in each instance, sums of money were offered to be used in any way for a gateway to a cemetery, for a plaque, for flowers, or for the Memorial Day service itself. Because of those unsolicited contributions and the suggestions accompanying them, it gradually became evident that there was a strong desire on the part of the public for a permanent memorial here in Hawaii.

Capt. T. C. Miller, former chaplain for the Fourteenth Naval District was among the first to recognize this, so he talked to the women's group at some length on the subject. He was certain that Pearl Harbor would become a post-war shrine—a place to which pilgrimages would be made—and that either by an Act of Congress or through some other power, a great memorial would be established here. He urged that The Women's National Patriotic Organization be that "other power," thus centering and maintaining in Hawaii, where it belonged, the nucleus of the structure that probably would become national in scope. He did this realizing that with our national affiliation we would be in a position to reach into every little hamlet and village throughout the length and breadth of the United States.

Before accepting the responsibility of this great project, we consulted many prominent business executives, all of whom reacted most favorably. We were urged to undertake the project and were assured full cooperation in making Pearl Harbor Memorial a reality and not merely a dream.

Vice Adm. Robert L. Ghormley wrote us: "It is my sincere wish that plans may be drawn for such a memorial to be erected at an early date after the completion of hostilities, and my staff is ready to render any assistance you may need in attaining that goal."

The idea was then presented to the Attorney-General of the Territory of Hawaii, who was most enthusiastic and offered to advise and help. He suggested they form a charitable corporation under Territorial laws with a perpetual charter and petition the Governor for such a charter. The plan was discussed with the Governor, who, after careful consideration, said that upon petition he would grant a charter as suggested by the Attorney-General.

The group next turned to Gen. Robert C. Richardson, Jr., who assured them of his warm approval and wrote them in part as follows:

"The conception of the Women's National Patriotic Groups to sponsor a movement to secure funds for a memorial to commemorate the heroism of our people at Pearl Harbor deserves the unqualified support of all patriotic citizens, which I already foresee.

In all our history, there is probably no day which will stand out for centuries to come as that of December 7, 1941, a day that unified our country as never before with a determination to be free men and women. I visualize the memorial which your group has in mind as a national shrine to which all Americans will look with reverence and visit with humility."

When Admiral Furlong expressed himself in similar terms, we felt that we had the support of the general public as well as the various services of the armed forces of the United States. So we set in motion the establishment in Hawaii of a National Memorial to the men who fought in the battles of the Pacific.

The Pearl Harbor Memorial Trust was given a charter by Gov. Ingram M. Stainback on December 9, 1943, and is starting out to acquaint each and every American with the Memorial plan, and to enlist his or her support. The group has set a goal of at least five million dollars and hopes that the privilege of being a part of this great Trust will be sought by all patriotic citizens and organizations.

We have received many ideas or suggestions and here are a few of these.

From Adm. Chester W. Nimitz:
"Would it not be possible, using the natural beauty of one of the small valleys or hillsides near Honolulu to plan, landscape and plant a memorial garden with paths winding among flowering trees and shrubs?

Such a memorial would not only be a fitting monument to the armed forces but also a lasting adornment of which the Pearl Harbor Memorial Trust, and the people of Honolulu might well be proud."

From Riley H. Allen, Editor, Honolulu Star-Bulletin:
"The nearest to a definite proposal I have at this time is that of a public auditorium—and I mean a really large auditorium, capable of seating, let's say, 10,000 people, which could be used for mammoth pageants, spectacles, conventions, etc. Manifestly, such an auditorium should be easily accessible to the majority of Honolulu's population,

which means it would have to be located in a central place, with excellent transportation and parking facilities. Such a building would be the visual demonstration of the territory's grateful remembrance of its heroes of World War II.

Such an auditorium would not, of course, preclude a memorial shaft or some other fitting symbol of our remembrance of the heroic dead of December 7, 1941, the symbol of the nation's gratitude.

Honolulu is one of the few cities of our size and character which lacks a public auditorium such as I have described. With this city a post-war center not only of travel, but of conventions, patriotic and otherwise, of local and international exhibitions, the need for a public auditorium will probably be even more apparent than now."

From Edgar C. Schenck, Director of Honolulu Academy of Arts:
"My own conception is that the Memorial should be an end in itself, rather than something which would be utilitarian, such as a theatre or some other useful public building. At the same time, our cities are filled with sterile sculptural monuments and I am afraid that any sculpture would fall into the category of "official art," and for that reason I am dubious about a sculptural form for the Memorial. It is also conceivable that many of the States might be interested in having a definite part in such a Memorial, rather than the contribution of a certain sum of money which would be lost in the total effect of a building or statue. It therefore seems to me, that a logical form for a Memorial would be a large, carefully designed park, with space for individual memorials in it, either sculptural or architectural, by States or other groups such as The Legion, the Veterans of Foreign Wars, the D.A.R., etc. A theatre could also be incorporated in such a scheme if it was desired, although the location of the park, which I feel naturally should be on the slopes of Red Hill overlooking Pearl Harbor, would militate against such a building, owing to inaccessibility from town.

It seems to me that the idea of a park as a setting for individual memorials put up by local groups is a large enough idea for nationwide acceptance."

From J. H. Brooks, Commandant, Navy No. 128:
"I have been interested in this subject for some time, and am very happy to express to you my ideas. I believe that this Memorial should be in the form of a beautiful and impressive chapel, or at least should

contain such a chapel if it is to be more pretentious than only the chapel building. In this chapel perhaps there could be a mausoleum where the unidentified dead would be buried. If it is not practical to remove the remains from present cemeteries, perhaps one crypt could be included similar to the tomb of the unknown soldier in Arlington Cemetery. I think this Memorial should be located in or near Pearl Harbor. If the chapel could be available for holding Divine Services for service personnel as well as for the special occasions on which it would be used, this would make it of greater value.

I do not think that secular or recreational features should be included in the Memorial; if it is to be erected in honor of the war dead it should be restricted to an edifice which would be a perpetual reminder of their sacrifice and their heroism. To those who visit the Memorial it should carry a visual message of reverent respect and worship."

From Brig. Gen. William J. Flood:
"Hawaii, as the 'Cross Roads of the Pacific,' is the logical place for such a memorial, it being not only the center of commerce and travel in peace time and the territory against which Japan struck, but also the base through which and from which passed much of the material and manpower used in launching the Pacific offensive."

From Capt. Thornton C. Miller, U.S. Naval Air Station, now at Corpus Christi, Texas:
"After talking the matter over with several older officers at this station, I should like to suggest that the memorial be an amphitheater for the world's finest artists and musicians, and surrounding it there be established and maintained tropical gardens. I feel that the amphitheater should be adequate to include a chapel and a memorial hall."

From Lt. Gen. Robert C. Richardson, Jr.:
"Although I have not had an opportunity to give any real study to a plan for the Pearl Harbor Memorial, as a suggestion it might be a civic center of surpassing architectural beauty so located upon the high ground above Honolulu that it will afford a panoramic view from Diamond Head to Pearl Harbor. The location, however, should be accessible and in a zone of good weather.

In the group a Campanile might form the central motif. In the tower would be the finest bells, whose music would be heard all over the city. As a suggestion, the group of buildings might comprise: a civic auditorium of ample proportion for concerts, plays, and assemblies; a memorial hall in which there would be a separate room for each state, territory, or possession of the United States. Here each state, territory, or possession would memorialize in bronze the name of every native man or woman of the armed forces and merchant marine who gave his life in the war, either killed on the field of battle or as a result of wounds, or drowned at sea in line of duty. These rooms would offer to each state, territory, or possession a repository for trophies, portraits, etc., of native sons. The group could also include a museum showing the culture of the peoples of the Pacific Ocean."

❖ The American Institute of Architects, Hawaii Chapter, has presented a beautiful idea for a memorial on Red Hill, and another group envisions one at the harbor entrance.

At present, no attempt is being made to select a definite design for a memorial. It is hoped, rather, that plans and suggestions will continue to pour in from all sides. And from these can be culled by the finest architects a memorial plan that will incorporate the most desirable aspects of the many ideas. It may be a great cultural center, an amphitheater for the world's finest artists and musicians, or here in these lovely tropical isles there may be established and maintained the most beautiful garden the world has ever known.

Inter-Racial Marriage in Hawaii

❖ Thirty-two percent of all marriages contracted during the past fiscal year in Hawaii were between persons of different racial backgrounds, the annual report of Edward Y. Z. Chong, acting registrar general of the bureau of vital statistics, says.

Of 4,947 marriages performed in the territory during the 1943–1944 fiscal period, 68 percent were of couples with the same racial background. This compares, for example, with 78 percent in 1939.

Almost one-half of the Caucasian men married women of other races, the report shows, and 9 percent of Caucasian women married men of other races.

Caucasian men married 371 part Hawaiians, 189 Japanese, 77 Chinese, 65 Hawaiians, 51 Puerto Ricans, 48 Filipinos, and 39 Koreans.

Caucasian girls, when marrying other than persons of their own race, married 39 part Hawaiians, 28 Filipinos, 10 Japanese, 10 Puerto Ricans, 9 Hawaiians, 3 Chinese, and 1 Korean.

Japanese girls, when marrying outside their race, married 189 Caucasians, 36 Filipinos, 31 part Hawaiians, 7 Koreans, and 5 Hawaiians.

Of the groups marrying outside their own race, the Hawaiians and part Hawaiians continue to lead the list.

Hawaiian, part Hawaiian, Korean, and Puerto Rican women are more likely to marry men of other races than of their own race, the figures show.

The report also points out that there were 1,497 Japanese brides and only 1,231 Japanese bridegrooms. Only 4 percent of Japanese boys married girls of other races.

Twenty-one percent of the Japanese girls married men from other

First published October 1944.

races. There were more brides than bridegrooms from every race listed in the report, except Caucasians and Filipinos.

Korean girls, according to the report, in addition to marrying 33 Korean men, married 39 Caucasians, 14 part Hawaiians, 6 Japanese, 4 Filipinos, and 2 Hawaiians.

About twice as many Korean women than men were married in the past fiscal year. (From the *Honolulu Star-Bulletin*)

Soldier and a Juke Box

WILLARD WILSON

❖ Honolulu is a strange, new place these days. The beaches are fairly clear now of their barbed wire, but streamers of dank seaweed still dangle from the twisted strands at low-water mark. The formerly gentle, spoiled way of life in Hawaii has given way to something quick, sinewy, and hard. Life has become direct and meaningful, though at times crude and rough. There is urgency in the air. It is the home stretch and we are tired of talk. The whole city is lean, nervous, and in a hurry.

We walk into stores to buy socks or neckties, and standing next to us is a boy who a couple of days before was squinting through a tube at a Mitsubishi or a Jap torpedo leap-frogging through the water toward him. We climb out of a shoeshine chair to make way for a sailor with a patch on one side of his face, and a wind-burnt squint around his eyes, who has been out in that no-man's land beyond Saipan on some job he doesn't talk about.

None of them say much, these boys. In spite of the noise they make, they're quieter than they were when they started the job. They're years older than they were last year. It's not that they are solemn or humorless; it's rather that their humor has been turned inward and has at the same time become impersonal.

This boy was a rather small soldier, with a sergeant's stripes on his sleeve and some wings embroidered near the turn of his shoulder. He sat quietly beside me eating a hamburger steak, faintly visible through a mass of onions, and drinking sweet milk from a tall glass. It was noon, and every seat in the dingy lunchroom was taken. There was noise—a violent clatter of dishes, shouting of Chinese waitresses, rasping of many voices in competition and, as a final insult, the burbling burp and glide of an infantile crooner emerging to life again from a juke box and telling us, "I'm Hot Stuff—Honey take a light from me!"

First published December 1944.

The place was hot, sticky, full of smells generated from many bodies in a close place, steaming food, stale cigarette smoke. Every time I lifted the iced tea glass to my lips, I had to swab its sweating sides with a soggy paper napkin.

The sergeant looked at me over the top of his glass of milk. "Some joint!" he said, and grinned. I nodded, and had another go at the dispirited salad before me. He pushed his plate away from him and slid a cigarette out of a pack with one finger of the hand that held it.

"Where'd you learn that?" I asked. "Tractor. Used to push a Cat around in west Texas, and I never had more than one hand loose at a time."

The music box had stopped. He signaled to one of the girls and gave her a dime. "I don't care what the record is, just so it's loud." "Good God!" I said. "Isn't there enough noise without it?" He turned and looked at me, and I was embarrassed by the slow, quiet, inward-knowledge in his eyes. "Look, Mac," he said, "war is a lonely thing. A damned lonely thing."

"Okay," I said wearily. "Okay, my friend. So war is a lonely thing. Only from where I sit it's pretty damned crowded." He gave me a curious look out of his deep, far-away eyes. The noise of the cafe beat around us and a couple of sailors, drunk more with the relief of shore leave than with the beer they had been drinking, bumped against us and proceeded on their way.

"I guess it does depend on where you sit, at that," he said. He was leaning back and I realized he was no longer really thinking of me. For him I was just part of the setting. He dragged deeply at his cigarette and let smoke spin out in thin strings from his nostrils. "Boy," he said contentedly, "this sure is nice! You don't really appreciate it until you haven't had it for a while. Jeez, you don't know how nice it is to have a lot of folks around."

At first it was hard for me to grasp what he meant. I had spent part of the morning listening to a barrage of complaints concerning the evils of over-crowding in Honolulu. One couldn't get a decent meal, people cleaned out the stores like a swarm of locusts, those who needed the fresh vegetables never could get them when they got to the markets late in the afternoon, there wasn't enough highball juice and beer to go around even for the weekly ration. In other words, there were just too damn many people of all descriptions on this damn rock, and something ought to be done.

"Me, I'm just a gunner on one of the big cookies. And Man, if you don't think the tail of a B-24 is one lonely place to be on a bright sunny afternoon over Truk or someplace. Baby!"

I mumbled something about there probably being little time for loneliness with Zeroes and ack-ack all around. "Yes, that's what you would think. But actually that's when you feel it the worst. When things are going off all around you and there you sit like a model in a store window with the Christmas rush on outside."

"Scared?"

"Well, not really, while it's going on. I read a story about a belly gunner who hollered and wriggled around when he was in a scrap, but I just largely seem to want to take a nice long spell in the gentlemen's room. Far as I can figure out, that's the way it hits me, just makes me want to go to the toilet—but that's just the way it gets me." He said it apologetically, and then added slowly, "And it's so damn quiet inside you that you can hear your stomach turning over."

He kept coming back to that feeling of loneliness. "What about the other planes? You don't often go on those strikes alone."

"It's not so bad if you're in the tail of the lead plane and can see the others strung out behind. But when you sit there with nothing but a couple of hundred miles of air in sight, and the empty ocean below, waiting for a Zero to come around the corner, then is when you want someone to hold your hand. Boy, that's when you really want company!" There was a lessening of noise from the mechanical music box. He fumbled in his pocket for coins, and gave me a deep, happy grin as he rose to go over and feed them into the plastic sunburst of a juke box in the corner. "Jeez," he said, "people are sure swell to have around."

The Year in Retrospect

LORNA ARLEN

❖ Except for its important role as the base from which the Pacific war's mighty offensive was launched, there were few outstanding events in Hawaii during the past year. It was mostly work and little play for residents of the Islands, both civilian and military. But in spite of the monotonous pattern of work and rest, there has been the stimulus of being at least a small part in the events that have taken our armed forces from the perimeter of the enemy's empire to his very doorstep.

As the year began, there was grim fighting in New Britain, with Bougainville and Cape Gloucester the names that flared in headlines. U.S. heavy bombers were blasting northern France and talk of invasion was in the air. Adm. William F. Halsey was in Washington making plans that have turned out to be so gloriously devastating to the enemy. Columnist Raymond Clapper visited Honolulu on the ill-fated trip that resulted in his death a month later. Seven thousand Texans joined their most distinguished fellow-citizen, Admiral Nimitz, in a "Texas Round-Up" at Moana park. The war department announced plans to draft Americans of Japanese ancestry because of the fine record set by volunteers; the flying boat *Mars* made its first visit to Hawaii; and relief for night drivers came with permission to remove paint from below the protective shields of headlights. This was followed by removing the ban on night parking until 10 P.M.

During the month of February, as the conquest of the Marshalls took place after heavy fighting on Kwajalein, Roi, and Namur, and while the desperate fight for Cassino held the spotlight in Italy, Hawaii was concerned about the plight of three thousand "strandees" on the West Coast waiting for transportation to the Islands, the alleged over-supply of doctors in Honolulu, and the announcement that all residents must be revaccinated with "booster shots" for

---

First published December 1944.

typhoid and paratyphoid before June 15. Students of McKinley and Kaimuki high schools made war bond purchases of $333,600 to purchase a Liberator bomber.

In March, hearings were begun on the controversial subject of commercial rent control, a record-breaking city and county budget for Honolulu was announced, and Rt. Rev. Harry S. Kennedy arrived to succeed Rev. S. Harrington Littell as Episcopalian bishop of Honolulu. Ernest K. Kai resigned as secretary of Hawaii, later succeeded by Gerald Corbett. Inter-Island Steam Navigation Co. bought out the shares of all the Inter-Island stock formerly held by Matson Navigation Co., the transaction involving more than a million dollars. The first in a series of monthly selective service drafts took place, the first company of Wacs arrived, and the legal controversy over martial law, involving the Lloyd C. Duncan *habeas corpus* case, began.

The political season began in April with the convening of Democratic and Republican conventions, both of which lacked their pre-war colorful atmosphere. The Hawaiian Tuna Packers, Ltd., announced plans for converting their plant for assembling accessories for naval aircraft.

Lei Day brought a refreshing reminder of the "good old days," for elaborate plans were carried out to recapture as much as possible the enchantment of the past. The almost prohibitive cost of leis, however, prevented many persons from wearing the fragrant garlands. All photofinishers, amateur or professional, were required to register with the central identification bureau as a security measure. The Work to Win campaign celebrated its first anniversary with a ceremony at the Honolulu stadium preceding a baseball game.

News of the invasion of Europe in June was received in Hawaii with intense interest but practically no public demonstrations. Nearer the hearts of the Islanders was the Marianas campaign, which focused attention on Saipan, Tinian, and Guam. In Honolulu there were three spectacular accidents in close succession, two being explosions of military supplies that killed and injured many, and the third a crash of two planes on Dillingham boulevard in Kalihi, destroying several homes and killing twelve. Chauncey B. Wightman succeeded Maj. Gen. Briant H. Wells, USA, ret., as secretary of the Hawaiian Sugar Planters' Association, and Kamehameha Day was celebrated not as a holiday but with some attempt to bring back the traditions of other years.

In July, Hawaii had one of its rare holidays, with fireworks banned,

On the rare occasions that leave was granted, fun-hungry men invaded the honky-tonk sections of Honolulu.

University students made up the Varsity Victory Volunteers. Eloise McInerny places a lei on each volunteer during a ceremony at UH's Hawaii Hall.

Volunteer AJAs of the 442d Infantry Battalion, about to make history, assemble for aloha ceremonies at Iolani Palace.

On March 4, 1942, Japanese bombs rocked Honolulu. Although Pearl Harbor was the intended target, the bombs landed seven miles off target on the lower slopes of Mount Tantalus, just one thousand yards from Roosevelt High School.

Tears of joy welled from Iuemon Kiyama as he greeted his son, Howard, when the 442d Regimental Combat Team returned home.

however. A six-hour alert in military areas on a Sunday morning created some excitement until it was learned that the "elements" had proven to be friendly. During this month General Richardson dropped the title of military governor, and the office of internal security replaced the former office of the military governor.

Unification of military and civilian regulations in a single manpower program was achieved in August by the War Manpower Commission and General Richardson, and island workers twenty-two years or over were deferred from military service for the remainder of the year because of the acute manpower shortage. Residential areas were closed to prostitutes, and a controversy began that ended a month later in the closing of Honolulu's brothels and the temporary cessation of an alleged $15 million racket.

September brought news of the invasion of Palau in the Carolines, and Hawaii's continued importance in the Pacific war was emphasized by the announcement that six thousand more workers would be brought to Hickam Field alone. The army announced that work would soon begin on a new $16 million hospital located on land formerly occupied by the Samuel M. Damon estate in Moanalua. The Naval Court of Inquiry was in session at Pearl Harbor investigating events of The Seventh, local recruiting of Wacs began, and it was announced that Waves, Spars, and Women Marines would soon be sent for duty in Hawaii.

Meanwhile, throughout the year, Hawaii's number one problem continued to be lack of housing. Figures show that at least five thousand additional homes are desperately needed in Honolulu and that twenty-five thousand persons are living in sub-standard dwellings, with resulting impairment of health and morals. In a series of articles in *The Honolulu Advertiser,* the living conditions of many sections in Honolulu were compared with the pest holes of the Orient.

The question of whether government-subsidized housing should be encouraged, and to what extent, has been thrashed back and forth. Plans to ask for $5 million from the Federal Housing Administration were endorsed by Admiral Nimitz and General Richardson, yet little has been done to relieve the situation. Gov. Ingram M. Stainback declined to "put the Territory into the housing business" by importing 100 pre-fabricated houses that had been advocated.

Rental of private rooms in homes has been complicated by legal restrictions, particularly the home exemption tax. The board of supervisors refused to allow public parks for use as emergency housing sites. A mass meeting was requested to demand relief for the "homeless" workers who are sleeping in parked cars, garages, and on the floors of damp cellars. The housing problem in Honolulu was described by a territorial official as the "most difficult and seemingly insoluble one I have ever tried to solve."

Rents that began to skyrocket even before the war have finally been prevented from further inflation by an OPA freeze, but the prices of homes continue to soar. Newspapers recently carried a story to the effect that a home in the Diamond Head area was bought for one hundred thousand dollars a few months ago and then sold for twenty-five thousand dollars more. Prices of vacant lots are up one-third to one-half over pre-war prices, but homes are selling for two and three and even four times what they would have brought several years ago.

The outstanding event of October was the lifting of martial law by proclamation of the President, ending a record-breaking period of three years under military jurisdiction.

1945

In January, the City and County of Honolulu refused to lease Ala Moana Park to the Army, citing a law that prohibited a transfer for such a purpose.

In late February, U.S. forces completed the capture of Manila. In March, Iwo Jima was taken by U.S. Marines, and, in April, the island of Okinawa was invaded.

On April 12, while vacationing at Warm Springs, Georgia, President Roosevelt died. Harry S Truman was sworn in as president.

On May 7 the German army surrendered to the Allies at Rheims, France, and President Truman declared V-E Day. The news reached Hawai'i at 3:30 in the morning.

On June 16, the Punahou buildings and campus were returned to the school by the Army Corps of Engineers. A week later, civilians were told to turn in gas masks.

On June 21, Japan surrendered Okinawa. On July 8, the Philippines were recaptured.

Curfew and blackout was lifted in Hawai'i in July. The following month, gas rationing and censorship ended.

On August 6, the U.S. Air Force dropped an atomic bomb on Hiroshima, Japan. The destruction was massive and horrifying. Three days later a second atomic bomb was dropped on Nagasaki, with devastating results. On August 14, war ended in the Far East. The news reached Hawai'i at 1:20 P.M. Two days later, all remaining orders administered by the office of internal security were terminated. Civil government finally had been restored. The Japanese formally surrendered aboard the USS *Missouri* in Tokyo Bay on September 2. A three-day holiday was declared.

Weary of war, the people of Hawai'i breathed a sigh of relief that the long conflict was over. But a return to the normal life of the old days was not to be. Hawai'i had changed greatly, and there was no going back to a past that was fondly remembered by only some of the people. On the first of September about twenty-one thousand workers on thirty-three Hawai'i plantations went on strike.

Territorial Plans
for Administrative Center

A post-war planning division under the Department of Public Works of the Territory was created by Hawaii Defense Act, Rule No. 87. Members of this division, after much research and study, recently published a prospectus on various plans for expansion of the Territory's administrative center, which will demand action by the forthcoming legislative session. The following article is a condensation of this prospectus, which was prepared for the consideration of Gov. Ingram M. Stainback, members of the Territorial legislature, the Post-war Planning Advisory Board, and all organizations and individuals of the Territory.

Plan 1—Bishop Street Extension

The area between Beretania St. and School St. from Nuuanu Ave. to Emma St. presents some exceedingly interesting possibilities for development of an Administrative Center. This plan envisages the extension of Bishop St. through to the proposed new Vineyard St. arterial, with the Capitol Building terminating this gently rising vista in the large area between Vineyard St. and School St. Bishop St. is without question the one street in downtown Honolulu of sufficient width for an adequate approach to an Administrative Center and is almost entirely unspoiled by unsightly, cheap, and otherwise inappropriate buildings.

With the probable improvement and enlargement of the sea-borne passenger terminal to include the entire waterfront at the foot of Bishop St., it is not hard to visualize the really impressive and startlingly beautiful vista that would be opened up to the incoming visitor to Hawaii.

First published January 1945.

First impressions are lasting impressions, so we are told, and it is certain that in this case first impressions could not be anything but decidedly favorable. With the fifty feet or so of added elevation afforded by placing the Capitol Building in the location shown, with the broad expanse of a really beautiful downtown boulevard opening out before the eyes, flanked by public buildings of dignified architecture in a setting as truly Hawaiian as it is possible to achieve, the Administrative Center in this location would be distinctively our own, unique in its conception and execution in the United States and a source of great pride to the Territory for all time to come.

The area available in this location is adequate for both present and all future needs of the Territory, and the City, County, and Federal governments. It is within a reasonable distance of the business district and the present Civic Center so that there would be no disruption of public activities during the process of transferal from one area to the other.

As this transferal is accomplished, not this year nor next, but possibly within the next twenty-five to fifty years, any buildings that are not to be preserved for historic reasons in the present Civic Center thus vacated, and the property on which they stand, could be converted to other uses; quite probably they could be sold for private business, thus enabling the present business district to expand in the direction in which it has already shown a tendency to move, and returning to the Territory much of the cost of constructing the new Administrative Center.

It removes from close proximity to the center of the city an area that is already well on the way to becoming blighted and replaces it with a highly developed, beautiful termination to the best appearing street in the city. It undoubtedly will stimulate improvement of adjacent areas that are beginning to show signs of deterioration and should encourage substantial development of these areas. The amount of land required for the initial work necessary to make this plan a reality is relatively large, and the expenditure of money is considerably larger than would be required for some other areas under consideration. But if an enlightened public opinion finally determines that this is the area in which the future Administrative Center of the Territory is to be built, it is not believed that the price is too high to pay to provide a development that will be to the lasting credit to the citizenry of Hawaii.

Plan 2—The Harbor Entrance Plan

At the entrance to the Honolulu Harbor and directly outboard of Ft. Armstrong is a very large expanse of scarcely submerged tide land that extends in a general Waikiki direction all the way to Kewalo Basin. This entire area could be filled and could provide many acres of additional waterfront for the use and enjoyment of all Honolulu.

By opening up the entire area between Keawe and Coral streets, through the present Animal Quarantine Station and up to Queen St., a most interesting framework could be built on which could be super-imposed the elements of an Administrative Center adequate in all respects to meet all present and future needs. With the Capitol at the upper end, and the lower end possibly the site of a suitable memorial to commemorate those who died in this war, the picture presented to incoming visitors to Hawaii would be one never to be forgotten.

In reality, an extension to the present Civic Center would be conveniently adjacent during the transition period. By developing this area for the Administrative Center, many unsightly buildings would be removed and the entire vicinity would undoubtedly profit thereby. It is true that the land in this area would be slightly more expensive than one or two of the other proposals, but the difference in square-foot cost would be so slight as to be negligible.

Here also, as in the Chapter Plan, the objection may be raised that this development encroaches upon an area already zoned and to a certain extent developed for industrial uses. But zoned areas have been re-zoned to meet changing conditions, and this is not an insurmountable obstacle. Also, the author's conception of the uses to which the new land along the waterfront might be put would conflict with certain other very utilitarian uses proposed for this area, namely the incinerator and sewage disposal plant, as well as possibly one or more new fish canneries. It would appear that if at all possible such activities should not be incorporated in Honolulu's front yard to the permanent detriment of our very limited waterfront area.

The majority of the area is rather low and relatively flat, ideally suited to the kind of treatment suggested in this plan, but rendered somewhat more expensive in that suitable stable footings for large buildings would have to be constructed by underwater work. If, however, this plan should be the final decision of those charged with selecting the site for the Administrative Center, these difficulties could be overcome and the finished product would indeed be "a thing of beauty and a joy forever."

Plan 3—Present Civic Center Expansion

In presenting this plan, it seems apparent that no better description can be given than that prepared by the City Planning Commission in its report issued the latter part of September, entitled *Report On Proposed Honolulu Civic Center*, and released for general distribution.

"The City Planning Commission is of the opinion that the Territory and the City and County should cooperate to develop something that will have not only the charm of old Hawaii but the dignity and beauty which rightfully belong to this chief outpost in the Pacific. It is believed this can best be accomplished by leaving the present Civic Center as it is with Iolani Palace being converted into an historical repository as the center. . . . This plan would preserve the historical centers of Honolulu and Hawaii and provide for the future expansion in an informal and picturesque design which will accentuate the tropical surroundings of a greater Honolulu."

"The site as proposed embraces the present Civic Center which is a part of Honolulu and Hawaii that is picturesque, beautiful, and expressive of much that has gone before. This center should be preserved and added to, rather than abandoned."

"The site as proposed is centrally located, convenient to the main commercial and business districts. . . ."

"The present street system within the proposed Honolulu Civic Center is well integrated to efficiently move motor vehicle traffic and mass transportation if sufficient areas for off-street parking are provided within the various building sites. . . . It is proposed to widen certain streets within the area planned for Honolulu's Civic Center."

"The proposed Honolulu Civic Center does not set up a barrier for the best use or expansion of the land adjacent to it; conversely it separates the Central Business District from the encroachment of industrial development and other types of business . . . and will allow for business to expand in the Waikiki direction."

Equally true is that the present delightful informality of building location and highway access would be continued and perpetuated by the expansion of this area, but also it would necessitate an extension of the present haphazard location and relationship of administrative functions, leaving much to be desired in the matter of efficiency. Iolani Palace would still be the dominating building of the entire group, whereas Hawaii has reached the place in its progress where it is not only fitting but desirable that the new Capitol Building should be the keystone around which to build the arch of a strong, stable, and efficient government.

By all means let us preserve the Palace as a fitting historical monument. Let us convert it into a historical museum and protect it and preserve it as such a monument, unique in the history of the United States. But let us not, in our sentimental attachment for by-gone days, subject the Palace to the inevitable wear and tear of continued use as a legislative assembly, as well as a place to conduct all the business of the Territory, as it now exists, and with possible extension due to an increase in our Territory in the western Pacific. Rather let us begin now to plan and build in a logical and efficient manner so that our Administrative Center will be able to function and conduct our official business without unnecessary confusion and delay.

Plan 4—The Chapter Plan

Several years ago The Hawaii Chapter of the American Institute of Architects, looking ahead and seeing the coming growth of Honolulu and the Territory and the consequent need for more room for the Administrative Center, held a competition within its own membership, and from this competition was evolved a plan for a future Administrative Center that has become known as "The Chapter Plan."

With, at that time, great daring and imagination, the Chapter envisaged the removal of the Administrative Center from the present location of the Civic Center and went rather far afield searching for an area that presented the necessary opportunities for expansion and orderly rearrangement of the governmental functions. The plan, as finally accomplished, suggested the possibility of connecting the present Civic Center area with the Ala Moana and Ala Moana Park by a long, beautifully landscaped mall, terminated at one end near Punchbowl St. by the new Capitol Building and at the other, or Waikiki end, by the oft-discussed Municipal Auditorium. This was before the war was upon us, but it has since been suggested many times that this could be fittingly called a Victory Mall.

The entire area suggested for acquisition is in a relatively sparsely developed area, and disruption of present business activities would be held to a minimum by virtue of this fact. In this plan, as in the Bishop St. Plan, already blighted areas immediately adjacent to the present administrative and business center of the city would be removed and replaced with a highly developed, dignified, and beautiful Administrative Center. Adjoining areas would undoubtedly benefit thereby, and it could be expected that substantial development of these areas would speedily come to pass.

The area between Kapiolani Blvd. and Ala Moana Blvd. has been zoned for industrial uses. This proposed plan would cut through this area along the diagonal of Queen St. and Halekauwila St., thereby cutting the industrial area into two parts. These areas have been rezoned many times in many places to meet changing needs and requirements of the community. The area necessary to be acquired to bring this plan into actuality is quite large, and the amount of money involved for initial expenditure is also large. But Honolulu and Hawaii are not impoverished. If, after due discussion and deliberation, the consensus is that this Chapter Plan presents the closest approach to a fulfillment of Hawaii's needs, the amount of money involved will shrink to its proper perspective, and the Territory can be justly proud in proclaiming to the world that we have started down the road of orderly, planned development.

Plan 5—The Thomas Square Plan

In casting about for suitable locations in which might be developed a new Administrative Center, it was at once apparent that the area both mauka and makai of Thomas Square and the Academy of Arts presented one possibility that fulfilled all the requirements admirably. Here there is ample land available without disruption of any existing business or industrial activities. It is reasonably accessible from the present business district and Civic Center, although farther removed than other locations that have been proposed. It is true that in this location quite a number of individual property owners would be eventually dispossessed, but generally speaking all dwellings in this area are relatively old and approaching obsolescence. The property is not expensive, as would be the case in other locations mentioned, and can be acquired with a minimum of legal difficulties.

Aesthetically, the setting is ideal. This plan proposes a new Capitol Building just below Prospect St. on the more gentle slope of Punchbowl. Terminating, as it does, a long vista extending from Kapiolani Blvd., and ultimately it is to be hoped all the way from Ala Moana Park and the ocean, the Capitol Building would be the dominating feature of this entire section of Honolulu. At an elevation of approximately two hundred feet above sea level, it would be visible for many miles at sea and would be among the first recognizable landmarks to greet the eye of incoming passengers, both by sea and air. The mall, extending from King St. to the Capitol, flanked on either side by architecturally fitting, beautifully landscaped public buildings, rising terrace on terrace one above the other, would afford a setting for our new Administrative Center that would be difficult to duplicate in any city of the United States. With the Academy of Arts forming the nucleus of a future cultural group as a minor focal point at the center of the picture, and a suitable Municipal Auditorium dominating the extension of the mall between King St. and Kapiolani Blvd., the grouping of the buildings, open spaces, and park areas would form a complete, harmonious, and entirely unified Administrative Center.

Here there is ample room to meet all present and future requirements of an Administrative Center that would combine Territorial, Federal, and City and County activities. True, during the transition period between the start of the new and the final vacation of the old, duplicate functions would of necessity be carried on for a while. But, if after careful study and deliberation by all bodies and individuals concerned, it should develop that this is the site that would best meet the needs of the present and future Honolulu and Territory of Hawaii, this inconvenience would be insignificant and would soon disappear in the sense of pride and gratification inherent in a good job well done.

Planning Honolulu: A Study

PHILIP FISK, ALLEN JOHNSON, JAMES MORRISON, VLADIMIR OSSIPOFF, AND ALFRED PREIS

A. I. A. ARCHITECTS

❖ Ethnographically and climatically, Honolulu has affinities with all countries and nations bordering the Pacific Ocean; geographically, it is their center. Air transportation brings these countries closer to Honolulu than to each other, with traveling time reduced to hours. These conditions and Honolulu's own charm and beauty predestine this city as a recreational as well as a cultural-educational meeting place for the entire Pacific Area.

The strategic position of Honolulu in war-time remains strategic in times of peace. The role Honolulu is playing in winning this war can be carried on to perpetuate a lasting peace. Honolulu can serve not only as the communication and administration center but as the site of a "Pacific" Memorial for expositions and festivals and as a forum for the development and exchange of ideas pertaining to peaceful, human relations and for making these the subject of scientific inquiry.

1. Cross island arterial from Keehi lagoon airport in direct line with Middle Street and the Kalihi Tunnel.

2. Kapalama Basin development continued with industrialization of surrounding areas, including Sand Island and lands makai of Dillingham Boulevard and Kamehameha Highway. The land mauka of the boulevard reserved for housing with Moanalua Gardens and Salt Lake as recreational areas.

3. Farrington High School, Bishop Museum, and Kamehameha Field Grounds retained, to form the community center of the Kalihi area, without being dissected by the Vineyard Street Extension.

First published January 1945.

4. Residential areas, redesigned so as to provide safe play areas, integrated with existing school grounds, forming neighborhood centers for educational, cultural, social, and recreational activities.

5. Mauka arterial traffic, carried as "one-way traffic," from the Kapalama Drainage Canal to the Waialae Golf Course via Vineyard, Captain Cook, Lunalilo, Bingham, King, Harding; and back via Waialae, Moiliili, Wilder, Prospect, Iolani into School, eliminating expensive condemnation and street widening required by "two-way" arterials. One-way streets are more easily crossed and require minimum traffic control.

6. Makai arterial passenger traffic from Pearl Harbor by-passes downtown via a new road of a traffic capacity equal to Dillingham Boulevard around the O.R.&L. terminal, completely separated from North King, Beretania, and Hotel feeder traffic; splits into one-way traffic each on Queen and Halekauwila Streets and unites again in a new street leading directly into Kapiolani Boulevard. At Kalakaua Avenue, a grade separation permits traffic to continue uninterruptedly on Kapiolani or Ala Wai Boulevards or Kalakaua Avenue, offering a solution for expected increased tourist traffic to Waikiki and to the new Yacht Basin and Ala Moana Beach development.

Continuous and distinct horizontal separation of heavy cargo and service traffic from passenger traffic maintained from Pearl Harbor to the Ala Wai.

7. Development of Nuuanu Stream as a parkway, with one-way traffic on each side, forming a mauka-makai arterial, ewa of the downtown area and leading into Nuuanu Avenue at Bates Street.

8. Commercial redevelopment, general rehabilitation of the downtown area, and prevention of inorganic decentralization of business through:

(a) Reduction of traffic pressure by arterial routing.

(b) The encouragement of traffic flow by a complete one-way system, thus relieving congestion.

(c) Elimination of vehicle traffic on King Street between Richards and Nuuanu, creating ideal conditions for a pedestrian shopping area with parking and loading facilities available from adjacent streets.

(d) Creation of adequate off-street parking facilities.

(e) The revision of the tax system to discourage the perpetuation of blighted structures.

(f) Rezoning of business districts along through-traffic streets in order to create organic neighborhood shopping centers, planned for concentric growth.

(g) Functional and visual integration with the Civic Center.

9. Civic Center—See detailed drawing.

10. The diversion of ewa-bound traffic on Kapiolani arterial into one-way Queen and Halekauwila Streets prevents the discharge of high density traffic into low capacity streets of downtown.

11. Punchbowl, with a green, a lake, an amphitheater, an auditorium, and buildings representing other nations, is proposed as the seat for the memorial as described in the introduction.

12. Development of a hotel and apartment area near downtown business-center, administrative center, cultural center, and new beach development.

13. Beach development through the intregation of Waikiki with the reclaimed Moana Peninsula and through the incorporation of Fort de Russy as a service men's recreational area. The Moana Peninsula with its new beach, club, and picnic grounds, the existing Moana Park, and the widened Kewalo Channel form a haven for Pacific-wide yachting.

14. Creation of a through street linking Manoa valley with Kahala district via University Avenue, Date Street, Alohea Avenue, and Diamond Head Road.

15. Rehabilitation of the Kaimuki Area through the conversion of alternate mauka-makai streets into neighborhood play areas, and elimination of through traffic by conversion of Waikiki-ewa streets into cul-de-sacs.

Punahou Goes Home

HUBERT V. CORYELL

❖ The boys and girls of Punahou are going back to their campus again. It was a big moment when, on Feb. 6, 1945, President Fox made the announcement at a special assembly called in the middle of the morning; and the thousand students present filled the air with their yells of delight. The earnest wish of every pupil, teacher, parent, and alumnus was to be granted at last. Honolulu's hundred-year-old school was going back to its own home, the home that its devout founders and loyal workers through each generation had built for it with toil and sweat and sacrifice.

Punahou has missed its campus. Day after day scores of Punahou people have peered through the ugly rolls of barbed wire that now surround the campus and swallowed lumps in their throats as they have watched strange men and women go and come.

Loyal Punahou-ites may have grouched over the school's loss, but these same grouchers know in their inner hearts that they wouldn't be holding up their heads now if they had not given up their home with reasonable cheerfulness when Uncle Sam's Engineers walked in on the morning of Dec. 8, 1941, at two o'clock, and took over. It was a jolt; but, when the people of Punahou knew the reason, they took it on the chin with the best smile that they could summon. When they learned what ideal working headquarters their campus had formed for an organization of fifty thousand men, spread out over the whole Pacific area, building fortifications, gun emplacements, pill boxes, storage tunnels, barracks, and other vital installations for the millions of our fighting men on the bloody road to Tokyo, they were proud. They are proud now to have helped—just by getting out of the way; but they are surely happy to be going back once more to their own.

Perhaps they will even cherish this campus of theirs more keenly because for a while they had to do without it. Some of those old buildings,

First published March 1945.

with their not too perfect classroom arrangements, will seem pretty fine to pupils and teachers who worked together in the early days of 1942 in makeshift quarters generously provided by parents, alumni, churches, and big-hearted people of Honolulu. Boys and girls who studied arithmetic in Mrs. John Doe's garage, with a single portable blackboard for demonstration purposes, will appreciate their big, airy geometry classroom next year, with its walls covered with smooth slate, even if they still sit in chairs and at desks that leave something to be desired in the way of comfort. And those who now dodge buses and passenger cars every time they swarm over to the University cafeteria for lunch, or pour out of chapel in a stream that inevitably spills over into the public street, will rejoice in having full and unlimited right of way when back on their own campus.

❖ As a matter of fact, it is a long time since Punahou students had arithmetic in a garage or social studies on a lanai or French in a Sunday school classroom; for those scattered makeshift quarters of the first off-campus months were left for more adequate ones as soon as possible. The school was drawn together once more in larger units. For grades nine to twelve, the school was fortunate to be able to rent the modern and well-equipped Teachers College building on the grounds of the University of Hawaii. Here, though the classrooms were relatively small, the Academy was able to organize the basic essentials of its curriculum once more and to restore much of the old feeling of unity and espirit de corps. The eighth and ninth grades were able to find good working quarters until June in Bishop Hall back on the old campus, and later joined the rest of the academy at Teachers College. Here all went reasonably well until the enrollment, reduced by war evacuations, began to swell once more with returnees from the mainland, and the school found itself in the distressing position of having to turn away many promising new pupils for sheer lack of space.

The Elementary School was fortunate in being able to rent from the University its newly completed Castle Memorial Kindergarten building, an ideal place for the instruction of smaller boys and girls and large enough to accommodate a full enrollment and to provide it with a rich and broad course of study. Indeed, sentimental reasons alone will make welcome the return of these small children to the old campus; for not until the new Elementary School—already dreamed of and planned for along with many other new buildings—can be erected, will the pupils of grades three to six have so fine a material set-up as they have enjoyed for the past three years.

Curiously enough the Primary Department, which was the only department to remain in scattered units after September of 1942, is, with the exception of the Kindergarten and one unit of first and second grades, already back on the campus—has been for a whole semester—and is already settled and happy. In the spring of '44, the school concluded negotiations for the return of Pauahi Hall. With floors refinished, walls repainted in cheerful colors, and a tall fence setting it off from that part of the campus still used by the Engineers, this old hall has been housing first and second grades, to their great contentment.

The Kindergarten groups have been and still are taken care of in large private dwellings in Manoa and Nuuanu, altered and refitted so that they serve their purpose admirably.

Punahou is going home, and for that reason all Punahou people are very happy. But those who have watched the school with an understanding eye will say unhesitatingly that these off-campus years— war years—have not been lost years. They have been mettle-testing years; but they have been good years. From the beginning, boys and girls and teachers and parents have been called on for reserves of mind and spirit. First there were the adjustments already described. Then there were the defense measures. Finally came active participation in civilian war activities.

Two or three weeks before the Japanese attack, a speaker representing the already existing civilian defense organization talked to a gathering of men teachers about the possibility of war and the need for preparedness plans. He pointed out to their complete dissatisfaction how important it would be to scatter the pupils in slit trenches dug all over the campus, in case of an attack. Leaving the meeting, one teacher said to another that the possibility of attack seemed too far removed to justify cutting up their beautiful lawns that way. Early in March that same teacher was superintending the seventh and eighth grade boys in the digging of two hundred yards of slit trenches below Bishop Hall. He and those boys had become so used to the idea of slit trenches that they never wasted a thought on the beautiful lawns that they were cutting up.

Teachers who had never thought of violence or death in connection with themselves and the boys and girls under their care took intensive first aid courses, learned how to stop profuse bleeding, how to make splints for broken bones, how to recognize "shock" and what to do about it, and how to make stretchers and carry wounded. They went to lectures on poison gases, learned to think about their deadly effect without shuddering too much, sniffed them from bottles so as to be able to recognize them, then went back to school and held endless conferences to devise the best means of protecting the children in their care from exposure to those poison gases, and to get them decontaminated if exposed. Gas masks were carried and children trained in their use. Air raid drills were planned and carried out with deadly seriousness until the victory at Midway eased the strain a bit. They are combined with fire drills now, but many students still call them air raid drills.

The Girls Physical Education Department turned itself for a year or more partly into a kind of service club, making all kinds of things for the Red Cross to distribute among the fighting men who needed them. Their amusement kits and "ditty" bags were sent to every post in the South Pacific. The school's print shop printed and bound thousands of copies of the game SALVO, which went and still go in great numbers wherever the Red Cross sets up rest and recreation units.

A team of ten boys and a teacher was recruited to serve at the O.C.D. medical unit in the Scottish Rite Temple on Wilder Avenue, actually sleeping there and being on call in case of emergency, day or night. Scores of boys and girls took on responsibilities with other branches of the O.C.D. in connection with possible attacks. Practically every teacher was giving his or her spare time to some form of war work—Red Cross, O.C.D., U.S.O., gas decontamination unit, military training unit, mass evacuation unit, blood bank, etc. Of course pupils and teachers in the other schools of the Territory were similarly active.

When the pineapple industry feared that it might have to fold up for lack of labor, students and teachers of Punahou joined the students and teachers of the other schools in helping provide pineapples and pineapple juice for the fighting forces. They learned to hoe, to pick pineapples, to break off slips for replanting, to pick up and sack such slips after they had dried, and to carry on numerous other activities in the prickly fields. They went forth clean and energetic in bumping trucks in the morning, singing—and came back tired and dirty at night—very often still singing. Those who did not go to the fields engaged in some other form of war work on "pineapple" days, such as cutting and rolling bandages.

Meanwhile the Engineers used the Punahou Campus for offices, shops, and living quarters. They made many changes in a number of buildings and to various areas of the campus. To some of these, they have given tremendous wear. However, except for those first days when nobody thought property damage significant as compared with the needs of the emergency, they have caused as little damage as possible and have maintained and cared for the campus conscientiously. If the splendid work done in restoring Pauahi Hall can be taken as a criterion, there is every reason to believe that the campus and buildings will be turned back to Punahou in good condition, in some cases perhaps even better than when they were taken over.

Yes, leaving the campus was a jolt to Punahou, and staying away so long has been a deprivation, and going back is going to be good; but still better, from the point of view of the teachers and pupils, is the sense of having sacrificed a little something to push the war to its conclusion, and of having taken a small part during these war years in the emergency labors that had to be performed. When classes start on the historic old campus next September, the boys and girls will be "in there pitching" according to their traditions, and will be just a little more dependable as human beings than they would have been if they had never been called up to leave.

A Pocket Guide to Honolulu:
Soldiers' Introduction to Hawaii

EILEEN O'BRIEN

❖ When Uncle Sam says to a soldier, "So You're Going to Hawaii!" he now has a practical method of letting the man in uniform know what to expect when he reaches the islands. It is *A Pocket Guide to Hawaii,* an attractive booklet that is issued to the men aboard the transports en route, and is something for which the Honolulu Chamber of Commerce ought to give three cheers.

Not that it is by any means a tourist-type glamour talk. On the contrary, it prepares the soldier for the wartime conditions that exist in Hawaii and debunks his preconceived notions of a hula girl under every palm tree. Thousands of service men have been bitterly disappointed in the contrast between Honolulu as it is today and the Hawaii about which they learned through technicolor movies and tourist bureau releases. If such a booklet had been issued to all service men, starting several years ago, there might be fewer cases of antagonism against "The Rock" among men in uniform.

The booklet is wittily illustrated by WO Robert Bach, who has been a frequent contributor to *Paradise of the Pacific.* He has had one-man shows at the Honolulu Academy of Arts, at Gump's in San Francisco and Carmel, and has exhibited in other leading galleries in various parts of the country.

It was prepared by the ponderous-sounding special projects branch, morale services section of the Central Pacific Base Command, and was produced by the army information branch, information and education division, in Washington, D.C. Although it is for military personnel only, we have been given special permission by the war department to quote from it.

After a "briefing" on the geographical set-up of the islands, the

---

First published March 1945.

guide points out that "the city of Honolulu is full of drug stores, department stores, soda fountains, movies, offices, and even Americans. . . . There are cops, public schools, dial telephones, churches, hot dog stands, public libraries, YMCAs, restaurants, daily newspapers. . . . So you're not as far away from home as you think."

A description of the outside islands follows and then the guide tackles Hawaii's unique racial set-up. "There's one primary point to remember," it states. "No matter what the color of their skin, no matter how they appear, the civilians you see in the Hawaiian Islands are Americans. They're just as proud of the Stars and Stripes as you are. Never forget that. You're going to run into a lot of Japanese during your stay. In 1941 there were 157,000 people of Japanese descent here. . . . Now get this straight. Most of these went to American schools. They learned to pledge their allegiance to the same flag you salute. They like American soft drinks. And one of their favorite radio comics is Bob Hope. They're Americans.

"What's more, many of them have husbands, sons and brothers fighting for Uncle Sam. These Japanese-Americans aren't just talking patriotism. Their battalions proved, in the battle of Italy, that they are willing to die for it. Don't sell them short.

"The native Hawaiians are a much smaller group. In 1941 there were only 14,246 pure Hawaiians and 52,445 part Hawaiians. These Hawaiians are fine folk. Don't let any fantastic fiction you may have read about them back home throw you off the beam. These people have certain fundamental ideals: They believe in strong bodies, in clean living and in democracy."

If more service men had been prepared in a manner such as this for the racial backgrounds of the people in Hawaii, there would undoubtedly have developed less antagonism between service men and local residents. Men in uniform have complained that the "natives" here are unfriendly, but they fail to realize that most non-haole islanders never know whether they will be treated courteously by service men or called a "dam-jap." The pocket guide will, therefore, perform a badly needed service in this respect.

"Keep this in mind," the booklet continues, "when you meet the people over here. They've been under attack. They've been living in a war atmosphere for a long time. They've been working long hours, suffering the inconveniences of overcrowding, curfew, gas rationing, and other necessary wartime restrictions. They haven't complained. . . .

But it hasn't been easy for them. So give them a break, and they'll meet you more than halfway."

A brief history of Hawaii follows and then short discussions of the hula, local government, industries, and the backgrounds of the various armed services in relation to Hawaii. Then the booklet gets down to the subject of Girls.

"Girls are scarce in Hawaii. When you've been off the boat for as long as 23 minutes, you'll find that telephone numbers here carry the same classification as war plans. They're marked 'Secret' and kept in money belts. If, by hook or by crook, you latch on to a few numbers besides the laundryman's (and his isn't as easy to get as you might think), you may wind up with a date. If this miracle occurs, the two of you can go swimming, take in a movie, or dance. If you're still numberless you can still go swimming, or take in a movie. Which is to say that a uniform here is about as novel as a light bulb in a prewar sign on Times Square. And there simply aren't enough *wahines* (gals) to go around."

Our only regret is that this well-written and cleverly illustrated booklet cannot be seen by members of all the armed services, as well as war workers, who arrive on Hawaii's shores.

Fixit Is Fine

STEVE CHIANI

❖ Miss Fixit is the sweetheart, mother confessor, and arbitrator of the Army, Navy, and Marines. For the past few years—four to be exact—she has been breezing her way into their hearts and minds through her popular question-and-answer column that appears daily in *The Honolulu Advertiser.*

This blonde dynamo, all of five-feet-three inches, has tenaciously clung to her sense of humor in spite of the tons of letters, some serious—some nonsensical—that come her way. "I don't want anyone to get the wrong idea," she said, as she pointed a red-tipped finger at the assorted reference books that are piled high on her desk. "I am not an adult quiz kid. All of my information comes out of sources like these, or from the library. And once in a while Hoibert pitches in with an answer or two."

Since she has caught the fancy of the public, she has lost twelve pounds from staying up nights doing research. Now that she has an assistant, a cute trick named Patsi, the researching has lost some of its gigantic proportions and Fixit's trim 105 pounds stays put. All branches of the service have apparently adopted her, and judging from the contents of her columns, she also enjoys a wide reputation among civilians as a sort of oracle.

Miss Fixit—or Ilona Bensczko Selle, as her friends know her—left her native Austria when she was five to live with an older married sister who was settled in Birmingham, Ala. She is the youngest member of a family of eighteen. Her first job was that of secretary to a medical director of an Insurance Company in Birmingham. Getting tired of routine work, and having cherished the desire to try her luck in Hollywood, she upped and headed west, after a short fling at her secretarial job. This was in 1931. Trying to break into the movies wasn't as easy as she had thought, and so she moved north to Seattle, Wash.,

---

First published April 1945.

where she lived for three years. Little did she realize when she left Hollywood totally disillusioned that one day her fan mail would top that of some of the current screen stars.

In 1937, her wanderlust took her to Shanghai where she became the fashion editor of the *Yankee Clipper* magazine and wrote fashion hints under the pen name of Alycia. Realizing that the Japs had little or no sympathy for the latest notes on what milady should wear, she got out when they took Shanghai and came on to Honolulu to live in 1939.

It wasn't very long before Ilona, or Alycia, got herself on the staff of the editorial department of the *Advertiser,* doing all sorts of odd jobs. Her golden hair, haloed in a braid that is worn coronet style, acted as a beacon—for she was constantly interrupted at her desk by streams of servicemen that would walk into the office and head straight for her, to ask all sorts of questions. These interruptions gave her the idea for the column, and after getting the "go" sign from Ray Coll, Sr.—the Boss—her first column, which was called "What, When or Where," made its appearance. It was only a matter of months until the response grew to such proportions that the Boss decided to play it up. The column was then changed to "Miss Fixit Answers"—and that's what she has been doing since March 1941.

Today she receives an average of a hundred letters a day and has had fifty proposals of marriage to date. One Army sergeant wanted to take her back to his Texas ranch as his bride, and "I can't even ride a horse," smiled Fixit. Her mail contains questions from men in nearly every theater of operations in the world. Many of the men who used to read her here have been moved on to one fighting front or another. She also gets mail from the families and relatives of the G.I.s, with requests from them to arrange a birthday party for their son, nephew, or cousin. This keeps Fixit plenty busy, for she arranges at least one birthday party a week, besides taking care of her thousand-and-one other chores. But she thrives on the thought that she has helped assure a lonely serviceman that his folks back home have not forgotten him. She received a letter from the mother and father of a sailor that she had birthday-caked recently. It said that their boy had sent them her photo and that it holds the place of honor in their living room. "And furthermore," continued the letter, "each day we look up at your merry eyes and infectious smile and bless you for the many things you are doing for our boys."

The most unusual request came from a soldier who barged up to her desk and said, "I want to get married." She didn't know whether he was nervous in the service or whether he was another lad that was struck by the romance of the Fixit legend. So she quipped, "I'm not in the mood, Joe." "Oh, I didn't mean you," he said blushingly, "I have my own girl. But I don't know how to go about it." From there on, Fixit took full charge and arranged the whole affair from flowers to preacher.

The word has so gotten around that no matter what is found on the streets—be it animal, vegetable or mineral—it ultimately winds up on Fixit's desk. "I've gotten beyond surprise stage," she said. "If someone brought me a lost elephant, I'd just take it in stride and try to find the poor beast his home." She receives thousands of lost articles a year, and more than 80 percent of them are returned to their owners. Wedding rings and wallets lead the parade. Her desk is usually filled with from twenty to thirty billfolds, most of them bulging with greenbacks. One of them was turned in with three hundred dollars nestling between the flaps. "It is thrilling to me," said Miss Fixit, "to see how innately good people really are. Often, little Oriental boys, and elderly men and women bring in these wallets with the money and identifications intact."

Miss Fixit makes a point of spending one day a week with the sick and the wounded in the Army and Navy Hospitals. Through her readers, she has furnished more than fifty recreational rooms in nearby hospitals and camps. The servicemen are so grateful to her for her friendly help that they have named bombers, tanks, and jeeps after her. One Marine bomber, named for her, saw action in Bougainville, and each bomb it dropped had the name of Miss Fixit scrawled across it in chalk. Any number of soldiers have come back from the various fronts with stories of the many fighting planes that are named in Fixit's honor.

Like so many of us, we were curious about Hoibert, but she wouldn't talk. "Say, Bub, that's a military secret," she said through a tingling laugh, "and anyway Sad Sack Hoibert doesn't like his private life delved into. So sit down and button your shoes, and let him be." It's amusing to hear this pert, attractive miss sling the G.I. lingo around like an old soldier.

Fixit likes to dance and can, if she has to, do a mean jitterbug. "But then when I let go—and cut a rug—I complain about my aching back for weeks after," she added. She much prefers Viennese waltzes and loves to listen to Wayne King and his orchestra. She says that a combination of Herbert Marshall and James Stewart is her ideal man—so don't get noivus Hoibert, because we doggies don't stand a chance.

When we asked Miss Fixit where she got her energy to be able to keep up with the splendid job of morale boosting she has been doing, her green eyes sparkled as she said: "I love being able to help the boys. They are a wonderful lot and I feel privileged to be able to ease some of the drabness out of their lives."

You can put this in your little black book, lady. The boys love you for it, and they aren't kidding when they say—Fixit is fine!

Troubles in Paradise

DR. RUBY T. NORRIS

❖ Sociologically, the Territory of Hawaii is part of the United States. When you arrive you feel at home almost immediately. It has the same religious system, family pattern, economy, language, and educational system. However, there are physical and social factors that set it apart and give it a distinctive flavor. Specifically, the Islands are a greater war zone, in common with other boom towns in mainland war production centers. They are set in the middle of the ocean—a chain of volcanic islands with inter-island travel infrequent enough to result in far less intercommunication than normally exists in a mainland community of this size. The invariable climate is distinctive also. At present the population has a highly unbalanced sex ratio. Finally, you have a permanent population only 25 percent of which is Caucasian. As merchants frequently say to us in the OPA, "Hawaii is different." I heartily subscribe to this statement, and from these distinctive characteristics a number of problems emerge.

Although we are in a war zone, we do not face the physical danger of invasion. However, we do face a danger of physical deterioration. People are living crowded together with many inconveniences such as lack of maids, curtailed delivery service and laundry service, and transportation difficulties. People are working who never worked before; others are working harder than they ever worked before. You cannot interview business men every day without getting a severe sense of strain among this group. They are working almost to the limit of human endurance. This is also true of other workers—even the bureaucrats are not immune!

We see the result in a restless search for high-powered recreation— not tiddlywinks—but something with a punch. I feel the Islands have not grappled effectively with the problem of providing mass entertainment. When people return from long, high-geared work days, they

---

First published May 1945.

want and demand a lot of varied opportunities for entertainment. Slot machines are not adequate.

I mentioned a number of physical characteristics of the Islands that are rather important. The climate is invariable, which makes for a sameness. The isolation from the mainland and the current lack of inter-island transportation cause people to live in circumscribed groups and makes for sameness of experience in communities. This creates a problem of stimulation for the individual. There is little impetus toward critical thought in the Islands because of the easy-going life in this climate. This again demonstrates a need for creative and inventive use of leisure time. Honolulu does a remarkably good job for its size. But all that we can do is none too much when we are set apart from each other by such barriers.

Another major problem at present is the unbalanced sex ratio in the Islands. Even before the war the only racial group that had a higher proportion of females than males was the part-Hawaiian. The war has accentuated this situation. Such unbalanced sex ratios have occurred frequently in American society—usually as a frontier phenomenon. You have it occasionally on the mainland where new industrial developments occur. The sociologists have a lot to say on this subject. Most human society throughout the world has been monogamous—chiefly because sexes are equally balanced. Often when you get a reference in history to polygamy, a closer study will reveal that the bulk of the population was monogamous, and plural spouses were the prerogative of the wealthy few, the chiefs or kings. However, it has sometimes developed that the sex ratio has been unbalanced by female infanticide or military decimation of the male population. When this occurred, plural spouses (formal or informal) are the almost universal development. At present the Hawaiian Islands have such an unbalanced sex ratio that unorthodox sex arrangements are quite prominent. You might say, at the moment, that the Hawaiian Islands, and indeed all of Polynesia, are slightly polyandrous!

The high divorce rates, flighty wives, sexual precocity, delinquency, and mental maladjustments among men are some of the results of this situation. The plight of the older man is particularly troublesome. The proverbial "wolf" is really rather a pathetic animal! Among the armed forces the same situation obtains. There are far more means by which the enlisted men can meet girls than exist among the older and higher ranking officers. I sometimes wonder whether the lonely atoll with an all-male population and the date-less community on the mainland are not better off than we are here. It will be easier to return from such isolation to the basic family and sexual patterns after the war.

I come now to problems of the Islands that arise from the peculiar racial composition. They are the most interesting, permanent, and difficult phases of the situation.

The Hawaiian Islands do not follow the mainland pattern of racial prejudice very closely. The picture here is interesting because of the minor degree to which resistance to new groups has been felt. There has at no time been a large Caucasian working class in competition with the newer groups. Here you have had a vacuum instead of resistance, because the planters introduced successive groups of non-Caucasian labor. As wave has succeeded wave, the new groups have become the majority rather than the minority. Business and cultural institutions tend to be less discriminatory under such conditions.

You must also give a great deal of weight to the religious and missionary background of the Islands. There is a humanitarian concern for health and social conditions on the part of the top management of these Islands that is extremely impressive. The pride with which they discuss the health campaign on the plantations is certainly distinctive in the whole of American agricultural economy. For whatever reasons, the extent of opportunity and the attitude toward other than white races in the Islands provide a most refreshing contrast to the mainland and to most other places in the world. The Islands' racial problem is so much less acute, and it is being treated so much more intelligently, that it is astonishing to a newcomer. It is not ideal here by a long shot, but discrimination here is in no degree such as exists on the mainland. There are a few clubs that exclude non-whites, but this doesn't come in the same class as the Jim Crow treatment of Negroes in the South nor California's attitude toward the Oriental.

The discrimination found here takes the form chiefly of a ceiling on economic advancement. On the plantations, certain races simply do not rise to managerial positions, and in most business houses, responsible positions are the prerogative of the haole. This is a vestige of Hawaii's plantation past and may have possibly been appropriate when the non-white races were largely uneducated and new to American culture. It is no longer warranted.

The war is bringing about vast changes in the economy of the Islands and dulling the edge of racial discrimination. The pre-war characteristics of the Hawaiian economy can be summed up by describing these as volcanic islands of remarkable climate on whose peripheral slopes good cane and pine soil has accumulated, providing the primary and basic cash income of the Islands. Next in importance to the money income from the exports of pine and sugar are the tourist income, government income, and return from local manufacturing. On the whole, the Islands represent an importing economy, drawing from the mainland a wide range of diversified manufactured products.

The effect of the war has been extremely startling on the economic structure and upon employment opportunities. Pine and sugar acreage in the aggregate has declined with the preempting of land by the armed forces and difficulties in getting labor. The Government services have greatly expanded. There has also been an increase in secondary manufacturing as scarcities develop and as the expanded population, with higher incomes, has more purchasing power. More people are in the service trades—entertainment, restaurants, and the like. In looking at the contemporary tremendous volume of business, it is apparent that, while big concerns have increased substantially, the little concerns, mainly Oriental, have come up even more rapidly. To their advantage has been greater ease in expanding personnel and greater flexibility of operation. The springing up of new enterprises is on an astounding scale. Further, there has been more rapid advancement of other races in haole concerns by dint of the breaking down of prejudice, loss of personnel, and general rise of wage levels. The rise of Federal employment has also fostered the granting of positions to people on a merit system basis.

In all parts of the Islands the wage level is increasing. The result is that, through the opportunities of the war and services needed here, the non-white races are lifting themselves up by their own bootstraps. It has often been said by some of my haole friends that the Orientals have gained so much in comparison with conditions in the Orient that they should be satisfied. The argument breaks down so easily—Orientals, like Occidentals, came to the United States to better themselves. A few generations don't change the logic of our Constitution and national ideals, which require that each should be allowed to stand on his own merits.

The elimination of racial intolerance is, however, one of the main crusades of our day and one of the main issues about which this war is being fought. You will see here in the future that the economic strength of this hard-working, intelligent, frugal, non-white population will cause the entire group to gain in every kind of way. The new soldier and worker population that is being added to the population here is accepting other races on an equal plane and will probably continue to do so after the war. I have always believed in the theory of race equality, but never have really seen the potentialities for its acceptance as clearly as during the year and a half I have been in Hawaii. The Island races on the whole have proved during this war to be hard-working, loyal Americans, and that is a role they will insist on in the future.

To conclude: Fatigue, tension, tightening of the labor market, the sameness of the community and sameness of the climate, racial discrimination, military adjustments, and disproportionate sex ratio— all are problems we face today. Racial discrimination and the sex ratio will of themselves improve because of inherent social and economic trends, but there is still plenty of work to be done in promoting social institutions. Energy, intelligence, and courage are needed to invent new ways and discard old ones to fit the needs of Hawaii's future.

Note: *This article is a condensation of a paper, "Current and Future Social Problems of the Territory," delivered by Dr. Norris at the twenty-fourth territorial conference of social work at the Mabel Smyth Memorial building, Honolulu.*

Colossus of the Pacific

LT. H. L. STICKNEY, USNR

❖ One of the greatest stories of the Pacific War concerns the almost unbelievable job that Pearl Harbor Navy Yard has done since Japan attacked it.

"The Yard" has become synonymous with tremendous effort and extraordinary accomplishment. The great base of today (a picture remote from the undermanned area that invited assault nearly four years ago) is intertwined with the lives of almost countless Honolulu residents, both kamaaina and malihini.

Much has been said of the Navy's job of salvaging the wreckage left by the Nipponese, and certainly it was a heroic job, but an even bigger and rarely mentioned task has been that of "keeping the fleet fit to fight," with all the tremendous problems of repair and supply that go with the huge amphibious operations now being carried out in the Pacific. Without Pearl Harbor it would have been impossible for the United States to maintain the Fleet that did the job at Kwajalein, Truk, Saipan, Palau, and Okinawa.

Under the direction of Rear Adm. William R. Furlong, USN, top ordnance and engineering expert, the Yard is now repairing and converting everything from PT boats to aircraft carriers, on production line schedule and in less time than it used to take to draw up plans. Its great shops are pouring out quantities of material for the Fleet and for the scores of new U.S. bases that are springing up in conquered territory to the South and Southwest. "Portable Pearl Harbors," the Navy's supply ships get much of their gear at Pearl. For instance, of the sheet metal shop's present output, it is estimated that approximately 20 percent is being shipped out to new bases.

Henry Kaiser could take a leaf out of Admiral Furlong's book on ship repair and construction. An early example was the aircraft carrier U.S.S. *Yorktown,* heavy contributor at Midway, one of America's

First published June 1945.

254

greatest sea victories. When the U.S.S. *Yorktown* dry-docked at Pearl Harbor that June 1st, she was badly damaged from a direct bomb hit, from a near miss and from another near miss. The word went out that the *Yorktown* was "priority," and fourteen hundred men swarmed over the vessel—shipfitters, machinists, welders, electricians, pipefitters, and shipwrights worked on different levels to restore bulkheads, stanchions, and deck plates necessary to restore structural strength and, as this work proceeded, to renew or replace the instruments, electric wiring, or fixtures that had been wrecked. Need for speed was so urgent that no planning was done and the job was brought to completion with planners and estimators working directly from the ship's plans. Men worked at exhausting speed, and on the night of June 3rd, two days later, she slipped out of the Harbor and joined Admiral Nimitz's force off Midway. What the U.S.S. *Yorktown* did after that is history. Her planes took part in the operation that sank two enemy carriers and disabled a third. She scored hits on many another Jap ship in that battle and helped turn back the threat to Midway and the Hawaiian Islands, probably the turning point of the Pacific War. Admiral Nimitz later announced in a speech at the Navy Yard that in the Battle of Midway our forces sank four of the six Jap carriers that had started the war by attacking Pearl Harbor.

More recently, the U.S.S. *Maryland,* after taking a torpedo in her port bow off Saipan, was overhauled and given a new bow, with revolutionary speed. When the extent of her damage was flashed to Pearl Harbor's Planning Section from Forces Afloat, a forty-nine day work schedule was proposed, which caused eyebrows to be raised doubtfully. There was little time for prefabrication, and work was scarcely begun before the *Maryland* arrived for dry-docking. In spite of this, a welded design, lighter and more durable than its riveted predecessor, was whipped into shape and fitted on by midnight of a day far in advance of her original deadline, and she was able to rejoin the Fleet in time for early action.

Many of the men who worked on the *Yorktown* and on the others repaired under similar conditions of urgency were new arrivals from the states and were pioneers in an expansion that has multiplied by more than six times the number of workmen at Pearl Harbor. Where the Jap raiders saw fields of sugarcane adjacent to the Harbor, there are now vast shops and storehouses and a great sprawling city of bachelors where thousands of mainland recruits live. Hundreds of these men belong to their own home-state clubs that compete for members with round the island tours, luaus, and other entertainment. When U.S. Senators Meade, Russell, and Brewster passed through Hawaii on their round the world junket, they went out of their way to speak to gatherings of their respective state clubs in the Navy Yard's Hall of Flags.

Pearl Harbor today is truly the melting pot of the world. Practically every known nationality and every state in the union is represented among its workers, including large numbers of Chinese, Filipinos, Koreans, Portuguese, and Hawaiians. There are lower numbers of Negroes, Puerto Ricans, Scandinavians, and others. A recent official survey disclosed that there are more than thirty-five nationalities represented.

Pearl Harbor's history is comparatively recent for, though her first dry-dock was opened in 1919, her real expansion did not get under way until 1940 when war clouds were gathering. Actually it was not until the Japanese attack that real impetus was given the program of expansion that, under Admiral Furlong's guidance, has since completely changed her landscape. One great new addition was the opening of Thomas Dry-dock in September 1943, one of the world's largest dry-docks and capable of handling any ship afloat or building. It is one of several Pearl Harbor dry-docks now servicing the Fleet. Of the ten miles of piers and wharves in Pearl Harbor, six-and-one-half miles have been completed since December 7th, at a cost of $35 million, and a number of new graving docks and a marine railway have been added to the Yard's facilities.

Even the harbor's shape has greatly changed since 1941 for, in more than one spot, coral from the harbor bottom has been sucked up and moved through pipes to fill an inlet. Now this solid ground is covered with military installations and tens of thousands of servicemen live in barracks and tents sprawling in every direction from the harbor. Only one thing remains the same in Hawaii. The beautiful weather is everything the malihini expected, and its year-round pleasantness is partly responsible for the high work output at Pearl.

Pearl Harborites work round the clock on military secrets, and to them Fleet movements are commonplace, but they don't talk about it much. They practically live with the shell-ripped warships that come back from the West. They see wounded American boys being carried from the hospital ships in the harbor and they see Japanese prisoners on their way to nearby prison camps. Pearl Harbor is much closer to the war than the mainland.

Great repair jobs come and go at the Yard, but lately hundreds of man hours are being devoted to tasks unusual even at this Naval base. As the Pacific war tempo has increased, the Army and Marine Corps have called on the Yard's skilled mechanics to install flame throwers on tanks or increase armor on the hundreds of invasion craft that bob up and down in the Harbor. Shortly after the release of the story about the Seabee bulldozer operator who covered up a Japanese machine gun nest with his blade, the Seabees asked Admiral Furlong if he'd be so good as to install armor plate on their bulldozers. The job was done by welders in the Shipfitters' Shop, and even they were just a little doubtful about it until they read where armored bulldozers were in the van of the attack at Hollandia.

The much publicized metal mattings, which aided materially in getting men and supplies across the volcanic sands of Iwo Jima beaches, were fabricated in Pearl Harbor. Many miles of mats and the sleds that carried them were assembled on high-priority job orders by the shipfitters, welders, burners, and sheetmetal workers at the Yard. Another unusual Pearl Harbor operation is a rubber manufacturing plant that uses crude rubber produced on Oahu and turns out such products as rubber gaskets for submarines.

The prefabrication found in all American shipyards is not new here. Huge ship sections are prefabricated with the help of reports flashed ahead from wounded ships, and as soon as the ship is rushed into drydock and damaged portions cut away, the new section is swung into place with cranes.

Battle repairs of such ships as the U.S.S. *California, West Virginia,* and *Nevada,* all sunk on December 7, sound like a history of the war in the Pacific. Some of them have been in and out of Pearl Harbor's drydocks more than once, and among them they have made a mockery of early Jap claims of their destruction. More recently, the Yard has completely repaired and made ready for sea in fourteen days a cruiser that had been hit in the bow and stern. Another cruiser has been refitted with a new prefabricated section in the record time of nine days.

On the occasion of American victories in the Pacific, it has been customary to remark, "that will help pay for Pearl Harbor." America needs no victories for this purpose. Pearl Harbor has avenged herself.

Gracious Tradition in the Home
of a Late Hawaiian Princess

ELLEN L. DAVIS

❖ Some months ago, when the USO learned that Uncle Sam's girls were coming to this doorstep of the Pacific war, it started looking around for an oversized welcome mat and a place to put it ... and found it in the historic old home of Princess David Kawananakoa on Pensacola Street. I'd met the Princess only once, when she came in her station wagon—as she so often did—to visit the Princess Home USO at Kahuku, which she'd turned over to us for the duration shortly after the war began. I remembered her rich, throaty laugh, the sparkle of pleasure in her eyes as she watched the G.I.s crowding the canteen and tearing around the beach playing games or swinging idly in hammocks.

And now she was to be godmother to the first USO club for enlisted women in the Pacific Ocean Areas. As Eleanor Wilson, special representative from New York who came out to help us plan our women's program, and I were driving over to see our new property, I was hoping that I would have a chance to hear that laughter again. But I didn't expect to find it right in our backyard! The big house stood on a rise in the lush green lawn, slumbering contentedly, like an old lady sunning herself in her memories. Our footsteps echoed through the great, high-ceilinged rooms. Eleanor's face, I was happy to note, was wearing that mingled expression of awe and astonishment we come to expect of Mainlanders who see Hawaii USOs for the first time. A thrill of pride in the accomplishments of a lot of hard-working people pattered quickly down my spine as she told me that nowhere else in the United States had she found USO clubs with so much beauty and spirit. "*And this!* Why this is the Hawaii people dream about. Look at the length of that patio."

"Lanai," I corrected absentmindedly, having promised to share my meager supply of knowledge with her. I was wishing the walls could talk. "There's a terrace out back, I understand, where the Princess used to have her hula troupes dance. Let's go see." We went around,

---

First published August 1945.

and there was the generous figure of the Princess, topped by a broad hat against the noonday sun, vigorously attacking the weeds in the border of flowers.

"Hullo," we called. She turned and that rich laughter I'd wanted to hear spilled between us. "I'm getting ready for the girls," she chuckled. ("The boys"—meaning any G.I. of any age—were always part of a great, sprawling family to the Princess. She was like a matriarch who was happiest when the clan gathered. She might forget a name here or there, but no matter. He was a boy in uniform, and he belonged. And now she was getting ready for the girls. Packing away personal belongings, pulling weeds, making plans.)

When we left later in the afternoon, I asked the Princess if she would sometime tell me about this house, where she had come, in 1902, as bride of Prince David Laamea Kahalepouli Kawananakoa Piikoi, a Prince of the Kalakaua dynasty and a descendant of ancient Hawaiian families of royal rank. "Any time, my child." When I phoned several days later, the Princess said: "Come right along. But you'll have to come in the back door; I've lost the key to the front door."

So the back door it was, and into a large room where the Princess sat behind a bridge table, writing busily. She was surrounded everywhere by crates and boxes. "Things from Pensacola Street," she explained, waving her pen in their general direction.

She talked more than an hour. Sometimes her voice grew husky, and sometimes it trailed off altogether, leaving us in a well of silence. She told of the flaming torches that used to line the long driveway and the carriages that passed between them, bringing guests to the house. Of gaiety and charm and color. Fragrance of flowers and the sound of sweet Hawaiian voices. Men in the uniforms of kings and princes, generals and admirals, their consorts and wives in evening clothes. Regal Hawaiian women in their stately holokus; brown-skinned youngsters in garlands of leis and grass skirts. The Crown Prince and Princess of Sweden, the Maharajah of Kipurthala, the Duke of Spoleta, Princess Maria Mercedes de Bourbon des Deux Siciles, Baron Maurice de Rothschild, Millard Tydings, John Nance Garner.

The sheen of polished wood calabashes, handed down from the days of King Kalakaua and Queen Kapiolani, was shut away in some of those boxes. In another was the jeweled royal order given the Princess by the King of Siam. I eyed the boxes wistfully, but I knew the past was too heavy with age to be disturbed.

We struggled back to the present, and as I rose to leave, the Princess leaned across the table and laid her hand on my arm. "None of those men and women who were my guests so long ago were more important than the girls who are coming. I want to welcome them as I would all distinguished visitors." But when "Hui Welina," as the Princess named the new club was opened some weeks later, she was not there to welcome the girls. She had gone to rest in the last crypt in the Royal Mausoleum in Nuuanu, the islands' valley of kings. Fulfilling an ancient Hawaiian tradition, Nuuanu skies had wept that day when the cortege had passed through the streets of Honolulu.

More in keeping with the spirit of the Princess, they had smiled sunnily the day Hui Welina opened. She would have liked, far better than the tears of her friends, the laughter of "the girls" she couldn't stay to meet. For she loved youth and romance and the tradition of gracious living, and all things about conspire to keep those things alive for young women who are Hawaii's wartime guests.

We can imagine her going about the grounds and the club. Smiling down at a young couple stretched out on lounge chairs on the lawn, the space between them bridged by their clasped hands. Pausing a moment under the plumeria tree she knew so well to watch young women in sunsuits gathering fragrant heaps of blossoms for leis. Watching a Marine who has spread out her material on the big yellow punee on the lanai and, brows furrowed and tongue firmly clamped between her teeth, is cutting out a slipcover for the dayroom back at camp. Looking in on a foursome having a dinner party in the private dining room the girls keep booked solid in advance. Glancing approvingly at a Navy girl who, having arrived some time before hot and disheveled from Honolulu's own battlefront—the shopping district— now enters the lounge immaculate in freshly pressed whites.

Standing against the background of banked flowers the USO arranges for all the many wedding ceremonies held at Hui Welina and listening as a girl in traditional gown and veil and a boy in uniform become man and wife. The Princess David is dead, but the heritage she left lives on in the big house on Pensacola Street. It will go back, after the war, to towns and cities all over the Mainland. And at the rate the marriages are piling up at Hui Welina, there are someday going to be a lot of round-eyed youngsters, far from here, who will want to hear, just once more "about when you and daddy were married at a Princess' house in Hawaii." The Princess would like that, too.

The Light Warden

WILLARD WILSON

❖ Some time ago we had a practice air raid alert and blackout. The sirens wailed, we again stumbled around in the dark for a few minutes, and malihinis made annoyed remarks. But as the sirens sounded their all-clear call, it occurred to me that here indeed, by the very "practice" nature of the blackout, was symbolized the end of a civic era. The sound of the dove was indeed heard again in the land, and the days of the light warden were numbered. Before he joins the dodo, Tojo, and other vanished relics of a past age, it seems to me something should be said in valedictory of the species—for the light warden was indeed a curious creature.

Whenever a person is singled out from the mob of his fellows and handed the truncheon of authority, whether he be merely a Sunday School superintendent or the leader of an impromptu night quartette, there occurs some subtle chemical change in his nature. Most people unconsciously resent the laws that they have helped to impose on society. Therefore, when one finds himself suddenly placed in the position of the enforcer rather than the enforcee, there is a temporary lift of the ego; a sort of "Now, by gosh, I'm on the other end of the stick!" as indeed he is.

It is a mood of exaltation that passes rapidly after he comes up against the dull realities of his job, however. Invariably he learns that the life of the ruler—however small the domain—is fraught with minute worries and uncertainties that lesser subjects know not of. Uneasy indeed is the head that wears a crown, even though the crown is merely a tin hat with a block "W" painted on the front.

I don't know how it is in mainland cities, but in Honolulu we wardens were for the most part a gentle race of men, ill suited to the speaking of a firm word or sharp command. A typical warden, I suspect, is one on whom either the finger of time has been laid or one who instinctively shrinks from the more public forms of war exhibitionism.

First published August 1945.

261

If he had been bursting with vigor, he would have joined the Business-mens' Military Training Corps and gotten himself a uniform, gun, and a series of physically devastating maneuvers that consisted frequently of crawling on his middle-aged belly through the hedges and gardens of Manoa Valley or guarding a sub-station of the waterworks. If he had been thirsting for both a uniform and immediate action, and for some reason was not in the regular service, he would have gotten himself into the Police Auxiliary, which still patrols the night in radio cars and has weird and dangerous adventures in the darkened purlieus of Waikiki and Kakaako. Being the man he is, however, an introvert and fawn-like creature, he seeks an outlet for his patriotic civic interest that will allow him to do a modicum of necessary service while attracting a minimum of public attention.

For this sort of person the corps of air-raid wardens, or as they were commonly called in this town "light wardens," was obviously created. Because of my apparent qualifications for membership, I was asked to join when I moved into a house on Rocky Hill. I could not very well refuse, for I had my evenings comparatively free, did not belong to the BMTC, and had never even remotely considered enrolling in the Police Auxiliary.

"We need persons of your type," I was told. "We need people who can keep their heads!"

I was vaguely flattered by the invitation, and to tell the truth rather anticipated the experience of dynamically keeping my head—of calling some neighbor's attention to the fact that his blackout paint was beginning to scale off a bathroom window, or that there was a beacon crack of light showing on the seaward side of the dining room. That was quite soon after the December 7 blitz, and our blackout was still excessively black. There was not yet any nonsense about allowing low-power "dim-out" bulbs, blackened on all sides and with a small aperture at the bottom that should be pointed either directly up or directly down, five feet from a window, not closer together than every ten feet, and answer to the provost judge if you're wrong, God help you!

Vague scenes flitted through my mind of a certain firmness with which I would speak to certain prominent citizens in my vicinity: "I'm very sorry, Doctor, but if you aren't more careful about that bedroom window I'll come in and bust the damn light over your head!" Or perhaps it would be the attractive blond down around the corner whom I had glimpsed a few times as she sleepily drew the blackout shades just at dusk: "I'm awfully sorry, Madam, but your light is showing— Oh well, perhaps I could come in and check things over for you— Thank you, a drink is nice on these warm evenings—Well—hm—."

So when the block head warden—or perhaps one should say the head block warden—asked me to join the forces banded together in protection of our homes and the enforcement of necessary restrictions upon the free life, after a proper hesitation I accepted the responsibility. I was assured it would not take much of my time, and that I would be doing a genuine and necessary service for my community. A man not in uniform is especially susceptible to any intimation of a lack of patriotism these days, regardless of the reasons for his civvies.

Here let me state, lest I be thought pharisaical in the matter, that I subscribe heartily to the praise that has been given the OCD and its dogged insistence upon the thankless task of preparation for disaster that everyone hoped would never come. Wardens and other volunteers usually perform their work quietly and without open reward, often at substantial sacrifice to themselves. With the exception of a few frogs who love to croak loudly even though it be in a small pond, most of the men and women in the corps were and are serious and intelligent about their chores, and correctly evaluate their importance.

Nevertheless, take it from me, this business of being a light warden is not what it was cracked up to be in advance publicity.

In the first place, I had to study things. I learned that the old English law that "a man's house is his castle" still applied. I was told to be polite and never on any account to enter a house unless I was invited by the tenant. I was told in effect that I had no real authority to do anything but march around, watch, and if I had any serious trouble to call someone else who would apply pressure. This rather knocked the props out from under the whole affair at first, until I had actually come in contact with a few householders who knew their constitutional rights—because they themselves were in a majority of cases also serving in some defense capacity—and were not inclined to be pushed around by a slight show of authority and a white armband.

It soon became apparent to me that my job was that of a psychologist and not that of a policeman. As soon as that was clear to me, the task took on new interest and I took on renewed importance in my own eyes. I began to study my neighbors furtively as I observed them puttering about their yards in the late afternoon. Because practically every one of my immediate neighbors was also a warden of one kind or another, I realized that they were also furtively watching me and wondering how they should approach me on the hypothetical night when I should inadvertently push a switch that would turn on some forgotten floodlight outside a house with which I was only vaguely familiar.

After my extremely brief period of indoctrination, I was assigned a regular beat that I was to cover two nights weekly. With green colored flashlight in my hand, arm band on my arm, and determination in my heart, I trod the path that first night. Nothing happened. Not a glimmer of light from any source troubled my journey, and when I checked in to precinct headquarters by phone I could report only nothing.

I have never known exactly what to say when I check in and am still vaguely embarrassed about it. Should one say, "Block nineteen—all quiet—Roger," or should one attempt to strike the informal note with something like "Block nineteen closing up shop. No murders, no bombs, no lights, no fun!" That small sense of anticlimax that I felt the first night has always haunted me as I have called in to zone headquarters.

For all I know, it suddenly occurs to me, there may be a correct way to do it with prescribed words and answers. As it is, I usually dialed the precinct headquarters and, when a crisp voice snapped at me from the other end, I fumbled for words for a few seconds and then ended up with the snappy statement, "Wilson, Block 19." I have never understood why I should say anything more than that, and I never would if the lofty individual on the other end of the line could understand plain English. His answer to that is invariably, "What's the name?" Then when I tell him it is still Wilson he says, obviously embarrassed himself at not having caught it the first time, "And what was the block, Mr. Wilson?" And so I tell him it is 19, and then hang up quickly.

I have tried once or twice to make some sort of pleasantry, and it may have been my imagination, but it always seemed to fall flat. The perfunctory laugh on the other end of the line seemed intended to remind me that this was war and that there might be some impatient warden somewhere champing at the bit to report an "incident" in his block. You see how the psychological aspects of the job worried me.

A Warden's Technique

WILLARD WILSON

❖ Getting down to the serious part of the job, and the thing that is really the heart of the whole problem of being a successful light warden, I found that the whole crux of the matter lay in a proper approach to the individual who inadvertently or carelessly violated the law. One had to approach him in a way calculated to get results, and at the same time one had to be extremely careful not to antagonize the transgressor. After all, the poor ignorant dolt is a neighbor of yours, and you are going to live in the same neighborhood with him for some time to come. To simplify the whole problem in my own mind, I catalogued roughly three general approaches a light warden might make to an illicit light and its owner.

One is what might be called the rationalizing approach. This is an exceedingly common dodge practiced by a surprising number of wardens who were not inclined to become embroiled in a technical argument. It worked something like this, as a mental state—at least it worked that way with me. I would be strolling along briskly, my green flashlight ready in my hand, my brassard on my arm, when I would come abreast of a house from which there was a distinct emanation of light. Actually I knew the light was too bright and I ought to do something about it, but native timidity might intervene between me and my bounded duty and I talked to myself somewhat as follows:

"In the first place, it is clear that the house is shaded from the vision of any possible enemy plane or ship by a dense hedge of trees. Even if the light were twice as bright, it wouldn't be dangerous. Not very dangerous anyhow. And besides, I know those people, and they will be going to bed in a few minutes—probably before I could get up to the porch. In addition to that, if a plane is going to see that light and attack this island, it has already spotted the thing, because the light has probably been on for an hour. Anyhow, if there was going to be an attack we would have enough warning from the sirens to enable us to

First published September 1945.

black out the entire city long before the raiders got here." By that time I am generally so far past the house that, looking back, I can see nothing, and so conclude that just as I predicted, the light has been switched off.

Once or twice my wife honored me with her company on my nocturnal patrol, and she invariably tried to force me into some overt act in justification of my existence as a warden. Especially did she insist that I "do something about" one neighbor of mine who since the beginning of the thing had maintained an oversupply of light in a rear bedroom that could not by any chance be seen from anywhere but one spot under an overhanging tree at the turn of the road. I pointed out that no invading plane was going to get into that highly disadvantageous spot, but her answer was always quite direct: "You're just scared. Just because his brother is the Fire Chief or something you don't dare tell him!" Because quite frankly she had something there, I did not encourage her to go patrolling with me.

Another approach commonly made by a warden to an obvious violation of blackout rules is a step beyond the actual avoiding of the violator and can be employed when one has been goaded either by his wife, neighbors, or his conscience into direct action. It is what one might call the academic or reasonable social approach. I may as well warn you, it is a lot better in theory than in actual practice. It consists of a frank, cheerful discussion of an illumination error in which a warden attempts to lead the violator, by the Socratic method, to the better life.

I employed it one night with notable lack of results in the case of the most chronic offender in my block—a gentleman who had been reprimanded by experts but who persisted in flooding his front room facing Waikiki with an illicit glow. In answer to my knock he came to the door, pleasantly invited me in, and asked me to be seated. Directly over my head, and apparently not worrying him in the slightest was, instead of the single dim-out bulb allowed at that time by law, a veritable chandelier of them. To my eye it looked like a cluster of baby spotlights.

"Lovely view from up here," he said by way of introduction, and I, not wishing to miss an opening, said yes, it was a lovely view of the ocean, and no doubt a ship at sea had just as lovely a view of us.

"Yes—except that there are no ships at sea any more the way there used to be. It would certainly be a beautiful sight—a fully lighted liner pulling out beyond Diamond Head there in the dark!" I tried tactfully to murmur that perhaps the darkened naval vessels on patrol could enjoy the lights on shore better now, but he missed the point, or rather conceded it gracefully.

"Yes, I guess they do. Pity they don't let us have more than a measly little bulb in each room. We could make such a beautiful sight for them. I always thought Hong Kong was a lovely place at night with its lights speckled all the way up to the top of The Peak. Ah, I expect that is blacked out now."

"Yes," I said pointedly, "probably better than Honolulu."

"Well, what can you expect—the Japanese are in control there."

Feeling that the oblique approach had somehow betrayed me and that we had come to the point, I said quite bluntly, "I notice that you have three dim-out bulbs in your chandelier. I don't suppose you generally use more than one at a time?"

"Oh, yes," he said blithely, "I turn them all on. I don't like a stuffy room and so I sit out here with the windows open at night. I found that it was uncomfortably dark with just one of those bulbs, and so I got a few more. It really makes it quite pleasant."

After which I retired. I somehow had the feeling that even if I quoted the letter of the law to him, he would smile and re-interpret it to me. He quite obviously knew the regulations, but he quite as obviously intended to do nothing about them. And for reasons that perhaps are clearer to one who has been a warden than to other mortals, I was stymied. I reported him in a routine way, but I noticed the next night that the bulbs were still there and still functioning. I expect that even the dull and heavy-handed thrust of a regular policeman would be parried by such suave admission of the obvious. And there in practice, as I say, one has the social approach (retreat is a better word) to the problem of the offender. Stated bluntly, it is do nothing, but explain your lack of inaction to yourself. Whether you can explain it satisfactorily to your wife is another matter.

A final method of dealing with such troublesome situations as may arise is undoubtedly the logical and natural one. It was that most commonly in force in the two weeks immediately following Pearl Harbor, and I must say it was effective. It undoubtedly would become popular again were we to suffer another raid in these peaceful Isles. It is best symbolized by the cry that we heard often in the jittery stillness of those watchful early war nights as we crouched in our hastily blacked-out rooms, never quite sure that a blanket hadn't slipped somewhere and exposed a whole ghastly square inch of illumination: "Turn out that damn light or I'll shoot it out!" From internal evidence I will testify that it was effective. We often turned the light out abruptly just in case something had slipped.

I recall one dark night out on Black Point, where I was living when the thing started, when I was given evidence that any visible illumination was dangerous to anyone in its vicinity. I had been sitting reading in my blackout den, which happened by necessity to be a five-by-four bathroom, when I heard a scratching and scuffling on the concrete walk outside the window. Quickly I switched out the light, scuttled to the door that opened out toward the impenetrable blackness of Waialae bay, and spoke into the night, making my voice as firm as voices went in those days.

"Looking for someone?"

"Oh hello there, Buddy," drawled a Panhandle voice from the murk—and suddenly to my horror a leathery face sprang out of the nothing not three feet from me into the frightening glare of a struck match.

"For God's sake come into the hallway for your smoke!" I said, horrified. "Don't stand there like the Diamond Head lighthouse."

"Okay," he chuckled. "Everybody seems to be so damn nervous around here. Just like these two guys I got on duty with me here tonight." He jerked the glowing stub toward two more intense blobs of darkness that lurked in the background. I could see a sinister glint of moonlight on the steel of their bayonets, and there was a solid unison thump as they dropped the butts of their rifles to the concrete.

"Well, sir, I'll tell you. I got myself a couple of machine guns set up down here at the turn of the beach. And some of these boys of mine shore have itchy fingers. So we are settin' there tonight a while back and one of them looks up here about where this house is and says, 'There's a light up there. By God I'm going to plug it.' And I grabs aholt of his machine gun just as he was swinging it around this way, and I says, 'Aw, let's take a walk up that way before we start plugging anything. It might be just the moon shining on a window or something. So we come up to look it over. And by John it was the moon!"

I tried to convey to him the idea that I was deeply appreciative of his wise decision in the matter.

"Well," he said deprecatingly, "some of the fellows say I'm soft, but that don't hurt me. You don't stay being a sergeant in the regular army for ten years if you're really soft. But I always say, 'Take a look before you shoot, boys. Else sometime you might hurt somebody.' These dumb privates————," I caught a sort of mental gesture toward his two shadows, "they want to pull the trigger and then ask is anybody there!"

Yes, those indeed were the days when the guardians of the blackout were men of direct action. A strange nervousness comes over a person when he is thrust into the stygian blackness of a moonless night full of strange noises he has been too busy to hear, strange shapes and shadows he has always heretofore dissipated with electricity, and strange new fears concerning the freight that may be borne on the formerly friendly waters crunching at the coral beach. There was not in those times any legalistic inhibition about trespassing on another man's estate, or getting a writ of entry. All one needed was a temporary authorization from someone who looked as though he had authority, a shooting iron, and a finger to pull a trigger.

Why there was not a heavier mortality among civilians in those first evenings is a mystery that can be explained only by poor marksmanship and scarcity of game on the streets. A shadow moving by a hibiscus hedge, a wavering palm frond, a glint of light on the polished globe of a street lamp were adequate signal for challenge. A staggering percentage of the street lamps in Manoa Valley were blown to splinters in the first two weeks of the war—and because many of them have not had their wires warmed by current since the thing started, they have only recently been replaced.

I was in on a few of those early patrols, but I was, alas, armed only with a sawed-off length of broom handle. Surprisingly, that weapon gave me a tremendous amount of confidence. As I walked along half expecting a parachuting Japanese to land like a cat beside me, or creep like a weasel from the black shadow of a tree, I swished the thing back and forth and felt periodically as brave as a tiger. Surely there has never been a more ludicrous or symbolic spectacle than that of a dozen University professors "guarding" the campus at strategic points through those frightful long nights when nobody knew when or in what shape the enemy would strike—and we armed only with broomsticks. There would have been something ludicrous in the spectacle if anyone could have seen it—a dozen Don Quixotes going out to look for parachuting windmills.

Another aspect of it, however, was heartening and on the whole creditable to the men who were by tradition remote from acts of physical bravery. That was the readiness with which they did what they were told had to be done, not in a sheep-like obedience, but quietly and courageously. For it took courage of a sort to go out into the black alone and stand for long hours waiting, waiting for anything, armed with a wisp of wood and knowing that if anyone jumped you there would be time for only one good long screech of warning before the trained fingers of the enemy would throttle you!

That situation was repeated all over Honolulu, however. Men went out quivering with nerves, jumpy with uncertain fears of unknown things—armed with golf clubs, old hoe handles, and in one case that I heard of with a "plumber's friend" that had a nice heft to it. They actually risked their lives, because there were abroad in the land not parachutists but infinitely more dangerous amateurs with firearms. Doctors, preachers, salesmen, teachers, musicians, gardeners, storekeepers—they went out into the dark unarmed and afraid—but they went.

It was from that motley crew of gentle-men that the wardens organization was recruited. It is no wonder that they are so slow to violent action and so amenable to the reasoning of a psychologically alert mind. It is no wonder that they shunned parades and, practically alone of all wartime organizations in Honolulu, did not succumb to the lure of a uniform. They were a fine, brave bunch of fellows who may have been afraid of the dark and its denizens, but who faced it and did what had to be done if the need presented itself. They were the salt of the earth, and I am humbly proud to have been one of them.

Victory

❖ Word of the impending Japanese surrender reached Hawaii shortly after three o'clock in the morning. Hickam Field went wild with joy, with men racing through barracks awakening those who still slept and telephoning the news to their civilian friends in Honolulu. Radios were switched on and telephones jingled in thousands of homes, and friends exchanged the incredible morsels of information. Like the rest of the world, Hawaii was tense with suspense during the days that followed. Pearl Harbor's spectacular celebration occurred on August 13, when the surrender news was confirmed.

On Victory Day, when President Truman's announcement was made that the surrender terms had been accepted, it was about 1:30, Hawaii time. Deliriously happy service men swarmed through downtown Honolulu and Waikiki, making so much noise with shouts and tootings of auto horns that the terrifyingly loud air raid sirens announcing the event actually could not be heard. Although the demonstration was the most hectic one Honolulu had ever seen, it was without unfortunate incidents of violence.

Hawaii, which was affected by the war more than any other area in the country, could scarcely comprehend at first the far-reaching implications of the event, as far as life in this community is concerned. The first dazed reaction was simply one of joy that the countless thousands of men in uniform who have swarmed through these ports would no longer be facing death in battle, nor suffer much longer the anguish of homesickness.

Swiftly moving events of the days that followed gradually brought home the glorious reality of the end of war as practically all the restrictions that had so altered life in Hawaii were lifted. The army acted promptly, removing all the controls that were still left from the days of complete military rule. The waterfront area, which most civilians had not seen since December 7, 1941, was no longer a restricted

---

First published September 1945.

271

area, and action was begun to remove the camouflage from Aloha Tower and to repair the long-stilled clock. Announcements of ships' sailings were resumed, sailings and departures took on their almost forgotten atmosphere of gaity, and kamaainas wallowed in sentimental recollections of the days before the war.

Hawaii shared with the rest of the country the lifting of federal restrictions such as gas rationing and manpower control, but unlike the rest of the country reveled in many other restored freedoms. Liquor was no longer rationed and bars no longer were limited to the hours from noon to 7 P.M.

Honest-to-goodness "night life" seemed to be incredibly imminent. Memories of mass fingerprinting and registration, mass immunization, restricted areas, blackout, curfew, and censorship suddenly were only nightmarish memories.

Apart from the pleasure of newly restored freedom, thoughtful residents of Hawaii were aware of the many problems that face these war-battered islands. Practically every road and building needs repair or complete reconstruction; the traffic and parking situation will need a wizard's wand; and housing continues to be a dilemma. The exciting months to come will prove whether or not the post-war planning of various groups will be coordinated into an intelligent procedure and whether or not the civic and industrial leaders of the community have the wisdom and ability that are so sorely needed, if Hawaii is to assume her potential position as the "capital" of the Pacific.

New Jobs for Lei Sellers

THELMA LEONARD, CONSTRUCTION SERVICE, AND LT. RUSSELL GORDON, AUS

❖ The lei sellers, once—and no doubt soon to be again—the first attraction to meet the tourist's eye as he stepped ashore in Honolulu, have a new temporary job. It's their second new job since the war dressed Hawaii's visitors in uniforms. The first job, once of vital importance to the war effort, was the making of garland strips to camouflage Hawaii's installations from enemy airmen.

It was a happy choice because thorough knowledge of colors and strong, nimble fingers to weave the deceptive patterns were required. It also permitted the lei sellers to work together. Or better, to sing together, because blending their own soft voices is as important to them as blending their colors. When camouflage was no longer needed, it appeared that the "cotton pickers" would be disbanded to seek other employment. Their first loyalty was to the war effort, of course, but the leisurely, "Islandish" manner of their working seemed doomed to assume the prosaic seriousness of typical factory labor.

Then someone, somewhere, suggested making furniture. Tons of burlap no longer required for garlands were available. The "girls" had learned to blend dyes. They could sew. They could handle hammer, saw, plane, sandpaper, and varnish; they could easily handle the large chairs and settees.

So, at their same location, Cam 1.2 . . . near Ala Moana Road . . . the sheds of the old camouflage plant were turned into a furniture shop, with Harry G. Good as superintendent. From shaping the lumber to the finished product in its gay Hawaiian flower designs, all the work is done by one hundred women. Settees, arm-chairs, ottomans, drapes . . . all the furnishings that can convert a Quonset hut into a home for nurses or Red Cross workers, or a day room for enlisted men, are designed and built by the lei sellers themselves and shipped throughout the Pacific.

First published September 1945.

273

One order alone for a distant base comprised more than a thousand pieces. None of the materials required for the work is of critical priority. Discarded burlap and target cloth are used in making drapes and upholstery. Kapok from obsolete life preservers and the stuffing of old mattresses fill the cushions. Plaited rope replaces steel springs. Short lengths of lumber, unsuited to building purposes, supply the wood requirements.

Probably no group of workers since the days of the Menehunes, legendary builders of fishponds throughout the Islands, ever made less "work" out of their work. Singing and joking and teasing . . . maybe a bit of gossiping . . . go on continuously. On Saturdays and during the summer vacation, the kids come to "help Aunty." Many of the women have planted flower gardens in tiny plots behind the sheds. Everyone brings her own lunch and mealtime resembles a party.

This complete lack of restraint has never resulted in what is politely referred to as a "labor problem." Utter lack of disciplinary control has never been abused by the workers, and the factory could well be used as a sample of complete accord between labor and control.

According to Mr. Good and H. Hormann, his assistant, not all of the women will return to their flowers now that the war is over. Many of the women, having learned the trade of furniture making, will form the nucleus of a new industry for Hawaii. But, as one observes the lei sellers weaving and blending wood and cloth into attractive tropical furniture, the impression is received that the singing women imagine they are still sewing long strips of flowers into the famous leis of the Islands.

Horse Racing Returns to Hawaii

CAROLINE WRIGHT

❖ "They're off!" The old familiar race-track shout was a real treat to war-time Honolulu as the bangtails returned to the Kailua Race Track on July 1st at the Oahu Jockey Club Summer Meet. Several thousand G.I.s saw for the first time Oahu's top thoroughbreds running it off on the fast five-furlong track . . . exclaimed at the beautiful setting of mountains and palm trees . . . beefed about the two-dollar admission charge. The Oahu Jockey Club promptly lowered the charge for service men to one dollar and, along with Hawaii's other race fans, they've been coming back every Sunday to enjoy the ten-week meet.

Yank magazine characteristically dubbed it the Pineapple Derby. Many of the G.I. Joes and Janes probably were not aware that horse racing in the Hawaiian Islands has a rich tradition dating back to nearly forty years ago. At that time the Parker Ranch, one of the world's largest . . . located on the Island of Hawaii, began importing horses from the finest mainland and English racing lines to develop the thoroughbred breed in Hawaii. As a result, the thoroughbreds racing today in Hawaii are of the same top bloodlines as the prize horses in the United States and England. Vying for honors at the Kailua Track are many sons and daughters of Ormesby (by Sir Galahad III), Overall (by Peter Pan), Onomea (by Rogers by Sweep), Skymore (by Moonraker by Broomstick), and countless other descendants of racing aristocracy.

For the past twenty years Hawaii's thoroughbreds have been racing on Island tracks. Racing was brought officially to Oahu in 1939, when the Oahu Jockey Club incorporated and built the Kailua Race Track. The opening meet and all pre-war meets saw horses from the other islands competing with Oahu's best. Due to war-time conditions,

---

First published September 1945.

275

it was impossible to have inter-island competition for the opening Summer Meet this year . . . but the Spring Meet, scheduled to start next February, should see many outside Island favorites competing with Oahu's top thoroughbreds.

Two strings of Island race horses have already been taken to the mainland for racing, and some of the best performers of the present meet are more than entitled to make a bid for mainland fame. Manuel Freitas' prize six-year-old sorrel stud, Hapa Haole, has yet to be beaten in his racing career. As a two-year-old, Hapa Haole won four races at Kailua and has so far remained unbeaten in racing at the Windward-Oahu track. Hapa Haole's sire is the fine stud Onomea (by Rogers by Sweep). His dam is Francis D. who, as a two-year-old, won more than seven thousand dollars on mainland tracks before being brought to Hawaii.

Dr. A. G. Schnack's beautiful bay stud, Infinour (by Infinite out of Dark Hour), is definitely a horse to watch . . . along with Manuel Ventura's fast grey Herodiones gelding, Lepo, and Manuel Freitas' bay gelding, Akia. Both Akia and Lepo have chalked up new track records in the present meet . . . Akia running the six furlongs in 1:15 1/5 and Lepo racing the five furlongs in 1:02 1/5.

Among the newcomers to be watched in coming race meets are Race Chairman Marshall Wright's Lakana, a fast six-year-old by gelding by Overall out of Ookala. Lakana is a full brother to Nimu, recently taken to the mainland for racing by T. D. Collins, with Johnnie Carroll as trainer. Awala, a fast Ormesby gelding owned by George Moniz, was entered late in the race meet, but should be a real threat in the coming Spring Meet. These are only two of almost twenty thoroughbreds who ran for the first time this season and have shown real promise.

One thing, however, will be missing from the Spring Race Meet . . . watermelons! The entire inside area of the track this year was a huge field of watermelons that race fans hungrily watched ripen as the meet progressed. Temptation was great as each Sunday the melons grew larger and juicier. The Jockey Club officials were considerably relieved when they (the melons) finally ripened and were whisked away to Honolulu markets.

No Hawaiian race story would be complete without mentioning Tommy Kaneshiro, the 34-year-old jockey from the Big Island who was named the Star of the Week after his ten straight wins in the beginning of the race season. Kaneshiro has been riding on Hawaii and Maui tracks for many years, but this is his first season at the Kailua track, and it's a real treat to watch his skillful riding.

The Oahu Jockey Club is looking forward to the time when there'll be a mile track at Kailua, covered bleachers, a jockey and clubhouse, and really big-time racing for Hawaii's kamaainas and malihinis to enjoy.

The Territory's Schools
Did Their Share

❖ With the coming of victory, the Commissioners of Public Instruction have reviewed with pride the important part played by teachers, principals, and pupils in the historic days since December 7, 1941.

Before sunset of that eventful day, trucks rolled up to the doors of school buildings and unloaded great numbers of frightened women and children. Teachers, principals, and cafeteria managers were already setting up Army cots, preparing food, and taking care of small children and babies. Night came and with it "a darkness that may be felt," for which no person was prepared, no building equipped. Stifling curtains were hastily arranged to cover windows of rooms in which some light was indispensable. The school staff stayed on to patrol the halls in the darkness; some slept on the floor or benches in the cafeteria; some served food to troops or workmen who materialized from nowhere and required food.

For days thereafter, members of the school staffs worked on in many schools, scrubbing floors, cleaning rest rooms, making beds, cooking and serving meals, and washing dishes. The needs of many people were being met. The first selective service registration was entrusted almost entirely to school personnel and also the finger printing and registration, and the housing survey. These huge tasks, covering the Territory, were done almost entirely by teachers and principals.

Schools remained closed for almost three months. When they reopened, 876 school units had been taken over for military use. Teachers met their pupils in shops, basements, private homes, and language schools—anywhere that space could be found. Air raid drills were instituted; small children were shown how to use the gas masks they constantly carried. Instructions were given as to what to do in case of an air attack. Teachers huddled with frightened children in open, muddy, slit trenches.

First published October 1945.

The student-work program—a major contribution to the war effort—was instituted. Teachers regularly accompanied pupils to the pineapple and cane fields. The effort expended was great and the adjustments difficult, but no one complained that it was unbearable. Teachers who maintained their own homes first suffered from the shortage of help and then had to adjust themselves to the complete disappearance of full-time or part-time household assistance. Marketing, made difficult by shortages, was further complicated by gasoline rationing.

With the construction of air raid shelters, playground space almost wholly disappeared. Programs of recreation at school and during out-of-school hours were dropped to a minimum. There were no holidays; work went on steadily, week after week, year after year. Life was geared to a tense pace; time for relaxation was almost unheard of. During summer vacations, teachers worked in stores, canneries, and in various industrial establishments. Help was needed, and the large percentage of the teachers accepted the responsibility of doing what they could.

Teachers, school secretaries, and principals willingly shared the accounting and collecting responsibilities entailed by the school sales of war bonds and stamps. These responsibilities were large; Hawaii's schools made an outstanding record in comparison with mainland states. Teachers and principles shared in the responsibility of supervising and directing the Red Cross activities of children from the sixth grade up.

The tensions were eventually relaxed, and the strictest war-time regulations were modified. From the point of view of permitting normal home life, the gradual relaxation of the blackout was of the greatest help.

Now that the war is over, the Commissioners of Public Instruction and the staff of the Central Office have expressed their gratitude and appreciation to every principal, teacher, secretary, cafeteria worker, and janitor who experienced the tense war years and who met so magnificently the difficulties, problems, and responsibilities of those years.

In addition to the new and heavy war-time responsibilities, they carried on during this trying period an effective program of instruction for the children of Hawaii, giving them guidance and a sense of freedom from fear, tension, and uncertainty. All this has been done in a spirit and with a competence that can never be forgotten.

Red Cross "Re-Cap"

MARJORIE G. SULLIVAN

❖ Hawaii has the only Red Cross Chapter that was under fire in World War II. Perhaps that accounts, in part, for the sustained interest and remarkable accomplishments of its volunteers. They know how it feels to have an enemy at the door, the anxiety of wondering if he will return tonight, or next week, or ever. The Hawaii Chapter went into action on December 7, 1941, along with the Army and Navy. Motor Corps was on the road immediately. Even though complete organization of few other corps had been effected, women turned out in droves to make surgical dressings, to sew, to knit, to prepare and serve food, to assist in hospitals—anything to help dispel the confusion and bring relief to the suffering.

Before the war, Volunteer Special Services headquarters, sewing and surgical dressings work rooms were in Castle Kindergarten. On December seventh they moved to private residences, and Motor Corps replaced them. Temporary headquarters were established in the Dillingham Building until February 1942 when the Honolulu Academy of Arts consented to the use of its Oriental Court, an ideal place that has housed the Chapter ever since.

For a year prior to war, the Chapter had been storing, in widely separated sections on all islands, reserve supplies—knitting, surgical dressings, and sewn hospital articles, in case the storm gathering in the Pacific did not "blow over." December seventh justified the precautions.

The expansion of Surgical Dressings is amazing. Production of dressings for 1942 was 1,607,080. In the past sixteen months it has made 15,264,429. June 1945 showed the largest number of dressings issued in a single month: 1,153,979. An interesting feature of this department is the making and packing of dressings for the Penicillin Laboratory at Pearl Harbor.

First published October 1945.

The Sewing Department switched from refugee garments to orders for federal and civilian hospitals. In 1942 thousands of bunny gas masks for infants were cut, and in 1943 a variety of articles for the emergency polio hospital was made, many completed in twenty-four hours. The most difficult order was for hundreds of Army surgical tent nets, sixteen-feet square, with pitched muslin roofs and two openings. Each net required four days of work by four women. Since March 1944, this department has completed 135,274 items.

December seventh exhausted the chapter's knitting supply. Undaunted, knitters set to work, completing in 1942 a total of 39,881 garments. A great many sweaters, socks, gloves, et cetera, have been issued, especially to the Navy, with the recent addition of afghans made by combining mufflers of harmonizing colors stitched with contrasting bright yarn. These are popular in hospitals and hospital ships.

Motor Corps was fully trained on Oahu and Kauai long before the war. Late in 1941, with trouble apparently in the offing, additional training was given—more first aid (with emphasis on emergency delivery of babies), military drill, gas and chemical warfare, and blackout driving. From the blitz until June 1943, Motor Corps headquarters kept open twenty-four hours a day, seven days a week. At first much of the night work was transporting pregnant women to hospitals—and corps members were glad of the training in delivery. In addition to transportation, Motor Corps operates an important library service that sends reading material to service units all over the Pacific. Motor Corps hours from December 1941 to August 1945 were 116,605¼.

Canteen had its practical experience before training. Service began six months before war with picnics for convalescents and visiting "Aussies." Quite a contrast to the grim days after the blitz when it did twenty-four-hour duty feeding diverse people, from tired truck drivers to frantic women with small children. Canteen has rocketed to the establishment of three major canteens on Oahu, where "Country Lunches" are served to convalescents nearly every day, assistance at the Royal Surf Canteen, two air strip units that work regular shifts seven days a week, and daily duty at the Blood Bank. Hours increased from 5,000 in the first war year to 82,316 in the last. During the past fiscal year, 754,361 men were served in the Territory.

The adage "precious things come in small packages" applies to the Oahu Staff Assistant Corps of only three members. The two original staff assistants have earned the epithet used by a southern Negro to describe a versatile individual—"de all-roundest pusson." Their daily duties run the gamut from receptionist to minor stevedoring. Surely no other staff assistants have done such a variety of chores. The third member conducts daily shopping for hospitalized service men—interesting, but the mere thought makes one's feet hurt. Approximately six thousand errands were completed since May 1944—everything from black underwear for the girl friend to uniforms for the men. In 1943 the other islands inaugurated staff assistants who also tackle any and everything.

The first Nurse's Aides began work in April 1942. Since then sixteen classes have been graduated, 232 aides. Except for those on Maui, Nurse's Aides worked only in civilian hospitals until March 1945, when their services were requested for the 147th Army General Hospital. The importance of this corps in wartime Hawaii can scarcely be overestimated. The shortage of nurses is one of the Territory's most serious problems, and the Nurse's Aides' devotion to a tiring unglamorous job has been one of the outstanding contributions of the war. Their total hours were 66,207.

In April 1942, twenty-eight women formed the nucleus of the Hospital and Recreation Corps, which now numbers 356 "Gray Ladies" who have given 142,689 hours to federal hospitals. The value of this service in helping rebuild sick and wounded men cannot be exaggerated.

Three new corps were formed during 1944—Home Service, Air Force Cottage, and Dietitian's Aides. The first two gave excellent service, but, due to circumstances, were dissolved within the year. It is hoped that Home Service will be reorganized.

Fifteen Dietitian's Aides work in four civilian hospitals, assisting with tray service, special diets, et cetera. In a time of labor shortage, these volunteers have been of much help to overworked dietitians.

A vote of thanks is due the women who have coped with the problems of uniforms, a prosaic job with plenty of "headaches," which have been most efficiently handled.

In so short a resume, it is impossible to do justice to the efforts of several thousand volunteer women for almost four years. No one group can be singled out as being superior to another. All corps of Volunteer Special Services have marched in straight "company front," shoulder to shoulder, grateful for the chance to serve. Although the war is over, Red Cross work will continue.

The "Society Cops"

❖ In June 1939, Maj. Douglas King of Honolulu returned to his former home in England, hoping to be taken back into the British Army,
but was rejected as being over the age limit. He returned to Hawaii
and in May 1941, offered his services to his adopted country and was
appointed a "dollar-a-year man" with the Honolulu Police Department
in command of the Provisional Police. The Provisional Police consisted
of twenty-five-hundred-odd men who had been recruited and trained
by Mr. T. G. S. Walker. Generals Herron and Short thought these men
could be used in an emergency throughout Oahu as guards. Major
King doubted this because most of the men were key men from the
utility companies, large business houses, the plantations, etc., and as
it turned out afterwards, he was right. He conceived the idea, in conjunction with Chief of Police W. A. Gabrielson, of forming a Police
Reserve of Honolulu businessmen to serve with the Honolulu Police
Department in an emergency.

On July 28, 1941, 124 selected men from all walks of life started
training, and when the emergency arose on December 7, 1941, they
were ready and went on duty and have been on the job ever since. Each
man does at least one daily tour of duty every week from 4:00 P.M. to
11:00 P.M. and an additional tour of duty every sixth Sunday, so that
a team of at least thirty Reserve Officers is on duty in their own cars
as motor patrolmen seven days a week. They receive no pay and provide their own uniforms. The Department provides their equipment
and insures their cars, but not the men themselves.

All Reserve Officers receive nine weeks of training before going out
on the beat by themselves. After their training they are commissioned
as full-time Police Officers and have the same powers as Officers of
the Regular Force.

There have been 416 men commissioned in the Reserve since its
inception in 1941. The present strength is 187. The majority of the
men are haoles, but there are Hawaiians, Chinese, and Americans of

---

First published October 1945.

283

Japanese ancestry. Their ages range from twenty-five to fifty-five and, with the exception of the first class who were asked to join, all others have volunteered their services. Many officers who have left the Reserves have joined the armed forces or left the Territory; pressure of business has caused other resignations.

Major King is in charge and has a Regular Police Commission as Assistant Chief of Police. He is very ably assisted by Lt. Leon M. Straus and Sgt. Robert Kennedy, officers of the regular department, and his indispensable secretary, Mrs. Pang, known to all ranks as Bessie and to whose hard work and tact a great deal of the efficiency of the Honolulu Police Reserve is due.

Several large cities on the mainland have tried to form Police Reserves, but with little success, so Honolulu has every reason to be proud and grateful to a body of men, who have served since December 7, and are still serving, and who receive more "kicks" than thanks.

The Statistical Department's reports show that although the Reserve Division only works on one of the three watches each day, in 1942 they handled 12 percent of all cases handled by the entire department; in 1943, 19 percent of all cases; and for the first nine months of 1944, 17 percent.

Hawaii's Organized
Defense Volunteers

❖ The primary factor that influenced the formation of the Organized Defense Volunteers was the threat of attack during the uncertain months following December 1941. Several groups had organized prior to that time. They were called "Emergency Guard" and "Provisional Police." But during the early months of 1942, civic and business leaders throughout the territory began organizing defense groups on a large scale. They asked for Army sponsorship, so that they could be provided with weapons and be allowed to train with Army units stationed on the islands.

Oral approval for the formation of civilian-military volunteer defense forces was given on January 21, 1942, by the Military Governor and the Commanding General of the Hawaiian Department, Lt. Gen. Delos C. Emmons. Written orders followed, from time to time, authorizing units on the various islands. Terms of enlistment provided that volunteers would be ordered to duty as part of the armed forces of the United States only in case of an actual or impending invasion.

Strength of the volunteer units during 1942 is not accurately known. Reports were intermittent and rosters were changing constantly. However, officers familiar with the situation at the time estimated a total strength of twenty thousand (August 1942). Though these men were not highly trained, their morale was excellent, they were amenable to discipline, and they knew the terrain intimately. District commanders, particularly on the outlying islands, regarded the volunteer units as very important auxiliary forces.

As the hectic days of 1942 passed, decreased pressure on Army personnel resulted in better organization of volunteer forces. Physical examinations and oaths of enlistment were required; rosters were submitted regularly; and directives clarified details on supply, training, uniforms, and insignia. Volunteer ranks became more stabilized,

---

First published October 1945.

285

too, as many who joined in the first flurry of excitement dropped out because of increased civilian responsibilities, while others were eliminated for physical disabilities. However, many who left the ranks were placed on a reserve status. At that time, the Volunteers numbered approximately ten thousand and enrollment remained at approximately that level until termination of military control on July 4, 1945.

All Volunteers trained without pay, purchased their own uniforms, and gave freely of their spare time. Many came great distances to receive training, and a considerable number were without weapons until late in 1942. Their spirit and desire to learn were excellent.

Most officers commissioned in volunteer units had previous military training in the regular Army, the National Guard, Reserve Officers Training Corps, or Territorial Guard. Many of the noncommissioned offices of these units had prior training, too. The Army assigned officers as inspector-instructors to each regiment, many on a full-time basis.

All units were encouraged to participate in Army maneuvers and were offered the opportunity to go through the regular course (at Army expense) at the Unit Jungle Training Center (later designated as the Pacific Combat Training Center, operated by Central Pacific Base Command on Windward Oahu).

At a meeting on Oahu on 17–18 January 1945, all ODV unit commanders met with Lt. Gen. R. C. Richardson, Jr., and Maj. Gen. H. T. Burgin to discuss volunteer affairs. It was decided the need for the Volunteers had not yet passed. The Army encouraged volunteer effort by providing additional equipment for training purposes. Inter-regimental shooting matches were conceived, and this tourney served to stimulate volunteer activity throughout the territory.

With the cessation of combat activity in the European Theatre of Operations, and the progress of the war in the Pacific, Organized Defense Volunteers were released from Army control effective July 4, 1945. Appropriate ceremonies were held by all regiments, and individual service ribbons, individual Meritorious Service ribbons, and records of service (honorable discharge certificates) were awarded.

There is no doubt but what the Organized Defense Volunteers served a valuable purpose in the territory: In an emergency, they would have been of great value in augmenting military forces. The added strength of volunteer forces, almost twenty thousand in 1942, enabled the Army to send more troops to forward areas.

First Regiment Oahu Volunteer Infantry

Groups of business and civic leaders in the north sector of Oahu, appreciating the possibilities of attack and the need for local defense measures, organized other residents into groups for this purpose.

These units were originally known as "Hawaii Scouts" in honor of the Philippine Scouts who fought so nobly at Bataan. They were organized into three battalions totaling seventeen hundred members as of June 1942, in Waialua, Kahuku, and Wahiawa. On September 30, 1942, the separate battalions were given regimental status under the name of First Regiment Hawaii Scouts, the name being changed to Oahu Volunteer Infantry in January 1944, in response to a request from a majority of the regiment's component units.

Their designated mission was to assist the armed forces against attack, control subversive activity, and to perform any special missions necessitated by the military situation.

Missions assigned in April 1944 indicate the scope of training under the Provost Marshal: assist in the immobilization of persons designated by the Commanding General Central Pacific Base Command; Guard vital installations; assist in evacuating civilians from dangerous areas; assist in traffic control during evacuation; assist in execution of scorched earth plan; assist in all matters of local security.

Commanding Officers as of July 4, 1945, were: Col. Leo B. Rodby, Lt. Col. John H. Midkiff, Lt. Col. James N. Orrick, and Lt. Col. A. T. Longley.

Second Regiment Oahu Volunteer Infantry

Several units eventually comprising this regiment were formed in 1941 as provisional police companies. One unit of 123 men at Waimanalo went on guard duty at noon December 7, 1941, and served three days. Eighty-three of those relieved were then used as labor troops at Bellows Field, where they served for seven days more. Another group of 200 or more at Aiea, performed various duties from December 7 until January 31.

The separate battalions and companies making up this regiment were organized early in 1942. Public spirited citizens devoted considerable effort to these volunteer groups, and the plantation and sugar companies cooperated generously. Volunteer units were set up in accordance with geographic considerations so that most large communities in the south sector of Oahu had Volunteers for an emergency. They were divided into three general sectors: the Ewa, and Aiea, and the Waimanalo-Kaneohe sectors. From those areas were organized the "Oahu Scouts." Their strength, in August 1942, was approximately fifteen hundred. Various infantry units trained the Oahu Scouts until they were placed under the Provost Marshal in January 1944. At that time they were designated as Oahu Volunteer Infantry.

The units in the various sectors received instruction from cadres provided by regular Army units stationed in their sectors. The Twenty-fifth, Twenty-seventh, and Sixth Infantry Divisions were particularly active in this respect, and the Volunteers took advantage of many opportunities to participate in field problems, night maneuvers, and alerts.

Commanding Officers as of July 4, 1945, were: Col. Richard Penhallow, Lt. Col. Burt Bacon, Lt. Col. G. W. Groves, and Lt. Col. W. R. Dow.

Businessmen's Military Training Corps

Early in January 1942, Earl D. Bourland and twenty-two other patriotic civic leaders met in Honolulu to plan a volunteer defense organization of civilians living in the populous southeastern section of Oahu. Within a fortnight approximately fifteen hundred men had enrolled in the seventeen companies activated south of the Koolau Range between Makapuu Head and Pearl Harbor. Official approval for the regiment's activation was dated January 21, 1942. Four battalions represented the districts of Kaimuki, Manoa Valley-Waikiki, Nuuanu Valley, and Kalihi Valley. The regiment was placed under the Provost Marshal for training and employment.

BMTC ranks included executives, engineers, technicians, bankers, salesmen, carpenters, janitors, students—men of varied ages and occupations. As evidence of their sincerity of purpose, many executives who were unable to assume BMTC positions of responsibility because of the pressure of other business performed a private's duties. Final organization comprised a Regimental Staff and Headquarters Company, the First and Second Battalions.

During February and March of 1942, particular emphasis was placed on Pistol Marksmanship & Training. Almost two-thirds of the men had previous training, and the various units made rapid strides during the thirty hours per month devoted to this instruction. From April 1942 to May 1944, the regiment averaged about fifteen hours per month and this was coordinated by the regiment for all units.

The mission of the regiment was: immobilization of enemy aliens in Honolulu and environs; providing security and secondary defense for beach positions; acting as secondary troops for the Army; aiding the Provost Marshal in traffic control and riot duty; and guarding evacuation boundary lines and clearing the city.

Much of the early training was in the hands of officers of the Twenty-fifth, Twenty-seventh, and Seventh Infantry Divisions. Instruction was given in methods of resisting enemy landings and paratroop attacks. One unique feature of BMTC was the "Boot" school conducted by Edgar Rice Burroughs of Tarzan fame. From February until October 1942, "recruits" were trained for service with their companies.

This unit was alerted during the Battle of Midway and maintained continuous guard for three days. BMTC was called to duty again in July and August of 1942. In October 1943, it was assigned the guarding of a number of vital installations. Guards were posted nightly, performing this duty until July 9, 1944. In fulfillment of their mission to guard against possible internal disorders, the BMTC maintained an elaborate chart of their section of the city on which was recorded the density of races that might be hostile.

Commanding Officers as of July 4, 1945, were: Col. Willard L. Doering, Lt. Col. James D. Smith, Lt. Col. Alfred B. Henderson, and Lt. Col. Hugh W. Brodie.

Hawaii Defense Volunteers

Four months after Pearl Harbor, a group of Honolulu businessmen, comprising the various elements of Hawaii's mixed population, suggested formation of a volunteer unit to include the predominant loyal races. It was agreed that such a group would be valuable in handling a large part of the local population in an emergency, being on a common basis of understanding, language, and background, and that this group could readily differentiate between friend and foe.

Operating directly under the Provost Marshal, the HDV met for their first training in May 1942. They were 150-strong, predominantly Chinese, but including many of Filipino, Hawaiian, haole, and Puerto

Rican extraction. They soon reached battalion strength and were organized into four infantry companies, a headquarters company, and a medical unit. Dr. Min Hin Li was battalion commander, but he was replaced by Richard C. Tongg in December 1942. In November 1943, the battalion had grown to eight hundred men and was given regimental status.

Inasmuch as the HDV's sphere of operation was Honolulu, their training, in addition to basic subjects, emphasized guard duty, riot drill, street fighting, and similar subjects. They participated in OCD drills, practice air raid alerts, night maneuvers, and field exercises. Training and administration were under supervision of the Provost Marshal. After one year of training, HDV asked for actual duty and were promptly used as guards at vital installations, such as public utilities, engineer base yards, quartermaster areas, finance offices, and OMG installations; they relieved military personnel from those duties at night for ten consecutive months. HDV, in 1944–1945, actively recruited boys of sixteen to eighteen years with the purpose of giving them pre-induction training.

Commanding Officers as of July 4, 1945, were: Col. Richard C. Tongg, Lt. Col. Frank Wong, Maj. James Leong, and Maj. Young P. Kang.

Women's Army Volunteer Corps

The WAVC was a non-combatant component of the Organized Defense Forces. It was organized for service with the Army of the United States to make available the skill and special training of women in the territory and for the purpose of releasing, in an emergency, Army personnel capable of active military service.

Actual experience with volunteer workers during the occupation of Shanghai by the Japanese in 1937 caused Marjorie S. Holwill (now Mrs. George A. Breffeilh) to recognize the value of augmenting the service forces with non-combatant volunteers among working girls. With the approval of Lt. Gen. Delos C. Emmons, then military governor of Hawaii, Mrs. Breffeilh organized a group of twenty-six girls employed within the Office of the Military Governor. Basic training was begun on August 3, 1942. A WAVC unit was organized from women employed by the United States Engineering Department then at Punahou School. Total WAVC strength at the end of 1942 was 394.

Basic training, consisting of close-order drill, physical exercise, and military courtesy, started on August 3, 1942. All WAVCs took six weeks of this initial training. One-and-one-half-hour training periods were held thrice weekly. After initial training, the following subjects were covered: first aid, defense against chemical attack, stripping and assembly of weapons, operation of telephone switchboards and other signal communications, message center operation, elementary motor maintenance, traffic and evacuation, canteen and commissary service, and military correspondence. Officer classes were conducted on training, administration, and leadership.

The WAVCs assisted the public in filing income tax returns, assisted the OPA house to house educational campaign, furnished girls to help the OPA gasoline ration board, performed numerous emergency secretarial jobs for various governmental agencies, drove buses transporting Army personnel to recreation areas, and furnished details to the 147th General Hospital to help entertain patients.

Officers as of July 4, 1945, were: Marjorie S. Breffeilh, Gayle B. Gree, Kaaha O. Medeiros, Rachel L. Yap, Agnes S. Freitas, and Anne W. Kum.

First Regiment Hawaii Rifles

A group of citizens met at the Hilo Boarding School in February 1942 and agreed to form a company of volunteers to be known as Hawaii Rifles. A group of two hundred Hilo businessmen had already signified their desire to join such a group. Their first drill was on February 22. The men had purchased their own uniforms, and equipment was borrowed from the Territorial Guard.

Upon approval of volunteer organizations by the Hawaiian Department, plantations and several ranches in the Hilo and Puna areas (east side of the island) formed units. Their mission was defined as anti-sabotage, guides for troops, and action against the enemy when so ordered. As of March 31, 1945, actual strength was 91 officers, one warrant officer, and 1,632 enlisted men. On October 19, 1942, this unit was designated First Regiment Hawaii Rifles, with Col. Andrew T. Spalding commanding. Colonel Spalding had formerly commanded the 299th Infantry, Hawaiian National Guard.

As the Volunteers acquired the rudiments of basic training, they were able to participate in field problems with infantry units (elements of the Twenty-seventh, Fortieth, and Thirty-third Divisions) stationed on Hawaii. They were soon familiar with combat principles. On one occasion, Lieutenant Colonel Becker led his First Battalion on a night march over terrain usually considered impassable. The battalion marched twenty-nine miles and did not lose a man. At other times, units of the First Regiment patrolled twenty-two miles of coastline. Many units received Ranger Combat instruction.

That the men rapidly acquired close-order proficiency was evidenced at early parades and reviews. Their marksmanship was later proved by the Inter-regimental Shooting Competition completed in May 1945, when First Hawaii Rifles won undisputed first place with victories in thirty of thirty-six matches.

Commanding officers as of July 4, 1945, were: Col. Andrew T. Spalding, Lt. Col. George D. Becker, Lt. Col. Gilbert Hay, and Lt. Col. J. S. Beatty.

Second Regiment Hawaii Rifles

J. Scott B. Pratt, who later commanded the Second Regiment, formulated a plan for volunteer defense of the Kohala (northwest) side of Hawaii. He submitted the plan to the Army District Commander, Lt. Col. Victor S. Burton, who promised cooperation. Mr. Pratt immediately began organization of the "Kohala Battalion," which held its first drill February 15, 1942. Upon approval of defense units by the Hawaiian Department, additional companies, one mounted, were formed in the Kohala and Kona (west central) areas.

Actual strength as of March 31, 1945, was 74 officers, one warrant officer, and 1,239 enlisted men. Assigned missions were anti-sabotage, guides for troops, and action against the enemy when so ordered. On October 19, 1942, this unit was designated Second Regiment Hawaii Rifles, with Col. J. Scott B. Pratt commanding.

This regiment participated in field maneuvers with elements of the Twenty-seventh, Fortieth, and Thirty-third Infantry Divisions. Colonel Pratt asserted his regiment could be mobilized in one hour or less, due to completeness of organization and communications. A mounted unit, formed by Mr. Ronald K. von Holt, was included in the First Battalion.

They were about one-hundred-strong and were trained as combat troops as well as mounted scouts. This unit devised unique communications in case mechanical equipment failed.

Commanding Officers as of July 4, 1945, were: Col. J. Scott B. Pratt, Lt. Col. Ronald K. von Holt, Lt. Col. Laurence S. McLane, and Lt. Col. Roy Wall.

First Regiment Maui Volunteers

Col. Charles B. Lyman, Maui-Molokai-Lanai District Commander at the time, called a meeting of sugar and pineapple plantation managers on February 14, 1942, to discuss the formation of volunteer groups to aid in defense of these islands. The discussion revealed enthusiasm for volunteer defense units. Formal authorization for their organization was given on March 2 by Lt. Gen. Delos C. Emmons, at that time Commanding General, Hawaiian Department. Elwell P. Lydgate, Maui Pineapple Company, was asked to organize the Maui Volunteers.

Within the next few months, Colonel Lydgate, with the aid of other Maui citizens, organized three battalions and headquarters units totaling approximately seventy-eight officers and eighteen hundred enlisted men. Meanwhile, recruiting was proceeding on Molokai and Lanai. These units were divorced from the Maui District in December 1942, and details of their organization will be found in the history of the First Regiment Molokai-Lanai Volunteers.

The island of Maui consists of two extinct volcanic mountain masses, separated by a low sandy isthmus. The eastern mass is approachable from the south and east. The First Battalion was in that area. The isthmus, forming the most fertile and inhabited section of Maui, provided the Second (less Company H) and Third Battalion areas. Company H covered the east shore of the eastern mountain mass, Haleakala, from Muolea to Keanoe. "The Mounties" (horse cavalry) operated above the lowlands in the central and southeastern portions of Maui. Maui's pre-war population was 41,500.

Weapons training included bolo knives, bayonet, rifle, pistol, and shotgun. Maui Volunteers witnessed the operation of other weapons while participating in maneuvers with Army units. Supplementing the work of the Maui Volunteers were "The Mounties"—a mounted cavalry unit organized in March 1942 with an original membership of approximately seventy-five. These men, already schooled in horsemanship, accompanied Army units on field problems, performing scouting, patrolling, and reconnaissance.

Commanding Officers: Col. Elmore P. Lydgate, Lt. Col. John T. Moir, Jr., Lt. Col. E. Stanley Elmore, Lt. Col. Edward B. Hair, and Capt. Robert von Tempsky.

Molokai Battalion Molokai-Lanai Volunteers

The authorization of a volunteer defense force on Molokai was published in April 1942 by Col. Charles B. Lyman, Maui District Commander. The unit was originally designated as the Third Battalion, Second Regiment Maui Volunteers. Mr. L. Thornton Lyman of Kaunakakai organized the men of Molokai, and training started in May. By the middle of June, their aggregate strength approximated 750. There were four companies and a platoon of cavalry.

In December 1942, Molokai-Lanai Volunteers were placed under the commanding officer of that district rather than the Maui District. Re-designation as the First Regiment Molokai-Lanai Volunteers was approved by Lt. Gen. Emmons in March 1943. Lt. Col. L. Thornton Lyman has actively commanded this group since its inception.

Molokai is one of the smaller islands in the territory and had a prewar population of thirty-eight hundred. The Volunteers covered the island quite well geographically. Cavalry and infantry units were at Kaunakakai and East Molokai. Other infantry companies were located at Kualapuu, Hoolehua, and Maunaloa.

The Volunteers observed and participated in many of the 108th's maneuvers. Their mission at the time was to participate with the Army in a cordon defense of the island. Though even up to August 1942 the only weapons available were those borrowed, there was much emphasis on rifle markmanship. A machine-gun platoon from D Company qualified 90.7 percent of its thirty-three men.

In 1943, although the threat of invasion was increasingly remote and the labor shortage increased demands for workers, 23 officers and 566 men reported for seven and eight hours of training per week. This schedule was not reduced until December 1943.

Lanai Battalion Molokai-Lanai Volunteers

Dexter Fraser of the Hawaiian Pineapple Company organized a volunteer unit of 150 men in April 1942. He continued his active cooperation until Organized Defense Volunteers were released from Army control. This unit was originally under the Maui District and was designated the Second Battalion, Second Regiment, Maui Volunteers. In December 1942, Lanai volunteer forces were placed under the Molokai-Lanai District Commander. On March 3, 1943, Lt. Gen. Emmons approved the redesignation of this Battalion as the Second Battalion, Molokai-Lanai Volunteer Infantry. Lanai Battalion strength as of March 1943 was 17 officers and 336 enlisted men.

Lanai is one of the smaller Hawaiian Islands. Virtually all approaches from the sea are steep and rugged. The populated area is in the center of the island. Pre-war population was thirty-two hundred.

Members of this Battalion were predominantly Filipino. Despite long working days in the fields, the men looked forward to drill periods and were quick to learn. In 1942, Lanai Volunteers turned out for drill every evening and again on Sundays, with training supervised by cadres from the 299th Infantry and the 108th. The Hawaiian Pineapple Company built and maintained a range, and marksmanship training was very popular. That interest in training was high is evidenced by the fact that almost one-third of Lanai's total male population received volunteer training.

Commanding Officers as of July 4, 1945, were: Maj. Pedro de la Cruz, Capt. Meliton Lacamento, and Capt. Pio Hadulco.

First Regiment Kauai Volunteers

Two battalions of Kauai Volunteers were authorized by the Hawaiian Department in March 1942. Enlistments were opened on March 8, and before the day was over the two battalions were recruited and there were enough additional men to start a third. The Third Battalion was quickly authorized and brought up to strength. There were then approximately eighteen hundred Volunteers. One year later, the Kauai Volunteers were organized into a rifle regiment consisting of three battalions of four companies each, plus battalion and regimental headquarters, a service detachment, and three mounted units. Mounted strength approximated seventy-five and regimental strength was more than twenty-four hundred. In addition, a large number who had received basic training were inactive and held in reserve. Ninety percent of the regiment was Filipino.

Indicative of the interest in Volunteers on Kauai, was the campaign sponsored by the Kauai Post, American Legion, for shoes and fatigue clothing. In June 1943, $25,932 was raised.

Commanding Officers as of July 4, 1945, were: Col. Paul H. Townsley, Lt. Col. R. C. Williamson, Lt. Col. Fred Janssen, Lt. Col. James B. Costorphine, and Capt. Alan E. Faye.

Honolulu Symphony in the War Years

MARVELL ALLISON HART

❖ As the Honolulu Symphony Orchestra prepares for its first series of post-war concerts, it is interesting to review its activities during the four years of war, which, strange as it may seem, were the most successful in the history of the organization.

On the evening of December 6, 1941, tickets for the 1941–1942 series of four concerts were being carefully taken from their boxes and placed in envelopes to be ready for mailing to season ticket holders on Monday, December 8. Because it is never possible to finish this job in one evening, Mr. W. Twigg-Smith, the manager of the orchestra, with one assistant, had worked until eleven o'clock and then decided to resume work at nine o'clock on Sunday morning. By that hour on December 7, as we all know, it looked as though music might be blotted out of the lives of people in Honolulu for months, or maybe for years, and the half-completed task of designating tickets for the 1941–1942 season of symphony concerts was completely forgotten.

In March of that year, however, the Directors of the Honolulu Symphony Society met and unanimously agreed that the concerts should be started because they felt that at no time in its history had the orchestra been more desperately needed by the music-loving people of Honolulu. Accordingly they announced a season of four concerts for the months of April, May, June, and July. During that year it was often necessary to postpone a concert for a week or two when service men were "alerted" and were unable to leave their posts, but nevertheless, the orchestra managed to give four performances in spite of major difficulties.

Perhaps only those familiar with the organization and management of a symphony orchestra can quite realize what a courageous decision the Directors made in planning for these concerts. No orchestra is

---

First published November 1945.

entirely self-supporting. All must be subsidized in some way by the community, either by the city or by private individuals. In Honolulu, aid is given by a small group of sincere music lovers, most of whom have been supporters for many years. To plan and carry out a series of concerts at such a time, with no assurance of financial success, but guided only by a firm conviction that music was more than ever a vital need, was the task the Directors and the orchestra's conductor, Fritz Hart, undertook with faith and enthusiasm during those first grim months of 1942, just before the Battle of Midway.

The concerts were held in the auditorium of McKinley High School, and because of the curfew, which made it necessary for members of the armed forces as well as civilians to be off the streets at an early hour, they began at 3:30 P.M. From the beginning, the attendance was large and soon the "sold out" sign began to appear long before the concert hour. Even so, eager people stood in line waiting to pick up tickets that might be turned in by persons unable to attend the performance.

In the fall of 1943, a season of six concerts was announced, and tickets were sold not only to those who had attended these concerts for years, but to hundreds of service men and women who welcomed the opportunity to listen to symphonic music such as they had been accustomed to hearing in their mainland homes. Bach, Beethoven, Brahms, Mozart, Wagner, and compositions by modern American, English, and French musicians were played to capacity houses throughout the 1943–1944 and 1944–1945 seasons. Many who could not buy seats in the auditorium stood outside in the gardens to listen. These were indeed thrilling times for all those who had worked so hard for the success of the orchestra in lean years.

During all this time, rehearsals were held on Sunday mornings—the only time possible for musicians serving in the armed forces and civilians holding war jobs—and never more than five rehearsals, and usually only four, were possible. Nevertheless, splendid concerts were given and the warm appreciation expressed so spontaneously by the large audiences was deeply felt by the conductor and members of the orchestra.

Many of the players had been members of Honolulu's orchestra for years; others came from mainland orchestras where they had occupied "first chairs" in various sections. Indeed, at one time Fritz Hart was heard to remark that Honolulu was "overflowing with so much fine musical talent that we could have two symphony orchestras here." Among these visiting musicians were Harry Meuser (bassoon) and Arthur Gault (oboe), of the Cincinnati Symphony Orchestra; Lester Spencer (violin) and Harry Weiss (viola), both prominent in radio and motion picture work in California; Richard Beresowsky (cello), member of a brilliant musical family of California and New York; Albert Gillis (violin), a Juilliard and Yale School of Music graduate and leader of the Gillis Trio; John Ehrlich, a brilliant young cellist who played with Stokowski's Youth Orchestra prior to entering the army; Loy Jones (viola), from the Cleveland Symphony Orchestra; and many others stationed here on Oahu.

Soloists, too, were plentiful among the men of the armed forces, and those who appeared with the Honolulu Symphony Orchestra were Capt. Edwin G. Davis and Pvt. Louis Brechemin (pianists), Harry Shub and William Rusinak (violinists), Harry Meuser (bassoon), and Frederick Wilkins, a pupil of the late Georges Barrere, and one of the most distinguished flautists playing today.

Twice, compositions by musicians stationed here with the army and navy were performed, and on both occasions Fritz Hart invited the young composers to conduct their own works.

In the spring of 1945, the Honolulu Symphony Society joined with the Honolulu Community Theatre in presenting the popular comic opera *H.M.S. Pinafore* by Gilbert and Sullivan, with Elroy Fulmer of the Community Theatre as Dramatic Director, Fritz Hart as Musical Director, and Josephine Taylor assisting with the dances. Then public performances were given to crowded houses, in spite of the military off-limits order placed on Roosevelt High School auditorium because of the "flu" epidemic two days after the opera opened. Two free performances, for only service personnel, were given. This production was successful beyond the most optimistic hopes of its sponsors, and a second musical show, in which the Honolulu Community Theatre and the Honolulu Symphony Orchestra will again collaborate, is planned for the coming spring.

Today the Symphony is preparing for its 1945–1946 season of six concerts. Fritz Hart, the conductor, is returning from Australia, where he was invited in July to participate in the Jubilee Celebration of the Melbourne Conservatory of Music, of which he was director for twenty years. While in Australia Mr. Hart conducted concerts with the A.B.C. Symphony Orchestra and the Melbourne Symphony Orchestra, gave two performances of his Christmas opera *Even Unto Bethlehem,* and a concert of some of his numerous choral works.

Dates for this year's concerts by the Honolulu Symphony Orchestra are November 13, December 11, January 8, February 12, March 12, and April 9. They will be held in McKinley High School auditorium at 8 P.M.—the first evening concerts since 1941.

Here is the program for the first concert: Overture—"King Stephen," Beethoven; Symphony ("Drum Roll") in E-flat, Haydn; "Somerset Rhapsody," Gustav Holst; Two Interlinked French Folk-Tunes, Ethel Smyth; Introduction Act III: "Dance of Apprentices" and "Procession of Meistersingers," Wagner.

The war is over, and once again the people of Hawaii enter into peaceful days. The Directors of the Honolulu Symphony Orchestra, its conductor, and the musicians who play under his baton look forward to a splendid post-war season, confident in the belief that they have the whole-hearted interest and support of the music loving people of Honolulu.

Hawaii's Bid
as United Nations Capitol

Decision to propose Hawaii as the permanent site of the United Nations Capitol was made relatively late, after other cities had prepared elaborate campaigns to "sell" themselves. However, a highly effective presentation was prepared and shipped to London by Hawaii's committee and the contents of this presentation are of interest regardless of the eventual decision made by the United Nations as to its choice of site. . . . The huge volume was sent with an attractive cover with a tapa cloth and flower lei design and a decorative map emphasizing Hawaii's central location in the Pacific. It was mounted on a wooden standard for ease in reading. The word "Hawaii" was spelled out on the cover in letters hand-carved of wood.

RESOLUTION BY THE HAWAII
UNITED NATIONS CAPITOL COMMITTEE

Adopted at a meeting in the Senate Chamber of the Capitol of the Territory of Hawaii, September 26, 1945.

Whereas, the selection of a place for permanent headquarters of the United Nations Organization—the United Nations Capitol—will be under consideration by the Preparatory Commission at an early date, and

Whereas, the interests of the United Nations Organization will

---

First published November 1945.

best be served by a location within the confines of the United States of America and one which, from a world standpoint, is central and neutral in its geographical position and character, and

Whereas, the Territory of Hawaii, U.S.A. is noncontiguous to continental United States, remote from any national capital and therefore removed from concentrations of political and economic pressure; it has an equable climate and natural scenic beauty which makes it an inviting and physically suitable setting; and, by reason of the diversified racial origins of its population and its record of success in achieving racial harmony, it provides a uniquely appropriate environment for an organization dedicated to world amity, and

Whereas, the Hawaii United Nations Capitol Committee is truly representative of the people of Hawaii and qualified to speak in its behalf,

Therefore Be It Resolved

That the Honorable Ingram M. Stainback, Governor of the Territory of Hawaii, be and is hereby empowered, in behalf of the people of Hawaii, as represented by this Committee, to invite consideration of Hawaii as a location for the permanent headquarters of the United Nations Organization, and

That he be further empowered to tender a site within the Territory of such dimensions as are deemed requisite for a World Capitol and its auxiliary units, and

That he pledge that whatever hotel, transportation, residential and other facilities may be required to serve the needs and convenience of the members of the United Nations Organization will be offered by citizens of Hawaii, and

That he convey assurance that the People of Hawaii deeply appreciate the honor that would attend the selection of these Islands as the location of the World Capitol and that they pledge their cooperation to the utmost in meeting the responsibilities entailed by this high distinction, and

That, as Governor of the Territory of Hawaii, he transmit this Resolution to His Excellency, Honorable James F. Byrnes, Secretary of State.

Title Page
To the United Nations
Preparatory Commission

The people of Hawaii, whom I have the honor to represent, respectfully invite consideration of these islands as a suitable location for permanent headquarters of the United Nations Organization, and hereby tender a site of such dimensions as may be deemed requisite.

Outlined in the following pages are the facilities and special advantages afforded here, and the reasons why, from the standpoint of both geography and environment, Hawaii is in an unexcelled position to meet your requirements.

(Signed) Ingram M. Stainback
Governor of the Territory of Hawaii

"The forceful idea of our writer Pascal will no longer be belied: 'Strength without justice is tyrannical, and justice without strength is a mockery!'"
—The Honorable Joseph Paul-Boncour

Hawaii as the location of headquarters for the United Nations Organization would be uniquely appropriate. These islands are the home of a people of varied racial lineage, long and widely known for the friendliness with which they live together. And here also is situated—Pearl Harbor. Therein would perpetually lie a dual reminder, first, of what mankind can achieve in amity between different races and nations and, second, what can befall without a check on ruthless power.

"For all states, great and small, there are great opportunities for making contributions to the common cause . . . and the well-being and prosperity of all peoples."
—The Honorable A. A. Gromyko

The geographical advantage offered by Hawaii is implicit in the fact that these islands lie farther from any continent than any other body of land. Although an integral part of the United States, they are non-contiguous territory. They are located in the Pacific, theater of the most important international developments of the future, yet they are far enough from any nation on its rims to facilitate materially a detached point of view.

". . . to employ international machinery for the promotion of the economic and social advancement of all peoples."
—Charter of the United Nations

Hawaii's equable climate varies less than ten degrees between winter and summer and between noon and midnight. It has no extremes of heat or cold rain or dryness. It uniformly provides a mildness particularly welcome to elderly persons and suitable for outdoor recreation the year around. Members of the United Nations Organization will find here a climate conducive to comfort in both work and relaxation.

"Let us pray that, under God's guidance, what we have done here . . . will be found worthy of the faith that gave it birth and of the human suffering that has been its price."
—The Earl of Halifax

Hawaii is several thousand miles from the nearest national capital. It is far removed from any of the potentially explosive situations of the world, thus promoting an objective view of them. It is equally distant from large concentrations of industrial and financial power. Isolated from pressures, both political and economic, Hawaii fits the role of a neutral, centrally located, international capital more perfectly than any other place in the world.

". . . provide for periodic visits to the respective . . . territories at times agreed upon."
—Charter of the United Nations

Hawaii has the largest airport in the world. It is only nine hours flying time from the United States' West Coast and twenty-two hours from Hong Kong. Honolulu is a port of call for steamship lines of many nations on routes which radiate directly to mainland United States, Canada, New Zealand, Australia, South America, China, the Philippines, Russian and British Asiatic ports, and the Netherlands East Indies. Travel facilities to, from and within Hawaii will be found adequate in speed, capacity and luxury to meet the needs which a world capital will create.

". . . to save succeeding generations from the scourge of war."
—Charter of the United Nations

Hawaii is internationally minded. The inception here of the Institute of Pacific Relations, the activities of the Bishop Museum and of the School of Pacific and Asiatic Studies at the University of Hawaii, the cosmopolitan character of a constant flow of travelers, all bear testimony to this fact. Strongest factor of all has been the far-flung origins of her diversified population in developing a global consciousness.

"This Charter is a compact born of suffering and of war. With it now rests our hope for good and lasting peace."
—The Honorable Edward Stettinius, Jr.

Honolulu has complete cable, radio, radio-telephone and telephoto facilities capable of expansion to meet all requirements. It has two large daily newspapers, served by all the major press associations. In provisions for information and communications, therefore, it is well prepared; and it has had a long experience in receiving and accommodating international assemblies. Yet, with its predominantly agricultural economy it is remote from the congestion and turbulence of thickly populated industrial areas. It affords metropolitan advantages in a setting as tranquil as it is scenically superb.

"It remains for us to continue to foster mutual trust and friendly collaboration in order to make this, the greatest of international experiments, a great success in fact."
—The Honorable V. K. Wellington Koo

It is easy for people of all countries to feel at home in Hawaii—its wide diversity of races and nationalities tends to make this true. No community has a richer tradition of racial tolerance, and none has provided a more nearly perfect laboratory for the study of ethnology and interracial sociology, or used it to better effect. Here, then, is a community charged to a high degree with the spirit that must guide the world into permanent ways of peace.

Note: *As this issue went to press the issue was still undecided as to the permanent site of the United Nations Capitol. While other cities were putting on high-pressure campaigns to persuade the officials in their favor, Hawaii was waiting patiently, resting its case with the presentation described in the foregoing article.*

Five Hundred Men to a Girl

OLIVE MOWAT

❖ This article does not deal with the teen-age girl whose mother turned her loose at twelve. It deals with the girl whose parents want to know where the party is to be held, with whom she is going, and at what time she will return. It deals with the service men whose mothers and wives write two and three times a week, men who carry pictures of their wives and babies or their sweethearts, and show them at the slightest provocation. In Hawaii during the war, it was five hundred men to a girl, they say. Actually the figures are a military secret. Men from eighteen or less to thirty or more. Men. Good-looking, plain. Married men, single men, boys snatched from high school. Our teenage daughters meet them all, and parents deal in high explosives. Even though the war is over, the situation still exists.

Our girls meet them everywhere. On the beach, at dances, and at church. At clubs and on hiking parties. They became their confidantes. They hear from one that he is the recipient of a letter reading, "You have been away too long. I want a divorce." Another learns, "I have met someone else. . . ." They listen with sympathy to the problems of the men whose private worlds have crumbled, who feel suddenly that inspiration has deserted them, though they had still to face a battlefield. Or Sandy's wife is expecting a baby. Interest runs high and the first question on greeting Sandy is apt to be, "Is the baby here?"

The beach at Waikiki. It is so crowded with service men that the sand crabs have given up. One girl to ten men in any idling group. They are old beyond their years, these girls. They become adepts at character analysis. And they are aware of the difference in maturity between these men who pass through our town and the boys in the junior class at school. The boys have suffered by comparison. Parents do their utmost to foster and encourage companionship with the school group. But these boys haven't a chance . . . unless there is a

First published December 1945.

306

school dance where a Navy band is playing. Then the girls accept school invitations and spend the intervals talking with members of the band. The boys seem to understand the situation and are good sports in public, however much they might protest among themselves.

The girls gather groups of men and bring them home for the afternoon and evening, so at any moment, unexpectedly, there is a party. Mother has a son in the Philippines, or Guam, and a nephew somewhere in Europe. She wishes they might spend their liberty with a group at someone's home, with girls like these.

Some of the boys, or men, simply want to sit on the davenport to feel its roominess, to sense the luxury of springs. Others, become used to backless benches, choose the piano stool. There are three or four girls to sixteen or eighteen men. They dance, visit, giggle, play records, and sometimes go for hikes or ti-leaf sliding—a true Hawaiian sport—returning in time for supper. The boys talk of their families, of the girls back home, and their hopes and plans for the future. They all have futures. Sometimes they look our girls over and say, "I have a kid sister just your age." They see in them their own people. And they're all, without exception, homesick. But they do not often grumble. Sometimes they say quietly: "This is the first time in eighteen months that I've been inside a home." If you have a cat, they hold it. And they play with the dog. They come to the kitchen when supper is prepared, and we must dodge them in our duties. But we have fun. Sometimes they laugh and say, "This is just like home." Then we are happy.

Old-timers have holed in for the "duration and six." We go to town only when we must, for we dread competing with the milling crowds. Soldiers, sailors, marines, and seabees. The whistling. But we understand these whistles. A lonely boy from Arkansas or Weed or Talent who hasn't spoken to a girl for weeks, perhaps. Sometimes the whistles come from a convoy, beginning with the first truck and ending with the last. Our girls have learned to handle them. Never a glance, nor an alert look of recognition. But should a service man ask directions, our girls are courteous and helpful.

There are the dances, with hundreds of men to a handful of girls. Sometimes friends in the service invite them, then they blow and bounce in a glamorous jeep, thrilled and delighted. The majority of partners, however, are arranged for by groups whose business it is to supply girls for these dances. Busses pick them up, with chaperons, and they are taken to the party and returned when it is over.

And there is the telephone at night. It takes real understanding, this telephoning. It seems to the parents that all the men the girls have met during the day spend their evenings visiting with them over the telephone. There is also the situation of the lonely boys at faraway outposts. They rarely go to town. Once one of them met Mary. He telephoned every night until he left. Then he gave her number to his friends, and all winter long these boys talked with her. If, by chance, one was called from the telephone, another took his place and the first stood in line to get his turn again. She never met one of them.

School suffers. Mothers and fathers get irate. But these boys were interrupted in their studies, too, our girls seem to argue.

Hospital service is not neglected. On regular days our girls visit the returned wounded. They meet the men from battlefields—not through magazines, nor movies, but first hand. They spend time with those whose hurts will heal and with those who are injured permanently. They dance, if the men are able. Sometimes they play cards or write letters. These girls, in their middle teens, see more than gaiety in life. They see, and for the sake of the future, we hope they comprehend.

Sometimes instead of hospital visits, the girls meet at surgical dressing centers or care for babies at the local hospitals to relieve the shortage of nurses.

There is the somber side. We have had the full impact of it in Hawaii. Convoys leaving suddenly for battle. One day the boys were laughing in our home or chatting on the telephone. The next, there was a tangible silence. Ships have sailed away in the sunlight, or by the bright moon, or the dark of a tropical night, and the war has been very near. The war has been in our homes and in our hearts. We were the last touch of home for many of these boys. Our teen-age girls were quiet. "Mickey hasn't telephoned," they said, ". . . he must have left . . ." and silence everywhere. Listening for the telephone, hoping to hear.

Individually or collectively, they have gone—Sandy, Happy, Bill, Henry, Joe. They were not merely service boys who had come to stay with us for a while. They had become our friends. They had spent their liberty with us, stripped shoes and ties, even shirts, off in our homes. Oh, we run a respectable American home—but middies get tight and Honolulu is informal with the boys. We have extra beds, too, where they have slept on leave.

Our girls said good-bye. Good-bye, Sandy . . . in case you're called before you come again. . . . Good-bye, Bill. Good luck, Henry. So long,

Joe. See you when you come this way—be sure to call. . . . And those of us who have it in our hearts to weep at separation wonder if they understand and try to gather strength from them as we marvel at their strong serenity.

Then letters from the battlegrounds. Sometimes they were long in coming. Apprehension crept in. Has anyone heard from Happy? No? There has been time for a letter by now. And daughter was quiet, or jumpy, or irritable. But mother mustn't notice. Mother mustn't notice anything. Oh, Happy. . . . Then, one day, a letter, a shriek of delight. He isn't killed. He isn't missing. Happy is safe! There is homework to do, much of it. But Happy has written, and he must have his letter in reply at once. So he gets his letter, and the girl in the junior class gets a low mark for the day's work. Education in life. Julius Caesar can wait. . . .

Letters again. This time letters that never came. Finally one from Joe's mother or Bill's sister. Joe's submarine has been reported missing. Officially. Joe, ripping up the piano keys . . . Bill's plane crashed. Sandy has been killed in action. Sandy and Joan in our home, in stitches of laughter. No. Not Sandy.

Surprisingly, sometimes, the boys come back from duty on a routine trip. They are unexpectedly at the other end of the telephone, and wild hilarity runs over the wires. War nerves in Hawaii? Is it difficult to understand?

Our girls have been faced with that. We hope they are learning young, our teen-age daughters. We believe they are, as they helped us to gather the packages together that these boys had left us for safe keeping. We all have packages belonging to the stranger who has become our friend. And, if we must, we send them home.

Our girls have faced life and death. Not life and death separated by a stretch of years. But by a trip to Tarawa or Okinawa. We watched tight-lipped. But out of their hurt they carry on for the boys who are still here. Not the same boys, but the same service. They know first hand something of the tragedy of war. And the prayer in our hearts is that from their very young experience—an experience that has made them old in wisdom beyond their years—they will help to build a world in which Sandy and Happy and Bill, Henry and Joe and Honey may live unmolested to their three score years and ten.

1945—In Retrospect

EILEEN O'BRIEN

❖ Hawaii played an important but minor role in the world drama during the past year, one of the most eventful in history. Local news was relatively insignificant compared with the staggering headlines of war and peace. However, because Hawaii was affected by the war more than any other area of the United States, it reflected world events proportionately. Like the rest of the world, the Islands are experiencing the pains of transition from one era to another, and much of the future is unpredictable.

At the first of the year, while Patton was opening a mighty drive from Bastogne and Russian troops were battering at the German border, the road to Tokyo still seemed long and difficult. Superforts were attacking Nagoya and carrier planes were striking at Formosa and Okinawa, but the invasion of Luzon and the battle for Bataan and Corregidor was just beginning.

In Hawaii during January, Island Wacs left for mainland training and the first echelon of Waves, Spars, and Women Reserve Marines arrived in the Islands. The Christian Holmes estate at Coconut Island was leased to the army as a rest center for air force personnel, the musical show "Waikiki Diary" was presented by Pearl Harbor workers, and Mayor Petrie presented a budget for $11 million, 6 percent less than that of the previous year. Ernie Pyle was in Honolulu, en route to his tragic destiny at Ie Shima.

The same month *The Honolulu Advertiser* started a "Wake Up Washington" campaign in an attempt to ease the desperate housing situation. Honolulu housing, or lack of it, remained one of the top news stories of the year and is still one of this city's major problems.

In February, while world headlines centered on the "Big Three" meeting at Yalta, there was much public discussion in Hawaii about Honolulu's Civic Center, with several different proposals being launched, including the removal of the center to such sites as Punch-

First published December 1945.

bowl and the Ala Moana. However, sentiment prevailed for retaining and expanding the present buildings, poorly planned as they are, and the legislature failed to take action on the matter, so the issue is in abeyance until the next session.

The liberation of Santo Tomas prison camp the same month brought joy to many Honoluluans who had relatives and friends in the Philippines. Relief from Hawaii's wartime fish famine was promised with the first lifting of fishing restrictions, along the north shore of Oahu. The invasion of Iwo Jima was followed with special interest by the people of Hawaii because the Fourth and Fifth Marine Divisions, which fought the bloody and gallant battle, had trained on Maui and Hawaii and had spent passes and last liberty in Honolulu. February also brought the opening of the twenty-third biennial session of the territorial legislature.

World headlines in March were centered on the battle for Germany and the invasion of Okinawa, while in Hawaii there was still much sound and fury about the housing situation. The House Naval Affairs sub-committee on congested areas, headed by Ed V. Ezak, arrived in Hawaii and after a survey recommended immediate "remedial action." Work on the emergency housing area on the Palolo golf course was already in progress and, as a result of the Washingtonians' visit, plans were made for housing areas in Kapiolani park and Manoa valley. The latter is being brought to completion, but war's end stopped construction of the planned area at Kapiolani park.

An Easter sunrise service at Kapiolani park, attended by five thousand persons, ushered in the month of April in Hawaii. While Tokyo was being blasted with incendiary bombs, a test blackout in Hawaii brought reminder that military authorities considered the Islands not yet safe from enemy attack.

Hawaii's first parade since the start of the war took place in observance of Army Day, in spite of a deluge that soaked the troops and observers to the skin. Income tax investigators arrived from Washington as a result of "fraud prevalent in Hawaii." The month of April was saddened by the deaths of Ernie Pyle and President Franklin D. Roosevelt, but hope was brought to a weary world by the opening of the United Nations conference at San Francisco.

May brought world-shaking events climaxed by the defeat of Germany and longed-for peace in Europe. Victory in the Pacific still seemed distant, however, as thousands of American men were killed under the attacks of Japanese suicide planes off Okinawa. Events in Hawaii, mild by contrast, included the closing of the legislative session, additional lifting of restrictions on fishing, public debate over the location of piggeries, and authorization by the Federal Housing Administration for the construction of five hundred homes by private enterprise. Hawaii's traditional Lei Day was not officially observed because of the period of mourning for President Roosevelt.

In June, a probe was begun into an alleged black market in fish; Brother Paul Sibbing, president of St. Louis College, left for a new assignment on the mainland; and Capt. Mildred H. McAfee, USNR, visited the Islands. A water shortage brought a serious drought throughout the Islands, especially on windward Oahu. An influenza epidemic began, and theaters on Oahu were declared off limits to military personnel.

A labor strike at Theo H. Davies began a long series of difficulties that affected the Dairymen's Association, Ltd., Honolulu Construction and Draying Co., the Coca Cola bottling plant, and the Honolulu Gas Co.

July brought the welcome announcement that three hundred tons of meat for civilians would arrive, ending a practically meatless era of many weeks. This was followed by an announcement that Hawaii had topped the entire country in bond sales, being the only state or territory to have gone over its quota in all seven bond drives. In the last, Hawaii reached 186 percent of its quota.

Ten thousand men and women, organized volunteers for home defense, were released from army control and inactivated at a ceremony in the Honolulu stadium July 4th. These organizations, formed in the tense days after the attack on Hawaii, included the Businessmen's Military Training Corps, the Hawaii Defense Volunteers, and military battalions on all outlying islands.

This month was also notable for the final lifting of the curfew that had been in effect since the start of war. Complete blackout and curfew at nightfall prevailed until May 6, 1942, when the curfew was moved up to 10 P.M. In December 1943, full lighting was permitted until 10 P.M., and on May 4, 1944, the blackout was ended. Further signs that victory was approaching included the request that gas masks be turned back to military authorities, the removal of air raid shelters, and the announcement that the army would turn back historical Thomas Square after complete restoration. The navy lifted practically all bans on fishing.

The War Manpower Commission announced that Oahu was still short fifteen thousand workers, and the tax office stated that Oahu business was up 12 percent over the previous boom year. There were 4,796 cases of influenza reported.

The era-marking news of the atomic bomb over Hiroshima stunned Hawaii, as it did the rest of the world, in August, and this was soon followed by the breathtaking announcement of Japan's surrender. Hawaii went wild with joy, although its observances of victory were not marred by serious violence. War's end in Hawaii meant an end of mail and press censorship, security orders, control of aliens, air raid alarms, and countless other restrictions, as well as the controls that had applied nationally, such as gas and tire rationing.

Announcements were made that the army would return to civilian use St. Louis College and Farrington high schools, which had been used as hospitals, and Punahou campus, which had been headquarters for the army engineers. Other buildings and land parcels used by the armed forces during the war were gradually returned to their original uses.

A strike by employees of the Honolulu Gas Company created an inconvenient weekend for thousands of persons who ordinarily "cook with gas," but it was ended before the city was seriously disrupted. The Christian Holmes estate at Waikiki, where President Roosevelt stayed during his last visit to the Islands, was sold for $278,000 to a group that announced it would be the headquarters for a "Cosmopolitan club." The first "aloha" to an arriving vessel since the start of war was given the *Matsonia,* but welcomers were disappointed when military guards prevented them from using the piers' galleries, making them wait unseen by the arrivals until the latter got off the ship. Organized labor groups opened a canteen on Alakea street, opposite the post office.

As the memorable Japanese surrender ceremonies took place aboard the USS *Missouri* on September first, Hawaii began another month marked by more returns to a normal way of life. Liquor rationing was lifted and bars were allowed to return to pre-war hours, after being limited to sales of liquor between noon and 7 P.M. The city sponsored a five-day fete for eighty Recovered American Military Personnel, climaxed by a glamorous luau at The Willows. Chlorination of water was suspended, the move creating much public debate as to its advisability. The Inter-Island ship *Hualalai* was damaged by a seventy-five-thousand dollar fire.

The month of October was marked by several pleasant events, including the Chinese Double Ten celebration and lantern parade, the final performance of "This Is the Army," attended by Irving Berlin and thousands of civilians at the Honolulu stadium, and the aloha parade of Halsey's Third Fleet past Diamond Head, beginning the victorious voyage home.

Navy Day in Hawaii was celebrated in a spectacular manner, with the navy and civilians out-vying each other in hospitality. World-famous Pearl Harbor was open to all civilians for the first time since December Seventh, and an elaborate program of entertainment was provided, including demonstrations of amphibious landings and launch tours of the harbor. From the civilian point of view, the highlight was an opportunity to enter the Royal Hawaiian hotel for the first time since the start of war. Two events were scheduled there on Navy Day—a luncheon honoring Admiral Nimitz and a reception and dance in the evening, also honoring the great naval leader, both sponsored by the Honolulu Chamber of Commerce. The admiral was presented a Lionel Walden painting, a seascape in oil of the Waianae shore, the gift representing the aloha of thousands of individuals and practically all organizations in Hawaii.

The army announced that, effective November 1, its Central Pacific Base Command would cease operations and its functions would be absorbed by headquarters, army forces, middle Pacific. Maj. Gen. H. T. Burgin, commanding the base command, became commander of the Hawaiian artillery command, consisting of the Hawaiian antiaircraft command, Hawaiian seacoast artillery command, and non-divisional artillery specifically assigned or attached. This corresponds to the position General Burgin held under the Hawaiian Department at the start of the war.

Hawaii made its bid as the site of the United Nations Capitol, using as its chief argument the following: "... the Territory of Hawaii, U.S.A., is non-contiguous to continental United States, remote from any national capital and therefore removed from concentrations of political and economic pressure: it has an equable climate and natural scenic beauty which makes it an inviting and physically suitable setting; and, by reason of the diversified racial origins of its population and its record of success in achieving racial harmony, it provides a uniquely appropriate environment for an organization dedicated to world amity."

Although thousands of men in uniform left the islands for their longed-for journey home, service men and women still thronged the city's streets. There was a definite easing, however, of crowded conditions in restaurants, stores, and busses, and the employment situation in some businesses eased slightly. It was announced that there is an estimated $155 million worth of private construction waiting to be done in Honolulu and a public works program of many millions more. Labor supply continued to be far less than the demand.

Honolulu's much discussed cost of living continued to rise, the chief items in the upward trend being food, clothing, and recreation.

1946

Across the Mainland and in Hawai'i, labor demands to share in the post-war prosperity. Corporations turn a deaf ear and strikes occur. The Hawai'i Sugar Planters Association begins recruiting and shipping in Filipino workers. And statehood for Hawai'i gets a big boost when President Truman says he's for it.

On January 10, the first General Assembly of the United Nations meets in London.

On January 24, the United Nations establishes the Atomic Energy Commission to restrict atomic energy to peaceful uses.

On February 25, the U.S. Supreme Court says that martial law in Hawai'i was illegal.

On April 1, a tsunami strikes the Hawaiian Islands. On the five major islands, 159 people are killed.

On April 25, Big Four foreign ministers draft peace treaties for Italy, Bulgaria, Romania, Hungary, and Finland.

On May 17, stock is sold to finance a pro football team in Hawai'i. The first player to sign with the Hawaiian Warriors is Joe Kaulukukui. The twenty-eight-year-old quarterback stands five-feet-nine inches and weighs 155 pounds. The team colors are scarlet and gold.

On June 30, the United States joins UNESCO.

On July 1, the United States begins atomic bomb tests at Bikini, in the Marshall Islands.

On the Fourth of July, the Republic of the Philippines becomes a reality.

On July 15, wartime price controls are extended for another year.

On October 16, price controls are lifted on meat.

On October 23, Hawai'i loses its bid to be the home of the United Nations. Instead, that organization accepts a gift of $8.5 million from John D. Rockefeller, Jr., to provide a site in New York City for its headquarters.

On November 5, Johnny Wilson is elected mayor of Honolulu by sixteen votes. Republicans take both houses of Congress.

On November 9, controls on most consumer goods are removed.

On the final day of 1946, President Truman formally announces cessation of World War Two hostilities.

War and the Birds of Midway

HARVEY I. FISHER AND PAUL BALDWIN

❖ The leeward islands of the Hawaiian Chain are world renowned for their breeding colonies of tropical seabirds. Some of these seabirds breed in only a few other places in the world. Laysan and Midway are also widely known as the home of the Laysan Rail and the Laysan Finch. These latter species live, or lived, *only* on the most westward islands of Hawaii. Certain of these westward islands have been used extensively in the prosecution of the war, and rumors indicated that some of the birds were being ruinously decimated. The United States Fish and Wildlife Service and the Territorial Board of Agriculture and Forestry sent us to Midway to determine the fate of the Laysan Rail and the Laysan Finch and to make a survey of all the birds.

Our census figures (Table 1) offer some interesting and some disturbing food for thought. Why are some species such as the Christmas Island Shearwater, the Bonin Island Petrel, Bulwer's Petrel, Red-footed Booby, and Gray-backed Tern now limited to one of the two main islets making up Midway Atoll? Before the war they occurred on both. Unfortunately time was not available to study this problem.

Three species have been completely wiped out on Midway in the last four years—the Laysan Rail, the Laysan Finch, and the Brown Booby. Extinction of the rail on Midway probably means complete extinction of the species. Eastern Island of Midway was probably the last home of the rail, as E. L. Caum and Sgt. Lewis Walker, USMC, saw two there in July, 1944. The last rail observed on Sand Island was seen by men of the cable company in November, 1943. The main factor in the extermination of the rail was the over-running of both islets by rats that escaped to Midway from ships in 1943.

The present status of the Laysan Finch is incompletely known. It is gone from Midway, but may still occur on Laysan (the only other known habitat for it), where Coultas reported "at least 1,000" present

---

First published January 1946.

TABLE 1

	Sand Island	Eastern Island
Black-footed Albatross	36,000	18,000
Laysan Albatross	75,000	35,000
Wedge-tailed Shearwater	40,000	22,000
Christmas Island Shearwater	0	400
Bonin Island Petrel	25,000	0
Bulwer's Petrel	0	600
Red-tailed Tropic Bird	10,000	9,000
Blue-faced Booby	3	0
Red-footed Booby	0	450
Frigate Bird	60*	60*
Chinese Pheasant	2 or 3	0
Pacific Golden Plover	150	100
Bristle-thighed Curlew	12	8
Ruddy Turnstone	250	100
Gray-backed Tern	0	750
Sooty Tern	170,000	4,000
Noddy	0?	10
Hawaiian Black Noddy	1,350	750
Fairy Tern	15,000	5,000
Domestic Pigeon	50	0
Unidentified Dove	2?	0
Domestic Canary	30	0

* same birds on both islands.

in 1936. Hadden (Hawaiian Planters' Record, XLV (3):194) condemns the finch and states that it should be outlawed and destroyed at every opportunity. It is unfortunate that such an attitude ever existed on Midway. In all probability the rat and man are factors responsible for its extermination.

No individuals of the Brown Booby were seen on either island. In 1941, Hadden (*op. cit.*, p. 27) reported that this was the most common of the three species of boobies at Midway. Utilization of its colonial nesting areas for military purposes and, perhaps, the rat infestation are the factors involved in its elimination from Midway. Its loss on this one atoll is, however, unimportant compared with the loss of the rail and the finch, for this booby breeds throughout the western and central tropical Pacific area.

Other species now exist there in relatively few numbers. We saw only three Blue-faced Boobies. Consequently, for all practical purposes they may be considered extinct on Midway. This species breeds in the same general area as the Brown Booby and thus is in no apparent danger of extinction.

Despite careful observation we saw so few Noddy Terns that we thought the total number present did not exceed ten! It is questionable whether the Noddy was ever abundant at Midway. The extremely small number seen by us indicates either that this species is nearing elimination from this atoll or that the main body of birds was not present at the breeding grounds when we were there. The former is more likely because W. K. Fisher in 1903 found the Noddies beginning to lay eggs on Laysan between May 16 and 23. W. A. Bryan, in August, 1902, found but few birds of this species on either island at Midway. In 1941, however, Hadden reported about two thousand on Sand Island. If the population has indeed dropped, rats and destruction of nesting grounds are the most likely decimating factors. The Noddy was found breeding on all the leeward islands of the Hawaiian Archipelago by the Rothschild collectors in 1891, but nowhere in large numbers. It breeds today on certain islets offshore from islands of the main Hawaiian group, and is generally distributed on islands all over Oceania.

The Christmas Island Shearwater, Bulwer's Petrel, and the Gray-backed Tern are present in small numbers only. To some persons, the figure of 750 Gray-backed Terns on a small island may seem rather large. Actually, for this and related species, the number on Midway is very small, especially when compared with undisturbed colonies on other islands in other parts of the ocean. The single colony of this tern, located on Eastern Island, was just starting egg-laying. Formerly, we were told, some of these birds nested on Sand Island. Destruction of the scaevola shrub has probably had the most deleterious effect on this species. The population has been reduced since the war started. It is interesting to note that Rothschild in his Avifauna of Laysan states "The Grey-backed Tern was met with on all islands, *except Midway Island* (italics ours), and was breeding in great numbers on Laysan Island." Bryan reported that in 1902 he also could find no Gray-backed Terns on Midway. Consequently it appears that the present colony has been established since 1900. Extinction as a species is unlikely for it breeds throughout Oceania, from the Hawaiian Islands to the Fiji and Tuamotu groups.

Bulwer's Petrel we found in relatively few numbers, but it may have just been coming in to nest, and consequently our figures may be too low. Its absence on Sand Island is unexplained, unless it has been completely exterminated there. As late as 1940 it was present on Sand Island, but the rats probably affected its population severely, as they have on Popoia Islet off Kailua, Oahu. There is little or no danger that this petrel, which breeds widely in the Pacific, and also in the Atlantic Ocean, will become extinct, but there is the possibility that it will be eliminated from our Hawaiian Archipelago.

The Christmas Island Shearwater is apparently in about the same state as Bulwer's Petrel. Our chief concern is not about extinction of the species, but about its small numbers in Hawaii, if the colony on Eastern Island at Midway is representative.

Certain species are still present in such numbers that no great worry need be exercised about them, if no further inroads are made on them. Among these are the two species of albatross, the Wedge-tailed Shearwater, the Bonin Island Petrel, the Tropic Bird, the Sooty Tern, and the Fairy Tern.

The Black-footed Albatross is limited in breeding to the leeward islands of Hawaii and the Marshall Islands. The most important breeding sites for the Laysan Albatross are in leeward Hawaii. The Wedge-tailed Shearwater is represented on Midway by substantial numbers and breeds over a great part of the Pacific. It is in no danger of extinction, although its populations on various islands have no doubt been greatly reduced.

The subspecies or variety of the Bonin Island Petrel found on Midway breeds only in the western Hawaiian Islands and in the Bonin Islands. Hadden *(op. cit.)* estimated five hundred thousand "on the island" in 1941. Compared with our estimate of twenty-five thousand, this figure shows an alarming decrease. Rats living in their burrows and the use by man of so much of the surface of the island are the chief factors in the decline in numbers.

The subspecies of the Tropic Bird on Midway is likewise limited to the Bonins and western Hawaii for breeding. However, the birds seem relatively successful in their nesting and are apparently adjusting themselves to changes in the surface of the island, for we saw them nesting in highly artificial surroundings.

The Sooty Tern is so widespread over Oceania south from Hawaii, the Bonin Islands, and Marcus Island and is present in such numbers on Midway that the subspecies is relatively safe.

The Fairy Tern, or White Love Bird, probably has actually increased in the last twenty years. Except for possible damage to eggs and young by rats, this bird is perhaps the least adversely affected by war activities of all birds now on Midway. Bryan in 1902 found only a few on Sand Island. Hadden estimated three thousand on Sand Island in 1941, whereas our estimate for Sand Island is fifteen thousand.

Now, what are the factors induced by the war that have caused this shift in populations? We wish to discuss these factors in two groups— those factors causing physical disturbances to the birds and those causing psycho-biological disturbances. These groups are of course closely related and interdigitated. Throughout we wish to emphasize that we used Midway merely as an example of the effects of occupation by military forces and that similar or identical effects are likely on other insular populations.

Factors resulting primarily in physical disturbance are four in number. First, the removal of and injury to nesting and roosting sites by bulldozing for construction projects of many sorts, trampling everywhere by men, movement of vehicles of many types, landscaping of grounds for ornamental purposes, clearing of vegetation around utility areas, and the erection of barbed wire barriers and similar contrivances were major influences upon the birds. The method of operation of these is obvious: usurpation of nesting area by permanently constructed physical developments, churning and removal of top soil or sand, breaking of vegetation, and establishment and maintenance of many artificial cover conditions. Species affected include all ground and bush nesting species, or the entire birdlife at Midway.

W. K. Fisher in 1903 noted the vast numbers of birds breeding on Laysan and their severe competition for horizontal or surface area. There was also a vertical distribution of birds; petrels and shearwaters beneath the surface; terns, albatrosses, Christmas Island Shearwaters, and Tropic Birds on the surface; and boobies, some terns, and frigates in the bushes above. Schauinsland in 1899 had noted that seasonal distribution was an important factor in permitting the nesting of so many individuals of so many species. It is probable that on certain islands the horizontal, vertical, and seasonal distribution of the several species has arisen as an adaptation for survival, resulting from competition for breeding space. Populations on saturated islands are probably reduced in direct proportion to the extent of removal of space, vegetation, and soil from these islands.

Secondly, the killing of individual birds was effected by airplanes, ground vehicles, traps and pits, destruction of disliked species, target shooting, and construction work. Almost all species present were seen to be affected. The clearing of carcasses was a daily operation to keep down the flies and to reduce the food supply of the rats. Airfields, roads, gooney colonies, and pits were daily productive of carcasses. As an example, planes were seen to cut up about a dozen Sooty Terns in average approaches to a landing strip where a small colony of five thousand was situated. Dead albatrosses and Tropic Birds could always be seen near the mats. Night flying was especially destructive of birds and resulted in greater slaughter of the Sooty Terns than did daytime flying. Petrels and shearwaters were vulnerable at night also. Ground vehicles accounted for large numbers of dead, noticeably along roads, from which unwitting young albatrosses had to be removed each morning by the first driver, and near airfield mats, where vehicles occasionally ran through the edges of bird colonies. One such colony of Sooty Terns lost eighty-three birds to ground vehicles in one night and sixty-eight the following night. The death toll would have been greater had young been present. Foxholes and other types of steep-sided pits caught albatrosses, shearwaters, petrels, and Tropic Birds. Thus trapped, the birds were unable to crawl or fly out and were starved to death. Black-footed Albatrosses, and other species to a lesser extent, became entangled in barbed wire along the beaches. The "moaning birds," of which the Wedge-tailed Shearwater was the most dismal-voiced, were generally disliked by the men. They received little sympathy, burrows were purposely tramped down, and adults persecuted constantly. Many Bonin Island Petrels were in areas desired for lawns and consequently were destroyed. Bulldozing in certain areas must have killed thousands of shearwaters and petrels in their burrows.

Third, the destruction of eggs by factors already discussed and possibly by egg gatherers probably decreased the bird populations significantly. The collection of eggs for eating may be a serious matter. The extent of such collecting on Midway is unknown, but the practice was common throughout the Pacific. On small islands this one factor could mean extinction if carried on for several years.

Fourth, the exigencies of war have resulted in the use of certain small islands for bombing and strafing practice. Frequently these are small rocky offshore islands covered with bird rookeries or are reefs surrounding larger islands with airfields. With the cessation of hostilities the justification for the continued use in this manner should be re-examined. In battle zones many of the islands have been more or less completely denuded of their flora and fauna. This was unavoidable, but the effect was nonetheless disastrous.

Factors resulting primarily in psycho-biological disturbances are five in number. First, men walking through nesting colonies to take short-cuts or to see the birds caused disturbances that were almost perpetual. It is hard to conceive how the normal, complex, breeding cycle could proceed effectively under extreme disturbance of this sort in such species as the colonial terns. The Sooty Terns in their colonies were posturing, defending territories, laying eggs, and making a great noise throughout the day, as is their usual custom. This sight drew many watchers, and when one of them walked into a colony, the terns would rise in a wheeling, squawking uproar that was decidedly unnatural.

Secondly, rats inadvertently introduced in 1943 destroyed large numbers of small birds and their eggs. Mice introduced at about the same time probably exerted a much less drastic effect on the birds. Rat damage was greatly curtailed by an intensive poisoning and trapping program initiated on both islets in 1944, but the germ of a potential rat problem remains because we have no means at present of eradicating them completely. Control measures must be maintained indefinitely on all bird islands where rats exist, if the smaller birds are to survive. Because many of the Pacific islands offer no large quantities of vertebrate animal food other than birds and eggs, the pressure of increases in numbers of rats will be directly exerted upon bird populations. Rats may be held largely responsible for the extinction of the rail and finch on Midway.

Third, dogs and probably other domestic animals have complicated the ecological situation. Rabbits now kept in captivity may escape and cause additional damage. In view of the possibility of egg damage, psychological disturbance, and habits harmful to birds that might develop in dogs and other animals, it would be a wise policy to keep in force the pre-war practice of exclusion of mammalian pets.

Fourth, exotic birds may be an even greater threat than pets. As previously mentioned, it is a serious matter to complicate and jeopardize the nesting grounds of oceanic birds by attempts to establish game birds, song birds, and other continental birdlife at Midway. The environment there is highly unsuited to such birds; some require barnyard care to build up their populations. Another strong reason against bird introductions is that the oceanic birds are, as the Midway newspaper termed it, "the best entertainment we have on this island," and attempts to augment the avifauna are not in the best interests of recreation. Unknown and unpredictable psycho-biological reactions between the birds are almost certain to take place, and some will be detrimental to the native birds. Resulting losses may far outweigh any recreational benefits afforded by such continental species as have been introduced.

Fifth, changes in plant life have resulted from extensive clearing and extensive replantings. Grasses, shrubs, and trees have been planted widely on Sand Island. Dense vegetation may restrict the breeding of albatrosses, but it creates new sites for many other species. Grasses have been used extensively for sand stabilization; shrubs such as scaevola, tree heliotrope, and sea grape have been set out on sand dunes, and ironwood trees planted in great numbers. Sand Island has many more exotic plants than Eastern Island, where the main shrub is still scaevola alone. In some areas it was noticeable that grass and underbrush were removed for landscaping and rat control purposes. This removal destroyed the cover used by such birds as the Laysan Rail. As a whole, the changes have reduced the bird populations during the past few years more than they have helped increase the populations. When the new plantings are established, however, some of the birds should be generally benefited. A large-scale spatial readjustment of many bird colonies has been necessitated by the changes in the plant life and ground surface. Species unable to adjust rapidly have suffered.

Pan-oceanic breeders are naturally less liable to extinction from disturbances than birds breeding in only one archipelago or on one island. However, the activities of man are now so widely spread over the islands of the Pacific Ocean that even pan-oceanic island breeders should not be considered entirely safe from destruction as a species merely because they nest at widely separated localities. Careful and complete surveys are needed at present because it would be impossible on the basis of information at hand to list all the islets and islands where any of the oceanic birds discussed in the foregoing accounts are breeding. The fewer the islands used by any one species of bird, the more actively should protective measures be put into effect for that species. We do not know how much chance there is for any species, once exterminated from an island, to re-colonize it. We should watch the colonies of boobies and terns at Midway with this in mind.

Mono-insular endemics, or birds breeding only on one island, are in a precarious position. Immediate consideration should be given to transferring breeding stock of these species to other places to insure the longevity of the species. The species life of the Laysan Rail was prolonged some twenty years in this way without critical harm to any other birds on Midway, and the species would probably still be there had not rats been introduced. The Laysan Teal, Laysan Finch, Nihoa Finch, and Nihoa Miller Bird are mono-insular endemics that may still be in existence today.

Although there are seemingly large populations of certain species of seabirds at Midway, there is danger inherent in allowing breeding populations to decrease below certain as yet unknown levels. Work elsewhere has shown that small colonies of some species are slower to breed and are less successful in nesting than are large colonies of the same species, and that when too much reduced in numbers, no breeding occurs. A psychological interdependence exists among many colonial birds that is apparently an important factor in the initiation and completion of the reproductive cycle. It is important that population data be gathered often enough to make it possible to discern downward trends in numbers. Given that the extinction of birds living in small, circumscribed areas such as islands may occur with great speed, such surveys should be started before post-war developments are undertaken on the leeward islands and should be repeated at frequent intervals. Remember that just four years ago the Laysan Rail, the Laysan Finch, and the Brown Booby were abundant on Midway.

Since 1940 the degree and rate of environmental change on many Pacific islands have increased. War-torn islands have of course suffered most. News reports indicate that starving men on Wake Island ate all the gooneys they could get, and rats too. Before the war there was a rail endemic to that one island, but with rats, bombings, and starving men, there is little hope that it still lives today.

Midway shared briefly in the violence of war, but the birdlife there has fared relatively well. From Midway we have learned in detail what may happen on islands used intensively by man, but not subjected to combat conditions, and we have learned that the need for complete protection for bird islands is now greater than ever before.

Tourist Forecast

CLARENCE L. HODGE

❖ Hawaii can expect an influx of tourists in 1947 numbering more than 110,000, a figure unexcelled in the history of the islands, according to an estimate recently made by Mark Egan, executive secretary of the Hawaii Visitors Bureau. Before the war some fifty thousand tourists spent in excess of $20 million a year in Hawaii, and within five years Hawaii can expect to receive about $45 million from the tourist trade, Mr. Egan says.

One-hundred-ten thousand people is a sizable crowd in any man's language, and an annual income of $45 million is certainly worth cultivating because the huge wartime payrolls and spending of the armed forces in this area have dropped sharply in recent months.

These millions of tourist dollars will find their way into the pockets of local businessmen and residents of the community. After the first turnover from retail stores, hotels, amusements, restaurants, and transportation companies, these travel dollars will be used for payroll, rent, taxes, insurance, construction, and repair. These travel dollars will benefit every person in the islands and at the same time they will provide a cushion to sustain Hawaii's postwar economy.

This economy depends largely on four sound industries. They are the basic industrialized agricultural crops of sugar and pineapples, revenue from the armed forces and civil employees, and an expanding fishing industry. The annual income from each of these sources is estimated to run as follows:

Sugar and pineapples	$125,000,000
Armed forces and civil employees	53,000,000
Fishing	10,000,000
Total	$188,000,000

First published March 1946.

To this can be added a potential $45 million from the tourist trade, making an estimated postwar annual income from these five major industries of approximately $233 million.

This postwar tourist trade estimate is based on recent surveys made by travel organizations on the mainland that reveal that the average American family is all set for foreign travel. These travel agencies are receiving thousands of inquiries daily. "What countries can we visit now? When will passports be available? Can we travel by ship or plane? Are hotel accommodations available? How much will such a trip cost?" These are typical questions being asked by an American public itching to travel.

The average person has made good money during the war years and has put aside substantial savings. Wartime restrictions have prevented foreign travel, but at the same time war news has created curiosity and interest in Hawaii and the Pacific area. With the lifting of wartime restrictions, Hawaii can expect a tourist boom of great consequence to the Territory.

A travel survey made by *Town and Country* shows that 35 percent of all families interviewed want to go either to Canada, Bermuda, Hawaii, California, or Florida. Some mainland preferences were listed because of the present difficulty in securing transportation outside the United States. Another survey conducted by *Traveler Magazine* among fifteen hundred readers listed Hawaii as seventh preference for their postwar trips to foreign lands. Hawaii out-ranked all countries except Alaska, Canada, Cuba, Europe, Mexico, and South America. Hawaii will have stiff competition from these countries and must prepare to meet it.

Peacetime Honolulu was a regular port of call for steamship lines operating some sixty ships on regular schedules to this port. Transpacific lines provided passenger accommodations from moderate to luxurious. Ships running from Los Angeles and San Francisco to the islands made the trip in about five days. Besides the Pacific Coast–Hawaii run, Honolulu was a port of call for ships running from Japan; from Central America and the west coast of South America; for U.S. round-the-world cruises; and from the United States to Australia, New Zealand, and the Orient. At the outbreak of the war all scheduled services were suspended when American ships were taken over by the Federal Government for war service.

The ships of these various companies are being returned to their owners after their war duties. These ships will be ready for passenger trade as soon as they are reconditioned. New fleets of vessels are being constructed by several companies to handle the tourist trade. These vessels will provide regular runs between the mainland and Hawaii and throughout the Orient.

Pan American World Airways clippers are now operating daily flights from San Francisco to Honolulu. As new planes are received and travel to the islands increases, more flights and speedier schedules are to be inaugurated. Several airlines have petitioned the Civil Aeronautics Board for the run from San Francisco and Los Angeles to Hawaii. These airlines intend to use new four-engine planes in the Hawaiian service. These huge ships will make the trip in about nine hours. Air service to the Philippines, New Zealand, Australia, and the Orient is scheduled for later operation.

The airlines alone are expecting a volume of sixty thousand tourists to Hawaii in 1947; another fifty thousand can be expected to use surface transportation, making a total of approximately 110,000 one-way trips, or 220,000 two-way trips, annually, as Mr. Egan said. This is double the number of tourists in prewar days.

Trips to Hawaii will soon be within the price range of the average income group. Steamship lines are expecting to cut fares to the levels of prewar years, and bargain rates for special tours of all kinds are sure to follow. Just as soon as new fast fifty-passenger planes come off the line and are put in operation, air officials say that the San Francisco to Honolulu run will cost only $125 for a one-way trip. When these new rates go into effect, travel to Hawaii and throughout the Pacific will be within reach of masses of the people. And the time factor is important too. Job holders with only two weeks vacation could easily make a trip to Hawaii, spend ten days vacationing in the islands, and have ample time to get back to jobs in San Francisco, Chicago, or New York.

With the outbreak of the war December 7, 1941, Hawaii's tourist trade automatically closed, and the Tourist Bureau suspended operations in June, 1942. Looking toward a resumption of the tourist trade, the Hawaii Visitors Bureau has been revived. Mark Egan, a widely known hotel, convention, and travel bureau executive, was employed as executive secretary, office space was secured, and a peacetime program has been developed directed toward a vigorous promotion of travel to the islands when transportation and tourist facilities are available.

A monthly news bulletin, maps, booklets, news and feature stories, scenic photographs, and a twenty-five-hundred-foot kodachrome motion picture of Hawaii are being prepared for distribution to interested individuals and organizations throughout the world. A study of postwar tourist needs and facilities throughout the islands is being undertaken. Committees on each island are being organized to develop local interest in welcoming tourists, planning tours, making historical and scenic sites, cleaning up the beaches and parks, and encouraging the immediate construction of medium-priced hotels.

To hold this tourist trade, Hawaii must improve its hotels and recreational facilities. During the war its leading hotels have been extensively used by the armed forces. They need to be renovated, enlarged, modernized, and equipped to entertain and provide true Hawaiian hospitality.

At the present time there are only about 650 first-class transient rooms available to the visitor in Honolulu. When the Royal Hawaiian Hotel opens in late fall, another 350 first-class rooms will be added, making a total of only 1,000 rooms to handle an estimated flow of tourists of ten thousand a month in 1947. These people will not just stay overnight; they will stay a minimum of ten days, and many will stay longer. Based on a conservative estimate of ten days, these ten thousand visitors would need a hundred thousand room days per month, and our present capacity represents only thirty thousand room days, a survey by Mr. Egan reveals.

New hotels need to be built, and new public and private recreational facilities provided. If these accommodations are not provided by local businessmen, it is altogether likely that mainland capital will provide them. Public and private agencies must join the Hawaii Visitors Bureau in a Territory-wide cleanup program. Hawaii's beaches and parks and playgrounds should be cleaned up and made attractive. New parks and public beaches need to be developed. These facilities will provide more things for the tourist to do, add income to the Territory, and make life more enjoyable for the people of Hawaii.

The Japanese attack on Pearl Harbor and the war in the Pacific that followed focused the eyes of the world on Hawaii. It became internationally famous overnight and remained so throughout the war. The congressional investigation on statehood and the atom bomb tests being conducted by the Navy Department at Bikini Atoll in May have again placed Hawaii in the international limelight. In addition, thousands of

American families wish to visit Hawaii, Guadalcanal, Tarawa, Kwajalein, Saipan, Guam, New Guinea, the Philippines, Iwo Jima, and Okinawa because their husbands and relatives fought or were buried there.

These are postwar travel potentialities that should not be ignored. Hawaii must prepare now to take care of the host of visitors soon to visit its shores if it is to hold this lucrative trade against mainland and foreign competition. The tourist trade is Hawaii's third industry; it is up to the people of the Territory to keep it.

Housing Dream Come True

❖ A brand new town, complete from the garage of the last house on the last street to the drug store across from the community hall, is an event of importance. The territory of Hawaii is to have not only one such modern town but possibly a baker's dozen of them, and this isn't the dream of a visionary. In the midst of all the concern, discussion, and effort devoted to the problem of adequate housing and its accomplishment in both public and private projects, plans for the building of these new towns that will revolutionize rural life in the islands have been scarcely noticed, yet those plans are the most important from a community viewpoint of any in the entire housing picture.

There is a suite of offices in the Alexander & Baldwin building that doesn't have a sign on the door. Inside that suite men are bending over drafting boards every day, tracing out individual houses, groups of houses, business centers, and all that must go into a new modern town. The name of these offices is the Industrial Service Bureau. The man at the head of this organization is Theodore A. Vierra, and the organization is a department of the Hawaiian Sugar Planters' Association. The idea behind all this is to modernize plantation life, just as plantation work is being modernized through mechanization. Not only in Hawaii but in the mainland as well there is a drift of workers away from the farms. For years the youth of the nation has been going to the cities, and this has been a serious problem for agriculture, which must feed the nation.

One of the answers is to bring the cities to the farms and plantations, and to provide for the agricultural workers the things they want to move into town to get. Make the rural community complete and attractive and give its residents all the advantages of city life, without the disadvantages, and people will prefer to live there.

That's one side of it. Another side is that the plantations derive advantages from better arranged and healthier towns. Their man-

First published April 1946.

agement is more efficient and maintenance is easier. Then too there are the factors of safety and the general welfare that are just as important as the factors of efficiency in the fields and the mills.

The old plantation town was really a village; often a small settlement, with life centering around the general store. A majority of the plantation's people lived in the small outlying camps so that they would be nearer their work. With transportation what it is today, these camps are no longer necessary. All the people of a plantation can live in one larger town; and it follows quite naturally that the larger a town is, the more it can offer in the way of entertainment, social life, and recreation.

These new towns are to be equipped not only with the usual social facilities; they are to have the kinds of amusements the plantation people now go to the city to find. The big stores will be improved, there will be a better movie theater, a good pool hall, a good drug store, maybe with juke boxes. Churches, schools, and community centers will of course be included. In short, life will be amazingly complete for the size of the community.

One of the first of these complete new towns to be undertaken will be that of Olokele on Kauai.... Work will be started in the near future, depending upon the availability of workers and materials for building. There are to be 270 brand new houses, a new store, community center, theater, and all the other adjuncts. The streets are laid out for safety and convenience of traffic. Every house will have a sizable yard, and if the people who live in these new houses take pride in them, as undoubtedly they will, the new Olokele will be a beautiful town.

And Olokele isn't the only one. The engineers and draftsmen are already busy on other plans for other towns, and these are to be delayed no longer than present-day conditions make absolutely necessary. Not all plantations have to have completely new towns. Some already have good modern housing, which will be brought up to date through repairs and improvements.

There is another variation to this plantation community planning that will mean a lot to both the plantation towns where it is put into effect. This is the construction of new plantation housing adjacent to already established towns, so that an entire new town does not have to be constructed, and the plantation community becomes a part of the established town. Needless to say these towns will benefit greatly by these additions.

An example of this variation is at McBryde plantation, also on Kauai—and perhaps it should be pointed out that thus far Kauai seems to be leading in these new projects. The new houses for the McBryde plantation are to be built in an area adjacent to Eleele, and of course the business from this new "suburb" will flow into Eleele.

The individual plantation house to be built is something that will cause delight to anyone moving into it. The first two of the McBryde program have already been completed. During the real estate boom now on in Honolulu, houses offering the same space and accommodations would sell for around twenty thousand dollars. The new McBryde house has three bedrooms and none is smaller than twelve-by-twelve. There is a large living room and a large dinette. The kitchen and bathroom are also generous in dimensions, and the equipment is of the best. The bathrooms have separate showers and tubs, and the plumbing fixtures are of extra good quality. For each house there is a garage and an outside laundry.

Every stick of lumber that goes into one of these houses is seasoned and selected. If a board shows up with a flaw in it, that board is rejected and used for some other purpose. No better houses of this size and structure are being built anywhere in the islands. With proper care they will last and provide comfortable dwelling for fifty years.

Something else that should be mentioned is that the McBryde houses are not all to be alike. The old idea of a row of houses exactly alike in shape and color is passing. There will be something individual about each house—different colors, different designs, different shaped roofs, and different shaped lots. The lots incidentally are from eight thousand to ten thousand square feet in area. Any proud occupant can develop a beautiful home for himself and his family.

For all plantations, the housing program may extend over the next ten years. Some of those building complete new towns will do the job as a single project and complete it much sooner. At McBryde the schedule calls for two hundred houses to be built at the rate of twenty a year.

While this is going on, Honolulu and the other cities of the territory are going to grow. They'll become busier and more congested and less enjoyable places to live. Just as has happened on the mainland in the past, there will be a greater urge to get away from cities, especially among the people with families to raise, and enjoy the fuller, pleasanter life of the smaller centers. And it will be fuller and pleasant because those centers will have much more to offer. Hawaii's plantations have been leaders in scientific agriculture, in employee health, and in agricultural wages. The same farsightedness is now present in this planning for the plantation community of the future.

Hawaii—49th State by '49?

GEORGE H. McLANE

❖ Statehood for territories perhaps had its inception in 1787, when Congress, still under the Confederation, passed the Northwest Ordinance, bringing into existence the territorial form of government and providing conditions for transition from territory to state. Statehood for Hawaii has been brewing for more than a century. There was an American settlement in Hawaii before there was one in California. American civilization was transplanted to the Islands by American missionaries in 1820. Successive migration developed a harmonious citizenry of diverse origins.

In 1854, during the period of monarchy in the Hawaiian Islands, a treaty was proposed, though never ratified, that Hawaii come into the Union as a state, enjoying the same degree of sovereignty as other states. Again, the Hawaiian Commissioners requested, in 1893, that the consideration for ceding the Hawaiian Islands should be admission to the Union as a state. The treaty of 1897 repeated the request. By the time the Islands were annexed in 1898, they were intrinsically American. Today, the people of Hawaii do not consider themselves in the nature of an adopted group, but one for whom statehood would mean a natural heritage.

The Territory of Hawaii is a group of eight large islands and numerous islets in the Pacific Ocean, situated some two thousand miles west of California. The land area, 6,438 square miles, is larger than the combined areas of Delaware, Connecticut, and Rhode Island. The islands are of volcanic origin. From northeast to northwest, they are Hawaii, Kahoolawe, Maui, Lanai, Molokai, Oahu, Kauai, and Niihau.

In addition, stretching northwestward beyond Niihau more than 1,100 miles is an archipelago of rocks, reefs, and shoals that include

---

First published August 1946.

Midway. Likewise, 960 miles south of Honolulu and part of the City and County of Honolulu lies Palmyra, a coral atoll.

The population of the Territory grew from 423,330 in 1940 to an estimated 502,122 in 1945, exclusive of military and naval personnel. Its population is larger than that of any state at the time of admission with the exception of Oklahoma. Compared with the several states at the time of the 1940 census, Hawaii exceeded the population of the states of Nevada, Wyoming, Delaware, and Vermont, and its population was almost equal to that of four other states. The racial origin of this population, in addition to the native Hawaiians and the Caucasians from the mainland, is Japanese, Chinese, Korean, Filipino, and Portuguese. However, 86 percent of the population are citizens of the United States

For more than a century Hawaii has had constitutional government. The first constitution was established during the monarchy, having been granted by Kamehameha III in 1840. The Republic of Hawaii was established in 1894, and annexation was effected in 1898. Annexation was by voluntary action of the people and government of Hawaii and was the culmination of many years of negotiations. As early as 1854, during the reign of Kamehameha III, steps were taken by him looking toward annexation.

When Congress, by the Newlands Resolution, accepted the cession made on the terms that Hawaii should be incorporated into the United States as an integral part thereof and should be granted territorial status, Congress then and there committed the United States to the ultimate granting of statehood.

It has been through no lack of effort on its part that Hawaii has thus far failed to achieve statehood. Fourteen times, either by petition or by resolution, it has brought the matter to the attention of Congress. Ten times the territorial legislature has made appropriations to cover investigations by the Congress. On three occasions Congressional Committees have responded with noteworthy results. As far back as 1935, the Congress authorized the Committee on Territories to visit Hawaii for the purpose of holding hearings on the question of statehood for Hawaii. That committee, in its report to the Congress, recommended that the House and Senate give further consideration to the problem.

A thorough investigation of statehood for Hawaii was next made in 1937 by a Joint Congressional Committee. No stronger endorsement of Hawaii's qualifications need be devised than is contained in their report, which stated "that Hawaii has fulfilled every requirement for statehood heretofore exacted of territories," but recommended that the question of statehood be deferred on two grounds: first, that a plebiscite should be held, and second, on the grounds of the then-disturbed condition of international affairs. A plebiscite was held in 1940; the vote was 67 percent in favor of statehood and 33 percent in opposition.

Before the full significance of the plebiscite result could be registered in furtherance of statehood, war broke out and interrupted effective action until January, 1946, when a Sub-Committee of the House Territories Committee visited Hawaii and held extensive hearings throughout the Territory on the question of statehood. At the close of the hearings, this sub-committee stated that because:

1. The people of the Territory of Hawaii have demonstrated beyond question not only their loyalty and patriotism but also their desire to assume the responsibility of statehood; and since
2. The policy of the United States government is one of self-determination; that peoples be allowed to choose freely their own form of political status; and since
3. Hawaii's strategic location in the Pacific plays so large a part in our country's international position in this area; and since
4. The Congress of the United States has through a series of acts and committee reports indicated to the people of the territory that Hawaii would be admitted into the union when qualified; and since
5. The Territory of Hawaii now meets the necessary requirements for statehood.
It is the recommendation of this subcommittee that the committee on Territories give immediate consideration to legislation to admit Hawaii to statehood.

National impetus to the case for statehood for Hawaii has resulted from these hearings; Hawaii's qualifications for statehood are becoming widely known.

Gov. Ingram M. Stainback, early in the summer of 1946, appointed to a Citizens' Statehood Committee nearly three hundred citizens of Hawaii. The Committee is composed of five sections and is assisted in its functioning by an executive board of seventeen members, the chairman of which is the Governor of Hawaii.

Members of the territorial legislature, numbering forty-five persons, compose the membership of the first section; their efforts to aid the drive toward statehood will come from the advice and counsel stemming from the legislative branch of the government, particularly in the matter of legislating for funds for the national campaign. The Equal Rights Commission will perform its statutory function to assist and cooperate with the plans to accomplish the objective of admission of the Territory to statehood. The four heads of the county governments' section will be able to lend valuable support to the drive for statehood by coordinating the activities of the committee on the other islands. Of the two larger membership sections, the Organizations Section will strive to maintain interest in the objective of early statehood for Hawaii among the local members of the seventy-five organizations represented and to extend the interest in and support of such objectives as widely as possible among the mainland affiliates of such organizations. The Individual Citizens Section, through personal and business contacts, and by such other means as will be developed from time to time, will be able to foster the move for statehood on the mainland United States. The Citizens' Statehood Committee has been activated by the Governor and will be dissolved at the end of the next session of the legislature unless sooner terminated by the Governor.

Upon the opening of the Executive Office of the Citizens' Statehood Committee in Iolani Palace, data pertaining to statehood for Hawaii has been made available in quantity for distribution on the mainland, largely through the good will and ardent efforts of staunch supporters for statehood from the Hawaiian Islands. Nearly twenty thousand pieces of material have been distributed thus far. The most important educational work of the Committee has been the result of the large number of "Resolutions Favoring Statehood for Hawaii," which have been passed by the mainland affiliates of organizations represented on the Citizens' Statehood Committee. Such groups as the National Educational Association, the American Water Works Association, the Lions International, and the Daughters of the American Revolution have expressed their support of statehood for Hawaii during 1946. The Junior Chamber of Commerce, at their national convention, the Soroptomists, and the Zonta International have likewise, at national conventions in the mainland, supported Hawaii's desire for statehood.

Many business men and women have used the facilities of the Executive Office of the Statehood Committee for materials useful in making speeches at luncheon clubs and at other business gatherings during their necessary business trips to the mainland. One enthusiastic family has painted on the sides of their Packard roadster in large letters the words "Hawaii 49th State"; another chap attached a small statuette of King Kamehameha on his front bumper and likewise had emblazoned the words "Hawaii 49th State" across his car.

A group in the community has formed an organization known as the 49th State Athletic Association. This group plans to develop athletic teams both for local and mainland competition. One famous sports figure has been pictured with the Brooklyn Dodgers recently, with the words "Hawaii 49th State" across the chest of his uniform.

Although the Seventy-ninth Congress adjourned without taking action on legislation enabling Hawaii to form a constitutional convention, the Citizens' Statehood Committee has plans for a national "Statehood for Hawaii" effort to indicate benefits of Hawaiian statehood to the nation. A fair consideration of Hawaii's case should culminate during the Eightieth Congress in statehood for Hawaii.

"We Wish to Do Our Part"

❖ Because of the color of their skin, some of us forgot. Forgot that they knew about the seventh-inning stretch, read the colored comics on Sunday, liked apple pie a la mode. Forgot that they were Americans of Japanese ancestry—and not Japanese. Some of us said that color would tell, that yellow was yellow, and white was white. Others said, "The Japanese are fine people, but you just can't trust them." Because their faces were different, their names strange, their parents born in Japan, instead of in England, Germany, or Pennsylvania, some were sure they just couldn't feel as American as we did. Some pictured the Japanese in America as gloating over the crimson aftermath of Pearl Harbor—ready, one and all, to "stab you in the back."

America as a nation had been stabbed in the back. And Americans were determined to strike back, to fight for their country, their taken-for-granted freedom, the seventh-inning stretch, the colored comics, the apple pie a la mode. Americans of Japanese ancestry had even more to fight for. They had first to prove to the skeptical millions that they were Americans, that they had the *right* to fight for America.

In Hawaii, in December of 1941, there were 160,000 Americans of Japanese ancestry, bewildered, confused, suddenly held personally responsible for the actions of a country many of them had never seen. At the University of Hawaii were Americans of Japanese ancestry serving in the Reserve Officers' Training Corps. On December 7, the ROTC was called out and many of the men enlisted in the Hawaii Territorial Guard. For six weeks, through the crisis, these men guarded and protected the vital utilities and installations of the Territory. Then on January 19, 1942, all members of Japanese ancestry were inactivated from the services of the Guard with honorable discharges.

This was a paralyzing blow. The men had served the Guard and the United States loyally, with pride that they were doing their part for their country. And suddenly they were told that their services were no longer needed, when they knew there was a mammoth job to be done.

After the first wave of disappointment and frustration had passed,

---

First published December 1946.

342

the men realized that this was no time to sit passively by and bemoan their situation. They realized that they must find other ways to serve their country, they must prove themselves useful in some other part of the war effort. More important, they knew that they must prove to America her need of them and their own loyalty to her.

In the last week of January a small group of those discharged from the Hawaii Territorial Guard met with a few interested and sympathetic civic leaders and discussed with them their desire to serve. They asked themselves, "What can we do?"

They decided upon bold action—to petition the military governor, explain their peculiar situation, and offer themselves unconditionally for any service permitted in defense of their homeland and in the winning of the war. A meeting was called to mobilize as many of the former members of the Guard as possible—those attending the University and those in town. The petition, presented for their approval and acceptance, signed and delivered to the military governor, Lt. Gen. Delos C. Emmons, was an unconditional offer of loyal service:

Honolulu, T. H.
January 30, 1942
Lt. Gen. Delos C. Emmons
Commanding General, Hawaiian
Department, U.S.A.

Sir:

We, the undersigned, were members of the Hawaii Territorial Guard until its recent inactivation. We joined the Guard voluntarily with the hope that this was one way to serve our country in her time of need. Needless to say, we were deeply disappointed when we were told that our services in the Guard were no longer needed.

Hawaii is our home; the United States, our country. We know but one loyalty and that is to the Stars and Stripes. We wish to do our part as loyal Americans in every way possible, and we hereby offer ourselves for whatever service you may see fit to use us.

General Emmons accepted the men as a labor corps under the Hawaiian Department Army Engineers, to be housed as a unit and to work in conjunction with the army engineers. A one-day notice for preparation and mobilization was issued. The men left their jobs and withdrew from their classes to answer the call. On February 25, 1942, the group, calling themselves the "Varsity Victory Volunteers," assembled on the steps of Hawaii Hall, on the University of Hawaii campus, for a simple aloha ceremony given by civic leaders, college officials, instructors, and former classmates.

For eleven months the Varsity Victory Volunteers were known as the Corps of Engineers Auxiliary, were attached as a company to the Thirty-fourth Combat Engineers Regiment, and were therefore directly responsible to the United States Army Corps of Engineers.

Stationed at Schofield Barracks, the Varsity Victory Volunteers built military installations, roads, warehouses and dumps, quarried rock, and strung barbed wire. Their tasks weren't glamorous; they had no rank; they weren't flying planes or carrying guns; they weren't even G.I. After more than eleven months of service, the Varsity Victory Volunteers were inactivated, on January 31, 1943. They asked to be released so that they might enlist in the United States Army with the recently formed American-Japanese combat unit.

This, in terse outline, is the story of the VVV. It is the story of men who, because of the tint of their skin and because their parents migrated to America from Japan, had to prove they were Americans. They gave that proof, but in doing so proved more than the loyalty of 150 individuals. They proved to the United States that Americans of Japanese ancestry could be just as loyal to their country as Americans of any other ancestry. And their contribution will not be forgotten in Hawaii.

The majority of the members of the VVV served with distinction in the war theaters—with the 100th Infantry Battalion and with the 442nd Regimental Combat Team. Their roster had seven gold stars. Most of the men have come back from the fronts, and at least fifty-four of them have returned to the University of Hawaii, where they have organized the "Triple V Club."

Americans of Japanese ancestry in Hawaii are no longer under a cloud. Their Americanism has been proved beyond cavil. Familiar as the story is to many of us, it needs to be told to Americans everywhere, for one still hears of prejudice and discrimination against fellow Americans whose patriotic devotion is symbolized by the Triple V.

Note: *From the foreword of a pamphlet,* In Memoriam, *published by the University of Hawaii, and signed by Margaret Blegen, Charles R. Hemenway, and Gregg M. Sinclair, president of the University.*

1946—In Retrospect

EILEEN O'BRIEN

❖ Hawaii, like the rest of the country, groped its way through 1946, wrestling with grave problems such as a housing shortage and labor-management disputes. As the year comes to a close, these and other problems are far from solved. Cheering notes, however, have been the remarkable speed with which the disfiguring physical traces of war have been removed from the Islands and the sustaining optimism that eventually Hawaii is destined for unprecedented economic expansion as the air and sea crossroads of the Pacific.

The first of the year saw several "hangovers" from the war, such as the Pearl Harbor inquiry, investigation of irregularities in surplus property disposal, and the "get home hysteria" of service men stationed here. A protest meeting of fifteen thousand army men at Hickam Field was an orderly one, however, and the flare-up of men in uniform was not as violent in Hawaii as it was in Manila and other areas.

In January of this year, Hawaii's drive toward the goal of statehood was advanced a step by a visit of the U.S. House of Representatives' sub-committee on statehood. . . . While Mainland headlines concerned themselves with the shocking Degnan murder and strikes of electrical workers, packers, and others, Hawaii experienced its first approach to pre-war, ship-welcoming aloha when the *Aleutian* arrived here. Herman Wedemeyer, Hawaii's All-American St. Mary's football star, came home for a visit and was extensively leied and luaued by his fans. The same month, fifteen hundred Filipino laborers arrived to work in Hawaii's sugar plantations, which had experienced severe manpower losses during the war.

Heavy rains during February were the attributed cause of many cases of influenza, which for a while neared epidemic proportions. As the Mainland steel strike was ended, Hawaii continued to struggle

---

First published December 1946.

with the housing shortage, which was described by the Izac Congressional investigation report as worse than at any time and which still remains one of the most acute of any area in the United States. During this month the public schools of the Territory were given a citation by the United States Army "for exceptional and meritorious service in the war against Japan."

In March the first contingent of Operations Crossroads passed through Pearl Harbor en route to Bikini, and Honolulu made preparations to entertain the correspondents and official observers who would witness the atom bomb tests. Aviation milestones of the month were the first commercial flight of the giant Mars, bringing twenty-seven thousand pounds of freight and mail, and the arrival of the *Fluffy Fuz,* a B-29, which made a non-stop flight to the Philippine Islands and later set a record of seven hours, fourteen-and-a-quarter minutes from Hawaii to San Francisco.

During the same month a series of parties on all the Islands was given in honor of Earl M. Finch, a Mississippian who had befriended Americans of Japanese ancestry stationed at an army camp near his home. He continued his interest in these young men while they were overseas and after they returned to hospitals in the United States. At the close of his first visit to Hawaii, Nisei veterans and their parents presented Finch with $12,500 to continue his work of helping AJA veterans still in hospitals throughout the country.

A devastating tidal wave that struck all the Islands on April first took the lives of more than a hundred persons and caused damage running into many millions of dollars. Apart from the loss of lives, the tragedy was made more acute by the loss of many desperately needed homes and the difficulties of obtaining materials to replace them....

The first peaceful Easter in five years was highlighted in Honolulu by a sunrise service at Kapiolani park, attended by thousands. A newspaper headline of that day ironically carried the banner line, "Super Atom Bomb Claimed."

An outstanding event in the month of April was the observance of the centennial of the Catholic Mission on Maui with a "Century of Faith" ceremony at the Kahului fair grounds. This was attended by Archbishop Amleto Cicognani, apostolic delegate to the United States, who later officiated at a pontifical high mass in Honolulu stadium in observance of Damien day. The same month was marked by a visit to Hawaii of General "Ike" Eisenhower.

May Day is Lei Day in Hawaii, and the event was observed in a festive manner for the first time since before the war, last year's celebration having been canceled because of the period of mourning for Franklin D. Roosevelt. As the Mainland struggled with the railroad and coal strikes, Hawaii was concerned with the backlog of more than two thousand persons awaiting transportation to the Islands from San Francisco. In May it was announced that Coconut island, the windward Oahu home of the late Christian R. Holmes, had been purchased by a group of Mainland businessmen headed by Edwin W. Pauley, a California oil tycoon. The island was purchased for $250,000, and it was announced that $500,000 would be spent to convert it into an exclusive resort hotel. VE Day was observed quietly in Honolulu, the chief event being a service at Central Union church sponsored by members of the 442nd Infantry Battalion.

A temporary setback for Hawaii's statehood campaign took place early in June when the territories committee of the House of Representatives voted to defer further hearings until after the fall elections, eliminating chances for congressional action in 1946. Manoa war homes, a community of four thousand persons, was officially opened early in June, providing a slight easement on the pressure for housing in Honolulu.

In June, labor-management disputes that were to reach a gravely acute stage before the year's end began to attract public attention and, at the same time, the threat of a tie-up of Mainland shipping was temporarily averted. During this month the first wave of observers and correspondents en route to Bikini arrived in Honolulu and were extensively entertained.

While the atom bomb blasts made headlines in July, Hawaii was concerned with its own problems, chief of which was the threat of a general strike. This strike did not occur, however. A dispute over union contract renewal at the Honolulu Rapid Transit Company resulted in disruption of bus transportation over a period of several days. The controversy over the continuation of OPA was reflected in Hawaii as elsewhere, the rising prices being exemplified by the fact that the retail price of poi was up 100 percent.

In July, the airport on Lanai was completed, linking the "pineapple island" more closely to the rest of the Territory. A $3 million project to rehabilitate and beautify the war-created civilian housing area at Pearl Harbor was begun. During the same month a large group of

Aloha Temple members left for the Shriners' convention in San Francisco, and the first post-war South Seas cruise was begun with the departure from Honolulu of a thirty-four-foot schooner, *Myrtle S.* It was announced that Hawaii's civilian population had passed the half-million mark.

When Hawaii learned that members of the 442nd Combat Infantry Battalion returning from overseas would be given an official welcome in New York, the people of Hawaii decided to send fresh flower leis to the returning heroes. From all the Islands these leis came to Honolulu and fifteen hundred were shipped to New York in a special army plane. This "operation aloha" represented a spontaneous gesture on the part of Hawaii residents, and the fresh flower leis, when worn by the men in New York, created mild sensations. The 442nd was given a rousing welcome by Honolulu when the men returned in August. The battalion was deactivated on August 15.

In August, the first of a series of trials concerning alleged fraud at Pearl Harbor took place, resulting in a not-guilty verdict for the defendants. A spectacular "drone" flight was conducted by the army when radio-controlled Flying Fortresses were flown from Hilo to California. Ingram M. Stainback, newly appointed to a second term as governor of Hawaii, announced the formation of a committee to intensify the campaign for statehood in the near future, with a six-month budget of fifty thousand dollars.

A highlight of the month was the observance of Veterans' Day on August 15th. It was declared a territorial holiday and was marked by church services, dances for veterans, and a parade witnessed by eighty thousand persons. During the same month, juvenile delinquency became a matter of public concern, with special attention focused on escapees from Waialee school for boys and resulting investigations of conditions at that school. In August, Doris Duke Cromwell returned to her Diamond Head home for the first time in five years.

The chief event of September was the calling of a sugar workers' strike after failure of negotiations that had started in July. When months passed by without settlement, the strike had a serious effect on the economy of the entire Territory. Falling off of business was further complicated by the Mainland shipping tie-up, which prevented merchandise and food from reaching Hawaii.

September was marked by the arrival of the *Pacusan Dreamboat,* the B-29 that, after many delays, finally took off a month later and made a 10,030-mile non-stop flight over the top of the world to Cairo. The political season moved into full swing, with rallies resuming the colorful atmosphere of pre-war days. The Oahu Railway and Land Company announced that its narrow gauge railway would be abandoned next year and would be replaced by a trucking company for hauling sugar from the mills to the waterfront.

Throughout October the effects of the sugar strike and the Mainland shipping tie-up continued to have increasingly pinching effects on business throughout the Islands. A threatened strike of local waterfront workers was postponed. Primary elections took place on October fifth and, after a brief breathing spell, candidates of both parties launched their campaigns for the November fifth final elections.

The Waianae Company, Ltd., announced that it will go out of business, and its ten thousand acres of sugar plantation have been purchased by a local syndicate that plans to make available badly needed land for individual homes.

The highlight of November was a hotly contested election, which resulted in returning Joseph R. Farrington to Congress as delegate from Hawaii and putting John H. Wilson into office as mayor of Honolulu, succeeding Lester Petrie.

Among the prominent Hawaii residents who died during 1946 and whose absence is sorely missed in the Islands are the following: Laurence (Chu) Baldwin, Ernest Alexander R. Ross, Mrs. James Wilson (Grandma) Fleming, J. Gordon Wakefield, David Lee Austin, William Henry Beers, George Ii Brown, Dr. Arthur R. Glaisyer, A. LeBaron Gurney, Margaret M. Piltz Blaisdell, Rev. Fr. Herman Schrad, Arthur E. Restarick, Harold W. Boynton, Judge Francis M. Brooks, Mary Ellen Betters, Wesley T. Wilke, Mrs. Isabelle N. Thompson, Maj. Douglas G. King, John McCombs, Laurence H. Wolfe, Judge Daniel H. Case, William Peet, Francis (Alapaki) Smith, Elinor A. Langton-Boyle, James H. Raymond, Judge Lyle A. Dickey, and David William Anderson.

Afterword

The End of *Paradise*

Without Ma there, *Paradise* lost its kama'āina voice. Instead, editor O'Brien sought to exploit the military market by producing "special editions" as mementos—Navy Day Edition, Armed Forces Anthology, Victory Edition, Honolulu Today. But with troops heading home, the military was a dwindling market.

In July 1948, William Frederickson Sabin died, at age seventy-two. During his long journalistic career in Hawai'i, the versatile Will Sabin (he was also an artist and editorial cartoonist) wrote for the *Evening Bulletin, Hawaiian Star, Honolulu Republican,* and *Pacific Commercial Advertiser,* where he was that paper's first paid columnist. In 1942 he and his wife, Frances Ames, had taken over the *Hawaii Sentinel,* which he edited until his last illness. He was best remembered for his humorous poetry.

> HARK TO THE HIBISCUS
> When the night is blooming cereus,
> In the moonshine most mysterious,
> What flower in Hawaii makes a fuss?
> The "language of the flowers"
> Is unseemly at such hours,
> When we hear the little hibis-cuss!

After the war, Edwin North McClellan resumed his journalistic career in Hawai'i, becoming a thrice-weekly commentator *(Beyond the News)* on KGU radio. In April 1946 he also assumed editorship of *Islander Magazine,* a competitor of *Paradise,* but his name was off the masthead in August. In June of the following year, he became editor of the *Army-Navy-Veterans Review of Hawaii.* Later, McClellan wrote vignettes of Hawaiian history for *Forecast,* the members' magazine of the Outrigger Canoe Club. His column stopped in July 1955 when that monthly magazine changed format.

Eileen O'Brien occupied the editor's chair at *Paradise* until the close of 1954. By then the decline in military personnel and civilian war workers was dramatic, and the total population stood at just 544,000, a drop of 315,000 since the day O'Brien bought her piece of the company. Miss Harriet Ray, from the magazine's advertising staff, succeeded her. Earlier in her career, Ray had edited a small magazine in Hong Kong and worked in the advertising department of the *Advertiser.* O'Brien went to work as a copywriter for Tongg Publishing Co. and wrote a popular tourist pamphlet, *Kauai, Garden Island Handy Guide,* for them in 1957. The following year she again joined *Paradise,* as associate editor, from November 1958 to May 1959.

The number of tourists visiting Hawai'i approached a quarter million in 1959. Despite this rise in tourism, and consequent demand for information about Hawai'i, the magazine faced severe financial difficulties. It was taken over by a holding company, went through the motions of financial reorganization, and was declared insolvent in 1960. The name, files, and circulation list were bought by a Los Angeles businessman for seventeen thousand dollars. The printing plant was purchased by a local man for forty thousand dollars.

The magazine's new owner, Donald L. Bailey, part-owner of a Los Angeles circulation firm, brought Eileen O'Brien back as editor in June 1960. He named a "contents advisory committee" composed of two advertising executives and Joseph Feher, a senior curator of graphic arts at the Honolulu Academy of Arts. The new *Paradise* would be comparable to *Arizona Highways,* a spokesman said. That December Bailey decided to take over the editor's chair himself, promising to "include articles and features which will make *Paradise* truly Hawaii's own and only magazine." He put a new management and production team in place. O'Brien was relegated to the editorship of the Holiday Annual.

In 1961, the printing company of Watkins and Sturgis bought the business and kept it going until June of 1963. That's when celebrity travel writer Horace Sutton put together a *hui* to buy it. Sutton's interest lasted just six months. The new owner, Tongg Publishing Co., refocused the editorial content of the magazine, and in 1966 changed the name to *Honolulu.* David and Cynthia Eyre, owners of the Honolulu name, became coeditors. The new editors looked at back issues of *Paradise* and concluded, "the graphics were miserable, the printing mediocre, the photography scant, color plates scarce and editorial content . . . consistently dull."

The final *Paradise of the Pacific* was the May 1966 issue. On that last day of publication, the light rain blowing down Nuʻuanu Avenue probably included Ma's tears. Fortunate it was, for any prudish and prissy pedestrians, that the roar of traffic overwhelmed the emotions Ma may have "pungently" expressed.

About the Editor

Bob Dye is the author of *Merchant Prince of the Sandalwood Mountains* and edited two previous *Hawai'i Chronicles* volumes (both University of Hawai'i Press). He is a well-known freelance writer on local political events and Hawaiian history. His articles have appeared in local and national magazines, newspapers, and journals. He lives in Kailua on the island of O'ahu.